Yearbook 2004

YOUNG PEOPLE, SOAP OPERAS AND REALITY TV

EDITOR: CECILIA VON FEILITZEN

The International Clearinghouse
on Children, Youth and Media

Nordicom
Göteborg University

Yearbook 2004

Young People, Soap Operas and Reality TV

Editor:
Cecilia von Feilitzen

ISSN 1403-4700
ISBN 91-89471-28-8

Published by:
The International Clearinghouse on Children, Youth and Media
Nordicom
Göteborg University
Box 713
SE 405 30 GÖTEBORG
Sweden

Cover by:
Karin Persson
Printed by:
Grafikerna Livréna i Kungälv AB, Sweden, 2004

Contents

Foreword

The aim of the Clearinghouse on Children, Youth and Media is to broaden and deepen our knowledge of children, youth and media and, thereby, to inform relevant decision- and policy-making. We also seek to contribute to constructive public debate and promote children's and young people's media literacy. Hopefully, the work of the Clearinghouse will stimulate additional research on children, youth and media.

The basis of Clearinghouse activities is a global network of about 1000 participants in more than 125 countries, representing not only Academia, but also the media industries, politics and a broad spectrum of voluntary organizations.

Through its yearbooks, newsletters and survey articles the Clearinghouse has an ambition to contextualize knowledge about children, young people and media literacy, bringing together insights concerning children's and young people's relations with mass media from a variety of perspectives.

The Yearbooks present the views and findings of leading researchers around the world in a variety of specialities relating to children, youth and the media. Media violence, media education and media literacy, new media technology, media globalization and media regulations are some of the themes past yearbooks have treated. This year's volume is devoted to *Young People, Soap Operas and Reality TV*.

Children all over the world listen to and watch adult programming from an early age, albeit a more genuine interest in adult entertainment appears first around the age of eight. This exposure, combined with the transformation of the traditional soap opera into the extreme soaps and reality TV of today, has whipped up storms of controversy and aroused serious concern among adults. The Clearinghouse frequently fields questions like: What do children and young people learn from these series, the values and actions of which may run totally counter to those supposed to be taught by family and school? Is it not too early for children to gain such a direct, yet false, insight into adult life? And, are young people's conceptions of the human body and appearances, not to mention their own self-images and behaviour, influenced by the 'ideals' of these series? Some of these and other questions are addressed in the articles, based on current research findings, presented here.

Finally, on behalf of the Clearinghouse, may I express our gratitude and appreciation to all the contributors who have made this yearbook possible.

Göteborg in December 2004

Ulla Carlsson
Director

Young People, Soap Operas and Reality TV

Introduction by Cecilia von Feilitzen, Scientific Co-ordinator
of The International Clearinghouse on Children, Youth and Media

Soap operas have existed almost as long as radio and television have. And the *research* on soap operas and adults is rather extensive. One innovative U.S. study by Hertha Herzog, *What do we really know about daytime serial listeners?*, dates back to 1944 and was preceded by an article in 1941. The study focussed on the gratifications that housewives, the target group of such radio serials, received from listening. However, it was not until the 1980s that the soap opera genre, now on television, received intensive research interest. These studies were mainly carried out as text analyses, reception studies and cultural studies with women, as soap operas have long been conceived of (and looked down on) as a women's genre.

The term soap opera is, however, not used all over the world – in Latin America the most popular corresponding programme genre is the *telenovela*, and in Asia it is drama serials. There are also narrative differences between, on one hand, the soap opera and, on the other, the *telenovela* and Asian drama serial, of which one of the most conspicuous is that the soap is 'open', while the *novela*/drama serial comes to a 'closure' (see the introductory box *The Television Genre(s) of Soap Opera, Telenovela, Drama Serial* in this book, as well as the interview on *Latin American Telenovelas* with *Valerio Fuenzalida* and the article *South Korean Television Drama in Asia* by *Doobo Shim*). There are also many cultural differences between the serials, be they soaps, *telenovelas* or dramas, depending on the country in which they are produced, something that is evident from the just mentioned texts, as well as from many other articles in this book.

Recently, local and internationally exported soap operas, *telenovelas* and drama serials, often attracting large audiences, have become more and more common around the world, not least because of the explosive spread of cable and satellite television in the 1980s and 90s. In several countries, these fictional serials have also to a greater extent been addressing a wider audience than mainly women, that is, also men and young people. The U.S. *Dallas* and *Dynasty* (also for men) and *Beverly Hills 90210, Sopranos, Ally McBeal* and *Sex and the City* (for the young audience) are examples of such soaps, and there are similar tendencies among *novelas* and drama serials in certain countries, the reasons being that the women of today are more engaged in gainful employment than previously and that television in our contemporary media culture is subjected to aggressive competition from other channels and the new digital media. Many soaps, *novelas* and drama serials have also become increasingly daring – sometimes showing in a single or a few episodes more about sex, divorce, deceit, revenge, power struggle, shady economic transactions, crime, etc., than a person experiences in her/his whole life.

Moreover, the soap/*novela*/drama genre has recently been accompanied by highly sensational 'docu-soaps', 'reality game shows' or 'reality TV'. The definitions of this 'genre' or these genres are not commonly agreed upon and they have several historical forerunners – see the introductory box *The 'Genre' of Reality TV* in this book. Likewise, the authors of the articles presented here use the terms docu-soaps, reality TV, reality shows, etc., interchangeably. What the Yearbook and its authors focus on is more easily explained by referring to the recent generations of 'global events' reality TV from the late 1990s and the 2000s, which are popular among young people, namely reality game shows such as *Survivor, Big Brother, Popstars, Pop Idol* and similar serials. For the historical roots and main concepts of reality TV – including the fact that actors are replaced by 'ordinary people', that the 'story lines' are not traditionally scripted, that the contestants are recorded in most intimate detail during their hygiene routines, eating, sex affairs, stress, and conflicts by constantly running surveillance cameras, and that the audiences often are allowed to vote out the contestants according to unclear criteria – see the introductory box *The 'Genre' of Reality TV*. As *Lorenzo Vilches* writes in another box under the heading *First and Second Formatted Reality*, also included in this introduction, these new formats revolutionize the relationships with their viewers, with other programmes and with the media and cultural environment. However, as is also emphasized in one of the last-mentioned boxes, there is still an acute absence of *research* on reality TV.

Fact-based light entertainment programming – of which reality game shows such as the programmes named above have come to occupy the most central place – has developed in many forms since the 1980s and especially during the 1990s, as a response to the changing competitive multi-channel, multimedia and new information and communication technological landscape. Although often expensive, factual entertainment is nevertheless cheaper to produce than fictional long-running serials. The 'global events' reality formats have also proved particularly successful for export, as they can be adapted for the most part to local productions, which minimizes the risk of financial loss for the television channels and inventors of the formats. However, in order to attract and keep viewers' and advertisers' interests, the limits of the 'reality events' have successively been stretched by the television producers, i.e., new 'taboos' are gradually broken and the programmes are becoming increasingly 'brutal'. This is witnessed by the following small press selection from 2004:

Survivor (Expedition Robinson, in Sweden), formerly on the traditional public service network, is now aired on a commercial satellite channel, TV3. A well-known professor and media columnist says that 'the programme keeps its fascinating character of social-psychological laboratory experiment with human guinea-pigs, trigged by hunger for medial attention' but this introductory programme 'dissected [more] ghastly mentalities in the [contestant] collective' than any single episode in the earlier series, at the same time as 'the word democracy is used to market the programme' (Furhammar 2004).

Pop Idol (Idol 2004, in Sweden) is based on the idea that the winner will be recorded on a CD for an international music company. A media columnist writes: Contestants sometimes as young as 16 years of age and many performing poorly (singing out of tune and acting pathetically) are deliberately selected, so that the viewers can laugh at people making fools of themselves. The jury is 'honest', rude and mean towards the performers, which makes them feel bad and worthless (Croneman 2004). However, when accused, the representatives of this public service television channel (TV4) willingly pose in the newspaper, answering that it is quality TV, a completely new form within the genre, and that they want more and younger viewers (Boldeman 2004).

Today there are no limits to what TV producers may subject a never-ceasing stream of amateurs thirsting for fame to, another journalist writes. There are, for example, reality TV programmes in which the whole concept amounts to being awake as long as possible, winning money (*Shattered*, U.K.), or in which fat people on diets are locked in a house full of chocolate, cakes and other temptations, winning gold bars equivalent to the decrease in their weight (*Big Diet*, The Netherlands). There are also programmes in which women are subjected to a range of tests in order to decide whether they might 'succeed' in the pornography branch, winning money and a one-year contract with a distributor of pornographic films (*Can You Be a Pornstar*, U.S.A.); in which childless couples are scrutinized by a 16-year-old mother, the prize being her child (*Be My Baby*, U.S.A.); and in which young people aged 18 to 28 undergo plastic surgery in order to resemble their idols, with 15 minutes of fame as the prize (*I Want a Famous Face*, U.S.A.) (Sundholm 2004).

As will be touched upon later, and as is evident from the articles in the book, there are, naturally, clear cultural differences not only between soap operas, *telenovelas*, and drama serials over the world, but also between reality TV programmes in different countries. Although the recent reality TV formats have been hotly called into question in all places at which they have arrived, they have, as said, also been locally adapted, thereby not transgressing to too great an extent the borders of each country's specific cultural norms. In several nations, reality TV has also been regulated.

In sharp contrast to reality TV originating in the West, a similar but completely divergent trend exists in many 'southern' countries to deliberately use the format of 'edutainment', 'docu-soaps' and 'soap operas' in order to raise debate about social evils, contribute to solving health problems in society, etc. When searching in the data base of the information and communication platform *The Communication Initiative*, which is a space to share, debate and innovate concerning more effective development practice (http://www.comminit.com), several hundreds of concrete examples of drama serials, soap operas and *telenovelas* in the mass media can be found, the purpose of which are to tackle social problems in Africa, Asia and Latin America. Sometimes these entertainment-education strategies can be extremely candid, frank, reality-based and 'in your face', and have also been subjected to an intensive and questioning debate. The book will give a glimpse of this trend, too, further on.

Common questions to the Clearinghouse

What motivated this Yearbook is the fact that the transformation of the traditional soap opera into certain more extreme soaps, and the emergence of the recent 'global' reality TV formats have whipped up storms of controversy in a great number of countries, and generated worries about how such programmes are received by, and may influence, young viewers – because children from all over the world watch adult programming from an early age. The same is true of radio listening in areas where television is less common. Both soap operas and reality TV have, for example, been accused of striving for sensation by seasoning the contents with sex, nudity, promiscuity (especially in an age when HIV/AIDS is a great concern), bad language, and racism; they have been accused of promoting voyeurism and exhibitionism, and of contributing to new lifestyle standards that prioritize publicity, glamour, competition, heightened self-centredness, individualism, and oppressing other people – yes, contributing to mental violence. Reality TV, in particular, has also been under fire not only because it is called 'reality' when it, on the contrary, substantially constructs events, but also because it encourages bullying, harassment and degradation, in that the programmes and audiences humiliate and evict contestants, something completely contrary to ideals of tolerance, solidarity and peace in democratic societies.

In light of these circumstances, the questions to the Clearinghouse about soap operas and reality TV from many countries have been the following:

What do children and young people learn from these serials, in which values and characters'/'ordinary' people's actions often are completely counter to those that are supposed to be taught by family and school? Is it not too early for children to gain such a direct, yet mostly false, insight into adult life? And are young people's ideas and actions influenced by the values, actions and 'models' in these programmes?

These concerns and questions are justified, partly because of the contents of certain fictional and reality TV serials, partly because children do not distinguish between reality and fantasy in the same way as adults do. Even if children from early years, and almost all at the age of 5, can tell that a cartoon is only make-believe, a more 'realistic' drama series with live actors, for example a police action series, can be seen as reflecting reality even among children about 12 years of age (Rydin 1983). An Israeli study in the 1990s found that one possible explanation for why a disturbing amount of violent fights broke out among 8- to 12-year-olds specifically after World Wrestling Federation (WWF) programmes, emerged through children's discussions of their confusion over the fantasy and reality aspects of the series (Lemish 1998). Also, relatively many research examples, not only with children but, in fact, more often with adolescents and adults, show that people have a tendency to rely on media, including fictional contents, for their conceptions of facts and phenomena in reality that they have not heard about from direct personal sources or that they have no personal experience of. To mention but one example: Australian children aged 6 to 12, who were asked to estimate how often real life police engaged in different activities, tended to overestimate the frequency of certain activities and underestimate that of others, and these inaccuracies were in the directions predicted by television content. Among the activities that were seen as very frequent in real life police work were aggressive behaviours, such as dramatic chases and rough searches (activities shown frequently on television). In other words, children constructed their social understandings with reference to their most readily available source of information: television. However, children were less influenced by television when it came to estimating the frequency of police activities that they have opportunities to observe directly, such as routine patrols (Low & Durkin 1997 cited in Durkin & Low 1998).

The aim of this book

At the same time as the concerns and questions about young people, soap opera and reality TV addressed to the Clearinghouse are justified, the questions are, unfortunately, very difficult to answer. As underlined in the introductory boxes, research conducted on soap operas, *telenovelas*, etc., is mostly with adults, while research with young people and this fictional genre seriously lags behind. However, there are a few such studies from the 1980s and 90s, which will briefly be referred to below. But when it comes to the recent reality TV programmes, empirical research is (with very few exceptions) still generally lacking.

Thus, the primary aim of this Yearbook is to stimulate research on young people, soap operas and reality TV.

In order to do so, the Clearinghouse invited scholars from all over the world via the Clearinghouse global network to contribute their, although perhaps sparse, research knowledge on the subject as a basis for further research. We will in this context express our sincere and warm gratitude to all who contributed.

The research contributions in this volume shall therefore be regarded as case studies, of which some are exploratory, and their findings cannot be empirically generalized across borders. Also, the research approaches used in the case studies are mostly of a qualitative and short-term character, above all within the tradition of reception studies, where children or adolescents have been interviewed or asked to answer questions, often in their own words, concerning how they themselves perceive the programmes. Therefore, the book mainly contains findings from young people's perspectives, whereas there are no studies really attempting to discover long-term influences from an effect, cultivation, socialization or similar perspective. The need for further research is emphasized by several authors in the book.

With the existing contributions, the book nevertheless represents an attempt to give preliminary answers to at least some of the questions put to the Clearinghouse.

Whereas most contributing scholars have written either about soap operas or about reality TV, there are a few researchers who deal with both, as they found certain similarities between the genres, or had taken up soap operas as well as reality TV in their on-going or earlier empirical research.

However, it is not out of place to stress that we do not equate soap operas with reality TV. Even if one can find a few similarities between the genres, the differences are great. Also, there are many differences between single soap operas, *telenovelas* or drama serials – in the same way as there are many differences between single reality shows. And, as said and evidenced by the articles in the book, the programmes differ, sometimes strikingly, between cultures, as well.

The reason for combining these genres in the same book is, thus, not because of a view that they are 'all the same'. Instead, the book is grounded on the fact that it is these genres – in addition to factual and fictional media containing representations of physical violence – which over the past few years have increasingly troubled parents, teachers, media educators, media regulators and journalists in relation to children and young people.

How much do children and young people watch soap operas and reality TV?

The degree to which children and young people watch soap operas, *telenovelas,* drama serials and reality TV will, naturally, differ from one country to another, depending on, among other things, what kinds of programmes for both children and adults the existing television channels offer, the times at which the programmes are transmitted, and the age of the children – as well as on a whole range of other factors such as the young viewers' gender, socio-cultural backgrounds, interests, experiences, reception contexts, etc. We know, for example, that if there is an output of quality children's programmes at times suitable for children, the younger ones will also watch programmes specifically aimed at them, whereas the minor proportion of adult programming they also view is more a consequence of the small child's wish to be together with the family in front of television (or near the radio in areas where television sets are less frequent). For instance, in the Nordic countries, as well as in Australia and Japan, where there is a relatively rich supply of home-produced and diverse children's TV programmes of high quality at times appropriate for children, young children do indeed mostly watch children's programmes and also prefer to do so (Rydin 2000). However, even in these countries, a more genuine interest in adult programmes, mainly entertainment and fiction, appears when the growing child more definitely starts orienting her-/himself towards the peer group, in addition to the family. When this actually occurs may vary between cultures but happens, for instance, in Sweden around the age of 8 (e.g., von Feilitzen *et al.* 1989).

Research in the 1990s from a couple of Asian countries that produce very few children's programmes gave rise to other findings: In India, not a single of the few children's programmes recalled by a sample of young children interviewed was domestically produced, and most children mentioned programmes made for adults as the ones they liked – crime, thrillers, comedies and family serials. Of the 100 programmes most viewed by children between the ages 6 and 14 in 1994 on Malaysian television, only three were children's programmes. These were all foreign programmes (Goonasekera 2000).

In this volume, *José Ramón Pérez Ornia* gives in his article *Television Viewing among 4- to 12-year-olds in Spain* an exemplifying account of another kind of inadequate relationship between children's demand and children's programme offering: When children are most in front of the television set, few children's programmes are broadcast. Children's programmes in Spain – which, by the way, primarily comprise cartoons from the U.S. – are, above all, scheduled in terms of voids left by adults not watching television at certain times. However, these time slots are, in general, not appropriate for children either. As a consequence, children are largely forced to watch programming oriented towards adults.

This complexity of programme supply and broadcast time, in combination with children's age, produces a situation in which cartoons and fictional series for adults constitute the main television diet among 4- to 12-year-olds in Spain, along with a growing consumption of reality TV. The two reality TV programmes most watched by children of these ages during the 2002/03 season were *Gran Hermano* (Big Brother) and *Operación Triunfo* (Pop Idol), starting at about 9:30 p.m. and 10:30 p.m., respectively – 10 p.m. to 11 p.m. being the time period when most 4- to 12-year-olds in Spain view television. Due to relatively few *telenovelas* and long-running soap operas broadcast during 2002-2004, the *telenovela*/soap opera genre is watched by this child audience to a lesser extent. However, other fictional television products, such as certain Spanish prime-time (9 p.m. to 0 a.m.) series, have a significant child audience, not least those more family-oriented programmes including children in the cast and story lines. At the same time, almost one-fourth of what a Spanish child watches on television is advertising, sales or promotion of the channel and its programmes.

The youngest viewers within the 4- to 12-year-bracket in Spain view cartoons more than the older children, but even small children view some fictional series and reality TV. With increasing age, viewing of the latter two genres grows rapidly and practically exponentially within the age span. Regarding gender, boys watch cartoons more than do girls, who view adult fictional series and reality TV more than do boys – boys often prefer action and girls relationship dramas. And several recent reality TV programmes in Spain are musical contests (e.g., *Operación Triunfo, Popstars*) with young women competing. However, *Gran Hermano* also attracts boys.

Audience figures from another country – Germany – valid for 6- to 13-year-olds during October to December 2003 and representing the percentages of children who watch different adult genres 'often' or 'now and then' show that daily soaps come in third place with 67 per cent, while reality TV programmes are watched by 43 per cent. Roughly half of the younger children aged 6 to 9 watch soaps and roughly a quarter reality TV. Among the older children aged 10 to 13, some 80 per cent watch soaps and more than half reality TV. More girls than boys prefer soap operas, but the gender difference for reality TV is small, perhaps because this genre in the German study is exemplified in the questionnaire with *Big Brother* and programmes about accidents and other alarming events (Frey-Vor & Schumacher 2004).

The last-mentioned German figures are not presented in a special article in this Yearbook but are related here, since they – beside the Spanish findings presented above – constitute another fresh example of audience figures for adult genres among even relatively small children and such public data including preschoolers are rare. Returning to the Yearbook, a German example of the amount of slightly older children's viewing of soap operas and reality TV is briefly given by *Maya Götz*. Six to 8 p.m. is soap opera time in Germany, and, for instance, the German version of the adult soap opera *Good Times, Bad Times* (the concept of which has its origin in Australia) has a market share of over 50 per cent among 10- to 15-year-old girls. This means that every second young female adolescent viewing television at this time is watching *Good Times, Bad Times*, often five times a week for many years. Even some children as young as 3 years watch this serial. Maya Götz also says that the German version of *Big Brother* seems to be nearly as attractive to the 10- to 15-year-old boys as is the daily soap opera to the girls, a finding that corresponds to those mentioned above.

Even if quantitative measures on the amount of young people's viewing of soap operas and reality TV are not the main focus of other articles than the Spanish one, more audience figures are found here and there in the Yearbook:

Maria Dolores Souza gives evidence that the majority of the ten top-rated programmes among 10- to 14-year-olds in Chile are reality TV programmes and *telenovelas*.

Alice Y. L. Lee says that, on average, young people in Hong Kong watch television about three to four hours a day, and television drama serials are their most favoured programmes. Young people are also interested in foreign reality TV shows. According to one survey, 50 per cent of respondents between 12 and 16 years watched all drama serials broadcast in prime time (7 to 10 p.m.). Higher figures were, naturally, reached in another survey when young people who 'often' watch such serials were included.

Nayia Roussou and *Michaella Buck* exhibit audience ratings for the age span 13 to 54 years in Cyprus, showing that the recent kinds of reality TV programmes most highly attract the age groups 13 to 17 and 18 to 24 on the island.

There are also other instances of audience figures in the book and several authors underscore the high popularity among young people of the genres of soap operas and reality TV.

The meanings of soap operas, telenovelas and drama serials for young people

Why, then, are soap operas so popular among young people? One study on 6- to 19-year-olds' fascination with soap operas (all German or adapted German versions) is presented by *Maya Götz* in her article *"Soaps Want to Explain Reality":*
Daily Soaps and Big Brother in the Everyday Life of German Children and Adolescents. The author found that viewing of soaps is important in shaping the interviewees' everyday life. First, soap opera viewing assumes a *situational* function, as daily viewing serves to structure the course of the viewer's day. Second, the soap takes on *interactive* functions. Considerable talking about the events of the show takes place during the viewing, commercial breaks, and recess or (boring) lessons. Third, children and adolescents assimilate and interpret the contents of soaps and develop their *own thematic* understandings – everyone makes something different out of the soap opera. Maya Götz groups these subjectively experienced meanings into a variety of typical patterns, which in their turn are sorted into three main groups: a) children and adolescents get pleasure, they learn and get advice; b) they recognize themselves and are self-affirmed; and c) they complete or conceal what is missing in their own life-worlds (i.e., the soap viewing becomes an outlet for expression of feelings, para-social relationships and day-dreaming – or is used to fill time or gloss over a period of emotional emptiness, deficiencies or problematic situations).

The same author also finds an age-typical development of soap enthusiasm. For children aged 6 to 9, regular reception of a daily soap is integrated into the family routine as a 'bedtime story' and opportunity to exchange views on the more adult world. Increasingly, among pre-teens aged 10 to 13, the daily soap becomes an information resource, a kind of 'window on the adult world'. Slightly older children, aged about 12 to 15, recognize in the characters parts of themselves as well as

The Television Genre(s) of Soap Opera, Telenovela, Drama Serial

The text below is based on: Robert C. Allen (2004) "Making Sense of Soaps", in Robert C. Allen & Annette Hill *The Television Studies Reader*. London & New York: Routledge, pp. 242-257. Robert C. Allen is also editor of *To Be Continued... Soap Operas around the World*. London & New York: Routledge, 1995.

Fictional television serials constitute one of the most popular forms of storytelling ever devised. In some countries, such television series are a relatively new phenomenon, while in others – for example the U.S., Great Britain, Australia and several countries in Latin America – they have been staples of broadcast programming since the early days of radio. Television serials are linked by their distinctive serial narrative structure and have their media origin in the rise of the literary serial narrative in the eighteenth century – by the 1850s, publishing novels in magazine serials had become a standard. Serial comic strips and movie serials then helped to build a regular audience and consumer demand. Serial narrative was also crucial to the development of national broadcasting systems in a number of countries. Devised around 1930 as one programming strategy in the U.S. to lure women to daytime radio and advertisers to programme sponsorship, within only a few years soap operas proved to be one of the most effective broadcasting advertising vehicles (especially used for laundry detergents and household cleaning products, hence the word 'soap'). Soap operas have long had their most loyal viewership among women between the ages of 18 and 35.

In Latin America, *telenovelas* constitute a great deal of the total television output and attract more viewers than any other form of programming. Although U.S. serials are distributed widely around the world, there is even wider global circulation of serials made in certain other cultures, especially in Latin America and most of all Brazil. Australia and the U.K. are great exporters of soap operas, as well. With television spreading more rapidly over the globe since the mid-80s, not least because of cable and satellite channels, 'soapmania' has broken out in more parts of the world, for example, several Asian countries. One of the most striking demonstrations of the popularity of serial television was the serialization of the Hindu religious epic *Ramanyan* broadcast in India in 1987-88.

Although no other form of television fiction is attracting more viewers in more countries more regularly over a longer period of time, the serials have often been regarded as trash and largely been ignored in the 'serious' literature and research. Particularly it has been dismissed as waste-of-time women's trash or, sometimes, as adolescent trash. For a long period, social scientists mostly subjected television soap operas to quantitative content analyses comparing the construction of some aspects of social reality in the world of the soap opera with their bases in 'real life'. However, since about 1980, soap operas began to be taken seriously within European, Australian and U.S. research by means of text analyses (often related to theories of structuralism and poststructuralism), qualitative reception studies and ethnographical cultural studies – mostly within the context of feminist theory.[1] At the same time, Latin American research on *telenovelas* started to grow.[2] Issues considered in Latin American research have been, for example, the *telenovela's* relation to national identity, cultural authenticity, the relationship between television and everyday life, and the gaps between serials' representation of social reality and that experienced by serial viewers. In particular, television and *telenovelas* have been seen as an important instrument of modernity in Latin America: the economic, cultural, and psychic reorganization of society around the demands of consumer capitalism.

There are cultural differences between soap operas. For example, the longest running British soap operas have chronicled the lives of working-class people, while American daytime and prime time serials have more often featured the middle and upper classes. There are also 'open' and 'closed' serials. The U.S., British and Australian soap operas often continue for years, spread their narrative energy among a great number of plots and characters who move in and out, and are predicated upon the impossibility of ultimate closure, that is, problems are not solved and characters will not live happily ever after. Unlike the open serial, the Latin American *telenovela* and other forms of closed serial (such as the Asian drama, *editor's note*) are designed to end and their narratives to close – although this closure might not be achieved until after several months. Closed serials also offer viewers an opportunity, after closure, to look back upon the completed text and impose upon it some kind of moral or ideological order. In this sense, closed serials are inherently melodramatic in nature.

The serial is a form of narrative organized around institutionally imposed gaps in the text. These gaps leave plenty of time for viewers to discuss with each other both the possible meanings of what has happened thus far as well as what might happen next. Television serials around the world, more than any other form of programming, seem to provoke talk about their content among their viewers.

Since 1980, in countries where more women have entered the paid workforce, viewership concentrated among women between the ages of 18 and 35 has dissolved. (And many soap operas, *telenovelas* and drama serials have therefore widened their target audience by including more roles representing men, younger people, etc., *editor's note*.) Also, with increased competition between the many commercial television channels of today, games, talk shows, and 'reality' programmes – which are, generally, cheaper to produce and therefore less risky for channels to start – have become increasingly common and represent serious competition for soap operas in many countries.

Notes

1. See, for example:
   Allen, Robert C. (1985) *Speaking of Soap Operas*. Chapel Hill, NC: University of North Carolina Press

Ang, Ien ([1982]1985) *Watching "Dallas": Soap Opera and the Melodramatic Imagination*. London: Methuen

Buckingham, David (1987) *Public Secrets: EastEnders and its Audience*. London: British Film Institute

Dyer, Richard, Christine Geraghty, Marion Jordan, Terry Lovell, Richard Patterson & John Stewart (1981) *Coronation Street*. London: British Film Institute

Geraghty, Christine (1991) *Women and Soap Opera: A Study of Prime Time Soaps*. London: Polity

Hobson, Dorothy (1982) *Crossroads: The Drama of Soap Opera*. London: Methuen

Modledski, Tania (1982) *Loving with a Vengeance*. Hamden, CI: Archon Books

Tulloch, John & Albert Moran (1986) *A Country Practice: "Quality Soap"*. Sydney: Currency Press

2. See, for example:

Leal, Ondina (1985) *A novela das oito*. Petropolis: Vozes

Lopez Pumarejo, Tomas (1987) *Aproximación a la telenovela*. Madrid: Catedra

Martín Barbero, Jesús (1985) "Comunicación, pueblo y cultura en el tiempo de las transnacionales", in M. de Morgas (ed.) *Sociologia de la comunicación de masas*. Barcelona: Gustavo Gili

Mattelart, Michèle & Armand Mattelart (1990) *The Carnival of Images: Brazilian Television Fiction*. New York: Bergin & Garvey

Mazziotti, Nora (ed.) (1992) *El spectaculo de las pasión: Las telenovelas latinoamericanos*. Buenos Aires: Ediciónes Colihue

Ortiz, Renato, Silvia Herbera, Simões Borell, José Mário & Ortiz Ramos (1988) *Telenovela: historia e produção*. São Paulo: Editorio Brasiliense

Quiroz, Maria Teresa (1992) "La telenovela peruana: Antecendentes y situación actual", in Mazziotti, N. (see above)

Rector, Monica (1975) "A televisão e a telenovela", *Cultura* 5 (18), pp. 112-17

Rogers, Everett M. & Livia Antola (1985) "Telenovelas: A Latin American Success Story", *Journal of Communication* 35 (4)

their newly developing philosophy of life, while distancing themselves from other philosophies or personalities portrayed; they often identify with a particular character. It is primarily 14- to 15-year-old girls who develop a special emotional involvement with soaps and admit to being 'addicted' to them. In such cases, daily viewing of the soap opera becomes a vehemently demanded, zealously guarded retreat that young adolescent girls create for themselves (mostly watching the soap alone) in order to remain in contact with their own feelings and knowledge about relationships. In the older adolescents, aged 16 to 19, there is a 'lighter' appropriation of the genre together with a more distant attitude. The family now tends to be increasingly reintegrated into the sharing of enthusiasm for the soap, though the fantasies and emotional participation are remembered and continued.

While young people do not mistake soap operas for reality, it is especially the pre-teens who have the feeling that they learn much about reality from them, Maya Götz finds. Thus, she cautions against inappropriate female stereotypes and clichéd situations in soaps; against how the female body is portrayed; and against sexual violence directed at characters with whom the young viewers identify.

Helga Theunert and *Christa Gebel* report in their article *Reception of TV Series among Children and Teenagers in Germany* on another German study with 9- to 15-year-olds. The authors found that situation comedies and (German) soap operas definitely were the children's favourites – soap operas more among girls, who are interested in confusions in love life and daily experiences of young people, and sitcoms more among boys, who to a greater extent seek humour, exaggerations and breaking of taboos. In the third place, the children were interested in the suspense they find in action, mystery and crime series. (Reality TV programmes like *Big Brother* had not yet been launched in the country.) The programme preferences show what the age group in question has in mind: funny and exciting entertainment, and curiosity about the forth-coming period of adult life, especially as regards relationships and interactions in social communities.

Although interested in action, stories containing a great deal of physical violence were not favoured by the majority of girls and boys in the sample. However, mental violence such as insults, meanness, stepping on other people, taking advantage of them, bullying them – typical patterns of soap operas – were of interest to many children, as they checked to what extent such behaviour works. A general finding was that the series children in these ages prefer are a source of social orientation. A grave argument among the children for soap operas is their 'realism'. Another distinctive feature in the study is that the conception of soaps providing authentic insight into the everyday life is found particularly among young people from less intellectually stimulating milieus. Young people with a more intellectual background mention the soaps' attempt at being realistic, but do not, according to the authors, take such portrayals at face value.

Robyn Quin discusses, among other things, in her article *From Beverly Hills to Big Brother: How Australian Teenage Girls Respond* the sorts of meanings and pleasures that teenage girls in Australia take from soap operas as represented by the U.S. soap *Beverly Hills 90210*. The pleasurable returns of the studied 12- and 14-year-old girls' investment of their time in viewing the soap opera were multiple and various – but some pleasures were common. First, the genre and the girls' familiarity and expertise in the genre were a major source of their pleasure in the text. The second recurring theme in the responses related to respect. The level of deference the programme showed for the intelligence and maturity of its audience was a strong source of pleasure for the girls. They made frequent and appreciative mention of the fact that the programme tackled 'big', 'important' or 'serious issues', e.g., AIDS, binge drinking, parental extra marital affairs, breast cancer, cheating and shoplifting. The girls believed that the programme 'presented real problems' in 'realistic ways', avoided 'preaching' about behaviour and did not always 'pretend that every problem got solved like most American TV shows'. A third common theme in the girls' responses had to do with projection of themselves into, most especially, the evolution and dissolution of relationships and how they themselves would deal with the issues raised in the narrative representation of characters' relationships.

A project trying to discover how children aged 11-12 and 15-16 years in Norway experience the dual value influence from school and media, the 'parallel school', is presented by *Asbjørn Simonnes* and *Gudmund Gjelsten* in their article *Children Interacting between Values at School and in the Media*. At school children are taught normative, 'intentional' values. In media they encounter value profiles that sometimes are, quite obviously, the contrary. Focus in the article lies on two soap operas, the Norwegian produced *Hotel Cæsar*, which is the 11- to 12-year-olds' favourite, and the U.S. *Friends*, most favoured by the 15- to 16-year-olds. The researchers find severe differences and, thus, an obvious conflict between the values in these TV serials and the values and norms regarding relationships, attitudes, tolerance and problem solving stressed in the school curriculum. The absolute majority of the children in the study also seem to be aware of the different emphases on values between their favourite programme and the school. However, most children, and especially the older ones, remain comfortable with this situation, and do not feel they are in a 'crossfire' between the intentional school/upbringing and the media.

Generally, the children felt that their prime source for learning about what is right and wrong is their parents, and after that the school. However, 15- to 16-year-olds who express 'traditional' values concerning issues like sex and living together, family life, and violence, think they have been mainly influenced by their homes and the school, while those maintaining more 'liberal' views refer to influence from friends and visual media. And while some children declare very strongly that they are not influenced by media exposure, others admit quite openly that they are. To the extent that the children and adolescents use their favourite programmes to learn about adult life – and some children say explicitly they do – there is a risk that young people are also receiving an erroneous picture of the aspect of responsibility in adult life, the researchers say.

In Hong Kong, 12- to 16-year-olds and older young people are heavy viewers of drama serials, *Alice Y. L. Lee* writes in her article *Critical Appreciation of TV Drama and Reality Shows: Hong Kong Youth in Need of Media Education*. Hong Kong studies also indicate that such serials have great influence on youth attitudes and behaviour. Young people see, for example, historical drama series and drama series about professional groups of today as real reflections of life, say that they learn from the series, model themselves after their characters, and follow their ways of handling things. They also believe that 'deviant content', such as complicated love affairs, undisciplined sexual relationships, human conflicts and weakened marital relationships, frequently happen in everyday lives.

The author underlines the importance of media literacy training for young people in order for them to understand that the media construct reality, and how and why, to uncover underlying values embedded in the media constructs and to become critical viewers – without spoiling the youth's enjoyment of television drama. The media literacy initiatives in Hong Kong have been successful in these regards. While still enthusiastic about the series, students who received such training have learned how to recognize the hidden ideologies in the serials.

Turning to Britain, *Dorothy Hobson* relates in her article *Everyday People, Everyday Life: British Teenagers, Soap Opera and Reality TV* examples from her interviews with young people on different occasions. There are the unemployed 16-year-old boys in the mid-1980s, and the young men aged 16 to 20 in the mid-1990s who were in a young offenders unit. In 2004, there are 'ordinary' 13- and 14-year-old girls, and girls aged 17-18 years taking Media Studies and with sophisticated opinions about media production. Many of these young people were avid viewers of (British and Australian) soap operas. The overall pattern that emerges from these interviews is that the soap operas these young people watched, and the characters and stories they liked, are those to which they felt they could relate. Thus, the teenagers take information from the programmes, but bring to the viewing their own beliefs and behaviour systems. Not that the message inscribed by the producers does not have any effect, but the readings made by young people are overdetermined by what they bring to the media. For example, while some of the unemployed young boys who did not get on with their family chose to reject soap operas precisely because they were about families, the young boys in the remand centre saw the family representations in the Australian *Home & Away* as an unattainable paradise which they would never know. The girls also saw the value of the soap opera in giving information about the issues, which might relate to their lives, but they would have preferred information from other sources, as well. The researcher finds that soap opera is not a genre which should cause concern amongst, e.g., authorities, at least not regarding adolescents, for the fictional series both reflect the reality with which the young people are familiar and enable them to make their own judgements in relation to the fictional portrayals of that reality.

According to the Chilean researcher *Valerio Fuenzalida* interviewed by María Dolores Souza under the heading *Latin American Telenovelas*, there is a growing interest among children and young people in Latin America in watching especially the kinds of *telenovelas* which target the whole family in evening time, and therefore also include more different characters in the story lines – for example, more male and younger roles – than the traditional *telenovelas* aimed at women. Latin American *telenovelas* have a very effective capacity to produce social conversation within the family, peer group, at school, in the office, etc., and have, thus, a socializing effect. However, *telenovelas* are received in the family context, much more than, for example, films on television, so the consumption of *telenovelas* is social and the influence of them therefore always interacts with the communication within the family and other groups. The *telenovela* in itself does not have a sole, direct influence on behaviour, Valerio Fuenzalida says.

Thaïs Machado-Borges presents in her article *On Possible and Actual Lives: Young Viewers and the Reception of Brazilian Telenovelas* an ethnographical study of young viewers and *telenovelas* in Brazil, capturing precisely elements of social communication about *novelas*. She chose to focus on when the informants – mostly between 14 and 30 years of age – mentioned *telenovelas* in their everyday errands and conversations and observed that they were not only talking about the plots and characters, but also about the actors, their diets, spas, food, gymnastic programs, fashion and plastic surgeries, as well as about images, advertisements, magazines and diverse commodities interspersed with the plots of *telenovelas*. The article argues that viewers' engagement with *telenovelas* should be seen as part of the practices of coping and hoping that make up their lives. Their dialoguing with *telenovelas* is neither duped nor completely subversive or uncritical – it is a way for viewers to imbue their lives with fiction, images and fantasy, not only to momentarily escape from reality, but also as a way to hope and act in order to be embedded as a subject, as 'someone who counts', in a society where 'counting' is anything but self-evident for the majority of the population.

Television is a means to spread messages and information throughout Brazil, a country that is fractured by enormous social inequalities. Most of the informants were of the opinion that 'people watch [*telenovelas*] to learn' about 'new stuff', social issues, etc., gaining access to information that is otherwise unequally distributed. On the one hand, *telenovelas* introduce a myriad of commodities to millions of viewers, and in some cases consumption choices appear to form the basis for nationality as a collective identity. On the other hand, consumption of *telenovelas* seems to produce a feeling of collective participation in national rituals and national passions. However, viewers also play an active role in the reception of *telenovelas*, although the way they relate to this flow is coloured by the socio-cultural contexts within which they are positioned. For example, for those informants who lived under harder material conditions and had to confront prejudices and oppression on a daily basis, *telenovelas* were a way to find strategies to make their voices heard, to make themselves visible and recognizable as complex subjects. Through their reiteration of elements from *telenovelas*, they wanted to see themselves as complex subjects – not only poor (and black and rural) servants, but also interesting, intelligent, and seductive persons. Middle- and upper-middle class informants did not need to untether themselves from certain stigmatized social positionings but worked instead towards reinforcing their social status, e.g., by trying to make their lives and their bodies as 'beautiful as in the *novelas*'.

Young people may also actively influence fictional series in a more direct way, *Doobo Shim* says in the article *South Korean Television Drama in Asia*. In Asia, there is a new phenomenon called the Korean wave, referring to the recent popularity of South Korean TV dramas and other popular culture that have exploded across Asia. In Korea itself, audiences avidly consume these dramas, which often record remarkably high ratings and also have the highest advertising rates of all television genres in the country. The author discusses possible factors explaining the success of Korean dramas, with particular attention to young people. One factor could be the cultural proximity factor, as popular culture constitutes first and foremost the pleasure of recognition. Moreover, different cultural factors may be at work causing different countries to appreciate the dramas. Also, TV dramas provide audiences with opportunities to think about, discuss and debate their culture and social agendas, not least in relation to their own lives.

However, Korea is also the world leader in high-speed broadband access, with more than 75 percent of Korean homes having broadband. The author puts forward the theory that especially young people's use of the Internet has contributed to Korean television dramas' quality improvement and helped develop these dramas' export capacity, engendering the Korean wave. Young Koreans spend their time being connected to computers, watching television dramas, playing games, chatting, and attending virtual schools online. This means that the Internet has sped up the feedback process so that audiences submit their responses to a television programme even while watching it. Korean audiences also form Internet fan clubs of their favourite dramas and the main age group (19- to 25-year-olds) of these clubs overlaps with that of main online users. When fan club members dislike a synopsis of a drama serial, they pressure the producers to change it. And because these ardent fans are online opinion leaders concerning the programmes, and form the guaranteed market for the dramas' sales of video-on-demand, DVD and other secondary products, networks cannot disregard their fandom. In fact, television drama producers often invite fan club members to locations, arrange meetings with their stars, and even allow them to play minor roles in television dramas.

The meanings of reality TV for young people

Being able to interact more directly with television is also true of certain recent reality TV formats. Do the articles tell us anything about why reality TV is popular among young people, and how they construct meanings from these serials?

Four scholars introduced in the previous section, "The meanings of soap operas, telenovelas and drama serials for young people", also treat reality TV. *Maya Götz* included *Big Brother* in her study on 6- to 19-year-olds' fascination with soap operas in Germany, as young people paid attention to this reality TV programme, which is also edited according to the soap dramaturgy. Although *Big Brother* had been on just for a short time when the study was carried out (and enthusiasm for daily soaps often develops over and endures for years), Maya Götz found aspects among the children's and young people's meaning-making of *Big Brother* that were similar to the *situational*, *interactive* and *subjective-thematic* functions of soap operas. For example, for the younger children, regular reception of *Big Brother* was integrated into the family routine and sometimes aided by parents' positive attitude towards watching. Another motive for watching *Big Brother* was to be able to talk about it in school. Further, children found the serial pleasurable, felt they could learn from it, and that they got role models. According to the author, however, it is problematic that almost no children and adolescents in the sample seemed to understand that what they were viewing had been consciously produced and edited, but assumed that reality was actually being shown. Neither did most children see any ethical problems of the programme, and they

The 'Genre' of Reality TV

Since about 1980, but especially during the 1990s, a whole range of fact-based light entertainment programming has emerged on local and international television. Corner (2000) suggests that we may now live in a 'post-documentary' culture. In recent years, the reality game show has come to occupy a place at the forefront.

According to Brenton and Cohen (2003), the first reality game show (of the kind this Yearbook deals with) was *Expedition Robinson* broadcast in Sweden 1997 (based on a concept invented by British Charlie Paerson who sold the idea to a Swedish production company). The U.S. version, broadcast a few years later, was called *Survivor*. In these programmes, 'ordinary' people (though carefully selected by programme-makers) are isolated on an island for months and recorded by surveillance cameras. The participants are underfed and have to endure physical hardships and games in successively reshaping teams, as contestants are gradually evicted, until the last one carries off a large sum of money. Following these programmes was *Big Brother*, the format of which is owned by Endemol Netherlands B.V. and also sold to a range of countries over the world, where local adaptations are usually made. In *Big Brother*, the contestants are locked in a house, recorded by surveillance cameras 24 hours a day for a period of months, and gradually out-voted. Even if only parts of the recordings are edited and shown on television, in many countries all of it can be followed on the Internet and in some countries on digital TV channels. Several variants of *Survivor* and *Big Brother* have followed, for example *Temptation Island*, where married people come single to an island to test their fidelity to their partners at home (and without winning prices), as well as 'realities' especially for young people, such as *Popstars*, which started in the U.K. in 2000 and where young people compete to compose a pop music group. In the past few years, programmes have emerged in which the game, although still a competition, has more features of performance and learning, such as singing or taking dancing or singing lessons. The audience has become increasingly involved in these reality shows, as they are allowed to out-vote contestants by telephone, sending SMS messages to the TV screen, etc. An important fact is also that the formats are just as likely to have originated in Europe as in the U.S.

However, even if the surveillance cameras contribute to viewers' feelings of authenticity and trustworthiness, nothing is 'real' in these programmes besides the fact that there are no actors and no ordinary scripts. In other respects, the setting is constructed and heavily staged by the programme-makers.

The term 'reality TV' has previously been used for many other kinds of entertainment or factual-entertaining programmes in which the audience participates, for example, *Real World* on MTV from the mid-90s, and programmes based on footage of emergency service personnel (cops, ambulance drivers, doctors, etc.), which became a regular fixture in primetime schedules in the 1990s. The U.S. programme *Cops* (cops on the beat, staking out suspects, and making busts) is one such example. Another type of 'reality show' includes the many candid talk shows from the 1980s and 1990s. There are also several forerunners to 'reality TV', such as – to continue examples from the U.S., although there are many similar examples from other countries – *America's Funniest Home Videos*, which debuted in 1990 and captured, among other things, parents' recordings – often with the intent of showing comic aspects – of their tumbling toddlers and costumed cocker spaniels for the chance of winning US$ 10,000; *America's Most Wanted*, dating back to 1988 (presenting information about fugitives and re-enactments of their crimes, with the intention of tracking down the suspects); and docu-soaps of different kinds, for example, serials filming people's everyday life at home (such as *An American Family* in 1973). Other even earlier examples of programmes showing 'people being themselves' are *Wanted* from 1955 (which outlined the crimes of fugitives and interviewed their relatives and law enforcement officers working on the cases) and *Candid Camera*, which started in 1948 (where people's behaviour, often in staged comic situations, is recorded without their knowledge) and which also had a predecessor, *Candid Microphone*, on the radio in 1947. Over the years, there has, in addition, been a number of quiz shows in radio and TV, and many other game shows of different kinds (Rowen 2000, Brenton & Cohen 2003, Giles 2003, Holmes & Jermyn 2004).

With the popularity of the more recent entertainment reality TV programmes or reality game shows in the changing media landscape, many researchers have tried to define these hybrid programmes and position them in relation to their forerunners, as well as in relation to the soap opera/fictional drama and the documentary. There is, thus, much literature trying to disentangle the hybrids of 'infotainment', 'faction', 'real crime' shows, 'docu-dramas', 'docu-shows', 'docu-soaps', 'reality game shows', 'reality TV', etc. Holmes and Jermyn (2004) find, however, that producing a particular definition of reality TV, or even of the recent global 'event' formats, such as *Big Brother*, *Popstars* and *Survivor*, is perhaps too complex, considering the many hybrid guises over time. It is also worth noting, they say, that while early attempts to define reality TV emphasized the importance of a focus on 'real life' and 'real people', the more recent proliferation of reality TV has witnessed a move away from an attempt to 'capture' 'a life lived' towards the televisual arenas of formatted environments characterized more by display and performance. There is also an increasing focus not simply on 'ordinary' people, but also on celebrities. Perhaps, then, the authors conclude, it is possible to suggest that what unites the range of programming described as reality TV is primarily its discursive, visual and technological *claim* to 'the real'. It is perhaps not so much a shift in television programming as a promotional marketing tool.

Public broadcasters, on their part, often avoid specific definitions of these genres. Even programmes not found as factual, but mainly as entertainment by the audience, are classified as factual or documentary by the networks, which sometimes have to live up to public service quotas on factual programming. Or broadcasters use such terms as 'popular documentary', 'factual entertainment', 'reality formats', 'formatted reality', and the like (Hill 2004a, 2004b). Talking specifically of *Big Brother*, Jane Roscoe

(2004), who conducted interviews with the programme-makers of the Australian version, found that they prefer to call the programme a 'real-life soap', a smaller drama of everyday life. They also try to emulate the pace and grammar of the soap opera (when editing all hours of footage into what will be sent in the prime time slot). According to these programme-makers, then, *Big Brother* has a far stronger relationship to the soap opera than to the documentary or game show.

There are many reasons for the emergence of factual entertainment and of the new more extreme reality TV formats or reality game shows. Relative to a professional soap opera, *telenovela* or drama serial, reality TV is, although often costly, nevertheless cheaper to produce. Broadcasters have to struggle with an increasing competition for the audience in the deregulated international multi-channel landscape – and the recent reality formats reach many younger viewers (also because reality TV feeds several other programmes in the schedule with their contents). In interplay with new information and communication technology, reality TV is, as well, increasingly based on light cam recorders and digital technology, and exists in a symbiosis with the tabloid press and Internet, thus creating a multimedia platform and experience.

According to CanWest Global Communications Corp. in Canada, reality TV programmes such as *Survivor*, *The Bachelor* and *Queer Eye for the Straight Guy* have given advertisers a means to reach the young, affluent viewers they covet. An analysis covering the period September 15, 2003, to February 15, 2004, showed that eight of prime-time TV's top ten rated programmes in Canada were reality shows, led by *Survivor*, *American Idol* and *My Big Fat Obnoxious Fiancé*. Rick Lewchuk, CTV's senior vice-president of programme planning, said producing unscripted reality TV typically costs less than $ 500,000 an episode, much less than traditional scripted dramas. However, because repeats do not typically appeal to viewers, reality TV will probably change in coming seasons, for example, towards more reality shows with sports, romantic and makeover themes. It is also possible that reality shows will become more closely tied to advertising, with participants wearing special branded clothes, slaking their thirst with special branded drinks, and hunting treasures in the form of special branded products (Westhead 2004).

To keep and attract viewers and advertisers, the limits must therefore be continuously pushed, the boundaries between the public and the private more blurred, and new taboos broken. Representatives of the U.S.-owned and U.K.-based satellite channel Kanal 5 in Sweden say, in an interview related to the reality TV series *Extreme Makeover* (where people can apply for and undergo plastic surgery), that the channel's whole mission or business concept is the following: 'Kanal 5 is a company aimed at sales of advertising time on television and marketing of television programmes. By means of a programme output that clearly addresses modern people who are open-minded, we create a platform for effective communication for advertisers in Sweden.' That the channel addresses young people is reflected not least in the fact that the price advertisers pay for viewers over 44 years of age is the lowest (Granstrand & Berge 2004).

As Roscoe (2004) summarizes, then, hybrid formats such as *Big Brother* are rather a response to changes in international broadcasting contexts in which it is increasingly difficult to find sufficient numbers of drama productions, and where traditional documentary formats have found it increasingly difficult to capture audience attention in the competition among channels. The reality TV programmes can also be understood as a more general response to first-person media (cf., Internet and computer games) and to a changing media culture. Many of these new formats blur the conventional boundaries between fact and fiction, drama and documentary and between the audience and the text. They make the most of media convergence, spanning a number of media platforms (telephone, Internet, print media, radio and television), and they provide a central role for the viewer with more opportunities for interactivity. Holmes and Jermyn (2004) add that precisely the new recent reality TV formats are useful for export, as they can be combined with local production, which has a greater chance of success with domestic audiences. The accelerated importance of the format is clearly also shaped by a desire among programme-makers to minimize the risk of economic failures.

The recent reality TV formats have been subject to a heated public debate. At the same time, one must remember that the marketing of the programmes largely builds on a situation of synergy with the press. Public debate and critique must be started ('Will there be sex?' 'This is bullying television!' 'This is trash!' etc.). The best scenario for programme-makers is when the tabloid press is raging on the placards, which is why much of the debate is probably staged, as well (Furhammar 2004). The print media also play a crucial role in the construction of fame for the contestants.

In spite of much public debate, extremely little research attention has been paid to the difference between recent reality TV programmes, their relations to the changing media landscape, and why large parts of the audiences are interested in these programmes.

Because research, to date, has not told us why reality TV is so popular with parts of the audience, there are speculations: For the contestants there is the desire to gain fame and often money, to be someone, maybe coupled with an exhibitionistic vein. Viewers appreciate that the boundaries between the private and public spheres are crossed and blurred, that they can identify or para-socially interact with people who 'look like us'. Recording participants in intimate detail in real time arouses curiosity and contributes to a sense of 'liveness' and nearness. Possibilities of more interacting than usual (both via the Internet, telephone, etc., directly with the programme and in fan communities on the Internet) give a feeling of influencing the show (even if this interactivity has hardly changed the power relations between programme-makers and the audience). As Mark Andrejevic (2004) says: '[…] the promise of reality TV is not that of access to unmediated reality […] so much as it is a promise of access to reality of mediation […] The hallmark of the reality TV commodity is its translucency […] the behind-scenes feature.' (p. 215) A single, separate study from the U.K. conducted by Annette Hill (cited in

Brenton & Cohen 2003) shows that the majority of the British audience of *Big Brother* enjoyed seeing people live without modern comforts doing everyday things, witnessing group conflict, seeing the contestants visit the diary room and attempting the arbitrary and at times distinctly silly tasks set up by the producers. One third also said they enjoyed indulging their voyeuristic appetites. However, the viewers did not believe they were seeing 'real behaviour' but thought that contestants 'overacted for the camera' and part of the appeal of the reality TV experience was waiting for the mask to slip, in moments of stress and conflict, revealing the concealed 'true self' or 'real face' of a contestant.

References

Andrejevic, Mark (2004) *Reality TV. The Work of Being Watched*. Lanham, Boulder, New York, Toronto & Oxford: Rowman & Littlefield Publishers, Inc.

Brenton, Sam & Reuben Cohen (2003) *Shooting People. Adventures in Reality TV*. London & New York: Verso

Corner, John (2000) 'Documentary in a Post-Documentary Culture? A Note on Forms and their Functions', http://www.lboro.ac.uk/research/changing.media/John%20Corner%20paper.htm (retrieved January 2004)

Furhammar, Leif (2004) 'Demokrati à la 'Expedition Robinson' (Democracy à la 'Expedition Robinson')', *Dagens Nyheter*, 15 September, p. 21 (in Swedish)

Giles, David (2003) *Media Psychology*. Mahwah, NJ & London: Lawrence Erlbaum Associates

Granstrand, Lasse & Elin Berge (2004) 'Kanal 5 ser dig (Channel 5 Is Watching You)', *Dagens Nyheter. Sunday* 26 September, pp. 6-13 (in Swedish)

Hill, Annette (2004a) Seminar on British Factual Television at Stockholm University, Department of Journalism, Media and Communication, 8 September

Hill, Annette (2004b) *Reality TV: Audiences and Popular Factual Television*. London & New York: Routledge

Holmes, Su & Deborah Jermyn (2004) 'Introduction: Understanding Reality TV', in Su Holmes & Deborah Jermyn (eds.) *Understanding Reality Television*. London & New York: Routledge, pp. 1-32

Roscoe, Jane (2004) '*Big Brother* Australia. Performing the 'real' twenty-four-seven', in Robert C. Allen & Annette Hill *The Television Studies Reader*. London & New York: Routledge, pp. 311-321

Rowen, Beth (2000) 'History of Reality TV. 'Survivor II' and 'Temptation Island' lead the reality show pack', *Infoplease.com*, 21 July (http://www.infoplease.com – retrieved in July 2004)

Westhead, Rick (2004) 'Reality TV here to stay, study says', *Toronto Star*, 24 June (http://www.thestar.com – retrieved in September 2004)

showed no evidence of empathy for the participants voted off the show – instead the opposite.

Robyn Quin finds that the issue of projection, and the ways in which Australian girls used the soap opera *Beverly Hills 90210* to air and test their 'solutions' to virtual but potential problems in their own lives, has a corollary in girls' responses to reality television today. That is, the key to understanding teenage girls' pleasure in reality TV programmes seems to revolve around their interest in 'relationship-watching'. The author refers to on-going Australian research which shows that females in the 10- to 17-year-old demographic group are not only a signifi-cant fan group for (the Australian version of) *Big Brother* but major users of the web sites supporting the programme. It seems that reality programmes such as *Big Brother* create a space in which emotions, interpersonal relations and sexu-ality are scrutinized and examined. The kind of reversal of public and private life exhibited in *Big Brother* allows traditional expectations and assumptions to be questioned and problematized. The girls in another study say that what they find engaging in *Big Brother* is searching for ways to be themselves and still be ac-ceptable to their group – thus, viewing is about how you perform yourself. The programme is used by the girls to observe and analyse the behaviour of others, to check out what works and what does not, and to try to ascertain what sorts of behaviours bring the rewards they are seeking. *Big Brother* offers viewers a sort of 'relationship laboratory', where friendships, passions and feuds can be observed and contemplated, judged and criticized.

Besides talking with young people about soap operas, *Dorothy Hobson* inter-viewed British girls within the 13- to 18-year-old range about reality TV. These girls, however, were not particularly enamoured with reality TV, although they watched these programmes in order to be acquainted with them and obtain the cultural capital this knowledge represents. *Big Brother* and *Wife Swap* were cited as their favourites. The same pattern as for soap operas emerged for reality TV: Young people watch programmes to which they feel they can relate. Reality TV was, e.g., praised for telling stories that 'you can relate to in real life'. The girls chose to watch such elements that had a bearing on their youth, position in the family, etc. For example, they appreciated the role of the female participants in the reality series *Wife Swap* but saw them as mothers rather than wives as de-fined by the programme.

In Hong Kong, television stations have tried to copy the reality genre and produce their own local series without success – the Chinese participants have been shy of presenting themselves 'naturally' in front of the camera and the ef-fect was not 'real' enough. Therefore, imported U.S. reality series recently gained a foothold in Hong Kong particularly among middle-class youth, after simultane-ous bilingual broadcasting and Chinese subtitles were launched. *Alice Y. L. Lee* says that young people are particularly interested in foreign reality TV, here called 'true man shows', because they find themselves in an age full of curiosity about how normal people like themselves act under real, special circumstances. Moreo-ver, the reality TV programmes stimulate excitement. However, according to one study, young people in Hong Kong took the 'reality' for granted and were not critical about how 'real' the reality show was. In fact, they did not seriously think about this issue. Therefore media literacy training about reality TV is at least as important as training about drama serials, the author underlines. The media lit-eracy initiatives so far have been successful – the students who received such training are more critical about the 'reality' of these programmes than is the young audience in general. While still enjoying reality TV, they have also, for example, raised their concern about the promotion of the worst aspects of human behaviour in reality TV, and revealed that certain programmes strongly promote materialistic living styles and consumerism.

Other authors in the Yearbook focus specifically on reality TV. As has emerged, not only fictional serials but also reality TV differ between cultures. *María Dolores Souza* writes in her article *Chilean Tweens and Reality Shows*, that in Chile sex scenes and many other features of reality TV were important topics of public debate. However, Chilean television – as opposed to Argentinean and Brazilian TV – showed self-regulated products not at odds with Chilean society. There was, for example, no nudity or explicit sex scenes to see. Also, reality TV in Chile is mostly about taking lessons in song, dance, acting and other types of performances.

The author presents research on 'tweens', who also are salient in Chile, a rising social segment of children ages 8 to 13, who display the attitudes and behaviour one would expect of older children, but who are still quite young, 'in between' childhood and adolescence. Tweens want to see TV programmes targeted at older people, including adults, and have a special interest in the lives and whereabouts of young people on the screen. They want to find out the ways the characters interact with each other, handle their love and sex lives, and solve their problems. In this context, reality TV and Latin American *telenovelas* are the tweens' favourite programmes. The motives for Chilean tweens to watch reality TV are, first, that they want entertainment and excitement, associated with suspense and curiosity. Second, they identify with young people in the reality series – tweens look forward to adolescent experiences. Besides, there is a learning process. For some children reality TV is a way to 'teach' parents and other adults about the life of young people, at the same time as tweens want to learn social behaviour themselves. Finally, reality TV is instrumental to socialization: The reality programmes become a subject of conversation, helping tweens to exchange opinions, compare attitudes and integrate themselves in the peer group.

Even if Chilean tweens like watching reality TV and try to do so against parental rules, they are not uncritical of the programmes. For example, they perceive that some reality programmes induce conflicts among young participants so as to highlight drama, and show emotionality to its limit. The tweens feel sorry for participants in tears and distress, and resent the television industry, which, in their view, uses these instruments for getting higher ratings. However, tweens also criticize the way television generally (apart from reality TV) reflects people's lives. One objection refers to the black and white view of reality on the screen: the utterly negative view (poor people, crime and distress) and the utterly positive one (beautiful and popular people with shallow talk). Tweens want instead to experience a sense of proximity, programmes with nuances, reflecting real social life, real people and a real country. Another objection to television is the perceived general absence of youngsters on the screen and, specifically, the absence of average children and young people. Therefore, reality TV represents an alternative of seeing ordinary young people. Even though reality programmes have an entertainment purpose, they are complex, contain a certain reflection of everyday life, present contestants with diverse social backgrounds, and show that the search for success also means efforts, conflicts and rejection. Thus, reality programmes came to fill a gap that tweens had already identified on Chilean television, the author concludes.

Do young viewers 'learn' from watching reality TV programmes? *Annette Hill* considers in her article *The Idea of Learning: Young Viewers of Reality TV in the U.K.* the role of information in 11- to 18-year-olds' experiences of popular factual television in the U.K., such as *Popstars, Pop Idol, Big Brother* and police chase programmes. When asked, the majority of young viewers dismiss the idea of 'learning' from such programmes, because they perceive them as entertainment. Young viewers often associate learning with work, and work with school. However, they do differentiate between what the author calls informal and formal learning regarding television programmes. Formal learning is associated with primary features of a programme, whereas informal learning is more associated with secondary features – that is, what comes first is entertainment, and any secondary pleasures may include the possibility of learning, but are optional extras. For young viewers, if a television programme advertises itself as 'a learning programme' then it loses its attraction and becomes a teacher rather than an entertainer. Despite having a natural aversion to 'learning programmes', some young viewers are open to the idea of *learning about life and about people* as a by-product of watching an entertaining reality programme. For young people, watching the way others behave in social situations is potentially informative because they are still forming their own understanding of socially acceptable and unacceptable behaviour – and in this context reality TV deals with something that matters to them and that they can relate to. The research findings also suggest, according to the author, that young viewers are engaged in critical viewing practices when watching reality TV, not least because they might learn not to value learning from particular reality programmes.

Big Brother and its imitations have not met with success in France *François Jost* says in his article *Reality TV – The Mechanisms of a Success*. As this has instead been the case of *Star Academy*, the author theorizes in particular about why this reality serial has succeeded. *Star Academy* is based on the criticism that *Big Brother* shows idle young people, who become famous without doing anything. For television it is important to show the intimate details of the programme participants – but how can that be done, without giving viewers the feeling that it is the main part of the programme? Instead of everyday life being in the foreground and the games taking second place, as in *Big Brother*, being on television to demonstrate what one knows and learns is the first purpose of *Star Academy* and the invasion into private life is 'simply' the fallout of life in a boarding school. In this way, the entire family may also meet around the programme: By offering an image of an unreal, reconciled school, *Star Academy* gathers children who find their dream of a school where they would learn only what they like. By giving an image of rigour, the programme responds to the criticisms that parents often formulate concerning the laxness of current schools.

Another reason for reality TV's success is, according to the author's hypothesis, that the position of the TV viewer is sadistic, if sadism is seen as a demonstration of power against another person taken as object. The viewer takes a certain pleasure in contrasting the comfort of his/her own situation with the misfortune of others on the screen. And reality TV viewers in France have often voted against the explicit happiness of the candidates, making choices corresponding to what is expected from television narratives in general. This relation of domination over the person on the screen by the TV viewer is also connected to the fact that the contestants are human beings who look like us, with their failings and anguishes. Because reality TV glorifies the most everyday: getting up, dressing, eating and seducing, the viewers become the heroes of everyday life, and the mediocrity of the intimate behaviours shown also reassures the viewer of her/his own capacity. In this context the author refers to the device of reality TV to abolish the separation between what Goffman calls the 'front stage', where social representation takes place with actors and public, and the 'back stage', where the actors escape the glances of the public. If cameras are everywhere, even the toilet becomes a front stage. *Star Academy* is based on the idea that it is necessary to show all of what is usually hidden, something that ensures authenticity. What is to be avoided in society and in the usual front stage performance on television becomes here the standard. By putting the back stage in the foreground, reality TV legitimizes 'regressive' behaviour, as well, which partially explains the pleasure the young audience experiences. While children are sometimes excluded from the social scene by parents because of the possible impropriety of their behaviour, reality TV proposes a world just like the one in which they live in the back stage.

In Cyprus, reality programmes were moved to a later hour of transmission (10 p.m.), because the Federation of Parents' Associations lobbied against the shows in the House of Representatives, saying that these serials were demoralizing their children. Referring to Kellner, the Cypriot authors *Nayia Roussou* and *Michaella Buck* suppose in their article *Reality Shows in Cyprus: New Media "Fallout"?* that the way we perceive people is more and more mediated by media images, explaining why looks, image and style are becoming increasingly fundamental constituents of social identities, shaping how people are publicly viewed and defined. How, then, is the social identity of the younger generation affected by reality shows, where individual competition is raised to the level of adversity and the ethos of fair play is turned into a Darwinian struggle for the survival of the fittest in a game? Not only is reality TV in Cyprus extremely popular among young viewers, who, besides seeking entertainment, are insecure about social acceptance and want to learn rules of inclusion and exclusion in real life, but young Cypriots are also eager to participate in reality programmes.

Despite the lack of research, the authors find some preliminary support that looks, image and style are taking a meaningful place in the concepts and value systems of both contestants in reality TV and its young viewers. Among other things, the article portrays three contestants, a 19-year-old 'winner' (in *Super Idol*), a 24-year-old 'loser' (in *Popstars*) and a 20-year-old 'quitter' (in the middle of *The*

Bar). These contestants believe that the winner does not need to be the best, but needs to be attractive to the viewers. They also witness that the voting-out procedure was a traumatic experience, as were the oppressive behaviour of the media professionals/organizers, and the intrigue and bad language in the show. However, in the authors' opinion, the enormous appeal of reality series is found exactly in the out-voting process – the worse for the contestants, the better for the audience – as reality TV plays on our own fear of rejection and humiliation. Watching how others have to confront this fear, how they scramble to fit into a group and find their role and acceptance, makes us cringe, but on the other side brings us pleasure.

In South Africa, *Big Brother* is subjected to an age restriction (16+) and most of the controversial behaviour occurs outside 'open time' (two hours for the general public on the paid channel M-Net). *Nathalie Hyde-Clarke* says in her article *"But It's Not Real": South African Youth's Perceptions of Reality TV* than in spite of this, many younger people admit to watching *Big Brother*, and even if the age restriction is adhered to among some families, many are aware of the 'reality' events due to the public debate. Over time, M-Net has tried to increase audience figures and advertising sales by introducing more sex. After *Big Brother 1* and *Big Brother 2*, also heavily criticized for being racist, *Big Brother Africa* was transmitted to more than 40 countries, in some places on free-to-air channels for the general audience, which is why Malawi cancelled the show due to its 'immorality'.

The author reports on 16- to 19-year-olds' responses to some questions about reality TV and *Big Brother* in South Africa. The group was taking Media Studies and therefore probably aware of conditions of media production. More than half of these respondents found that there is little real about reality TV but that the scenarios are staged and constructed, thus manipulating the behaviour of the contestants. Many students also felt that the debate itself about *Big Brother* is staged so as to attract viewers. In addition, most respondents found that the contestants are not representative of South African society. Nevertheless, the students appreciated the shows for their entertainment value. Their comments also provided an insight into how young people may see reality TV as a reflection of attitudes and behaviour in society, and pointed to a generally cynical perception that the society may be represented in shows such as *Big Brother*. The respondents were displaying a 'take it or leave it' attitude, seemingly accepting such media content or resigning themselves to the fact that it is unavoidable in the world today. The author discusses the risk that young viewers may view the programme participants as role models or protagonists, and that this kind of reality TV may contribute to counteracting social improvement in societies in transition. Reality TV based on local content is attractive and offers an alternative to the largely stereotypical world of entertainment media imported mainly from the U.S. However, as with a large number of developing countries there is a genuine need for television content to transmit meaningful messages to youth, and the barrier between what is real and what is manipulated should be clearly defined for the youth in South Africa, the author says.

First and Second Generation Formatted Reality

Lorenzo Vilches

Reality, or formatted reality, programmes have not only become irreplaceable products in many television channels' programming, but also the most sustained successes, along with fiction series and football, and have caused major changes in the programming structures of both general interest and specialized television in the public and private sectors. The core importance of "reality" lies in its ability to revolutionize the relationships with its viewers, with other programmes and with the media and cultural environment.

According to Eurodata, which analysed programming in 72 countries with a total of 600 million viewers, the entertainment format of reality television accounted for 39 per cent of the highest audience ratings in Western Europe in 2003, compared to 35 per cent in 2000. Programmes such as *Big Brother* (Gran Hermano, in Spanish), *Pop Idol* (the most successful version in Spain being Operación Triunfo) and *Survivor* are now considered international television classics.

The publicity of reality TV highlights this format's capacity for change, as it was first developed as container programmes and talk shows in the 1980s. The programmes present situations of change in citizens' daily lives – a change in physical appearance, job or sexual partner. Today, producers present reality TV as an escape hatch in a world turned in on itself due to fear of terrorism, loss of employment, solitude and all types of nonconformity, including that of one's own body. In response to all this, television says it offers a change of life. (And the changes undergone by people in these reality programmes may be irreversible.) Examples of such "change of life" programmes are given by Gloria Saló in the magazine *Guion actualidad* (http://antalya.uab.es/guionactualidad):

> Reality makeover shows, which focus on improving participants' lifestyles and which brought into fashion the American format *Queer Eye for the Straight Guy*, in which a group of five gay men transform a young heterosexual man's lifestyle, continue to present new challenges. Among them are ideas like the Japanese *Ready to Date*, a mixture of dating and makeover, in which you can find a partner as well as improve your appearance; *Ten Years Younger*, in which with the help of a small facelift you can look like you did ten years ago; *Home Delivery*, in which individuals are physically and emotionally transformed; and *The Swan*, in which 60 women are transformed from ugly ducklings into swans. Relationship problems with the family, partner or colleagues have also been considered in programmes such as *Marry Me... Again!*, in which the aim is to give a couple with problems a second chance with a new surprise wedding; *Family Dinner*, which brings together family members to talk about their differences; *Five Things I Hate About You*, which gives family and friends the opportunity to help resolve couples' differences; or *Moving On* in which a specialist in self-help books analyses the problems and attempts to

provide solutions. The exchange of roles and "put yourself in my place" situations have been particularly fertile ground since the appearance of the English show *Wife Swap*, in which two mothers with very different lifestyles change places for a week. In *My Life in the Real World*, a politician becomes a housewife and lives with a limited budget, work and obligations that are far removed from his normal daily life, and which are those of a typical voter. In *Poor Little Rich Girls* three upper-class adolescents exchange their lives with three middle-class girls.

The latest trend in recent successful reality programmes has taken the form of key concepts such as the "twist", by which rules are created to make candidates confused, something that appears to be popular with viewers. The viewers' identification with the television participants continues its unstoppable progress. This is what happened in the United States, for example with Fox's *My Big Fat Obnoxious Fiancé*, which received 10 million viewers last season.

Another spectacular impact is due to the fact that television channels spread small fragments of the reality shows throughout the day like an oil stain. This means that a channel's entire programming is determined by the fortunes of a single programme (the reality show), which in theory should not last for more than two or three scheduled hours. Children have no alternative but to consume the snippets of the reality show broadcast during the daytime. Teenagers who had stopped watching television because of a lack of exciting programmes have been enticed back thanks to this format, because reality TV seemingly teaches them about life and relationships.

Adult programming schedules are saturated with celebrity gossip programmes, including a great deal of television's self-referential discussions. Television presenters take centre stage with those appearing in the reality shows. Then these programmes, made into clip format, become fodder for other programmes, and so on. In the first generation of reality shows, such as *¿Quién sabe dónde?* (Who Knows Where?), *La confesión* (The Confession), *Psyshow*, etc., the television presenter had a minor role. The central figure was the victim or villain who came to the studio to tell of his or her misfortune or misdeeds. In the second generation of reality shows, television professionals have taken centre stage and compete with competitors, becoming enemies or allies of some of them against others. Because of this, participants freely insult – or, on the contrary, cry on the shoulder of – the presenter of the programme once they have emerged from their confinement, i.e., when they have been evicted by public vote. As life in reality shows does not end with the programme, television professionals have had personal and emotional relationships with those taking part in their programmes, off the set.

The audience also participates extensively in reality shows. In the first generation formats, the audience was part of the set, seated and immobile in the studio chairs. Now it participates directly, voting against competitors by means of a telephone call system, which is the second major source of profits for television companies, after sales of advertising and merchandising.

The other media and the cultural environment have not remained impassive to all this. While serious newspapers and popular magazines have discovered that formatted reality programmes are an inexhaustible source of sales and therefore publish much information about them, writers and intellectuals put forward strident condemnations of reality shows on the same pages. However, as they are later invited to join in on discussions to talk about the subject, journalists, writers, sociologists and even philosophers end up tangled in the great reality cobweb. Politicians have also taken advantage of this format as a platform for their message. Among them is Alvaro Uribe, the president of Colombia, who requested a vote in favour of the national referendum, while sitting with the *Big Brother* housemates in 2003.

It used to be said that television contributes to social effects. However, this has changed radically. Television has become the cause of social, political and human events.

Several authors touch upon the commercial objective of most television channels to profit from advertising sales, which is why they – aiming at attracting as large audiences as possible – press the sensational and negative emotional elements of the reality TV series to the utmost and make the programmes increasingly 'evil'. An example from Nigeria shows that advertising may be interwoven with the programme contents in a more direct way. This is documented by *Eno Akpabio* in the article *Reactions of Nigerian Youths to the Reality Television Show Gulder Ultimate Search*. The country's first reality show was *Gulder Ultimate Search* aired in 2004 on several stations. During several weeks, the contestants – gradually out-voted – were living at a 'primal level of humankind' with the barest of comforts. They were subjected to many physical exercises at the same time as they were underfed, and their prime goal was to find a treasure on the island where they were isolated. The treasure, it turned out, was a bottle of Gulder beer. The whole contest was used to reposition and relaunch one of Nigeria's beers, which had started to lose its market share.

Gulder Ultimate Search elicited intense emotions from the respondents between 21 and 30 years of age in the researcher's study, and identification with the contestants in the programme occurred. The respondents also identified the various challenges facing the contestants as reflecting ups and downs in their own lives, and there was a consensus in the study that with determination and will power one can overcome obstacles to achieving ones' goals and ambitions. No respondent reacted negatively to the evictions; nor did any of the respondents see this as a blow to their goals and ambitions. They all uniformly focused on the motivation to succeed. The respondents' conscious attitude towards the beer brand remained unchanged (at least in the short term), but the author stresses that advertisers' expectation is creation of awareness and not measurable attitude change. Because the series ended up motivating these young Nigerian respondents to believe in themselves and more than before to achieve their goals and aspirations in life, there is a world of purposes to which reality TV programmes can be put from the purview of cultural norms, the author concludes and continues: Through selective presentation and tendentious emphasis on certain themes, the mass media are able to get impressionable members of society to pattern their lives after such presentation. The functionality of reality TV shows in tackling social ills and motivating young people needs further exploration in light of the effectiveness of *Gulder Ultimate Search* in achieving audience identification with the contestants and their challenges.

An example of entertainment-education

The functionality of media in tackling social ills and motivating young people is what is aimed at in many countries in particularly Africa, Asia and Latin America, where producers use the format (not yet of recent kinds of 'reality TV' mentioned above but) of radio and TV drama, soap operas, *telenovelas*, docu-soaps and other entertaining genres for *education*, that is, in order to raise debate and contribute to solving health and other problems in society. Within primarily non-formal education, the use of entertainment-education (EE) in an integrated manner and often in the form of multimedia initiatives has been growing significantly over the past decade, not least addressing health-related issues such as HIV/AIDS. Thomas Tufte (2004) writes that the ideal communicative scenario in this respect is 'communication for social change', i.e., to deal with the challenge of providing an information and dialogue-rich enabling environment where the media contents contribute to empowering the audiences in facing health-related and other social issues and fighting them in everyday life.

This book includes one example of such an entertainment-education series, seen from two different perspectives. The controversial and most watched South African youth-oriented drama series, *Yizo Yizo* ('This is it', 'This is how things are'), was first aired on the public educational channel in 1999. *Yizo Yizo* is, thus, *not* reality TV in the sense it has been treated here, but a drama series aimed at reflecting, and based on, reality – the first drama series in the country showing the lives of ordinary Black South Africans living in townships, a topic otherwise reserved for news and documentary series. The series, and multimedia strategy, deals with the impact of socio-economic factors upon children's experiences of formal schooling, including violence, sexual harassment and rape, and drug abuse. The TV programmes were intended to reveal the depth and complexity of the crisis facing South African schools, to model a process of action to create and sustain a culture of learning and teaching, and to stimulate discussion of key educational issues. Thus, the programme uses popular television formats to connect social issues to the everyday life-contexts of ordinary people – a distinctive approach to media citizenship that challenges the conceptualizations developed in the 'north' (Barnett 2002).

John Gultig writes in his article *"This is it": South African Youth's Reading of YizoYizo 2* about the second part of *YizoYizo* aired in 2001 (the third part was aired in 2004). *YizoYizo 2's* aim was to *inform* viewers of some of the critical problems facing youth and schooling in South Africa, *raise debate* about possible solutions and *social action* to change these conditions. Unlike many other educational dramas, *YizoYizo* producers decided that the veil had to be ripped off rather rudely: The drama had to be 'in your face' and controversial if it was to raise debate in the constituencies where producers felt debate was necessary.

Many of the issues *YizoYizo* set out to tackle are issues that communities are loath to talk about: rape, sex between teachers and learners, rampant drug use, the glamour of gangs and crime. *YizoYizo's* challenge was to find a way in which these things could be revealed as they were, in all their ugliness, while still sending out a message of hope and change. *YizoYizo 1* and *2* certainly did raise public debate in all forums and was in other media accused of being too sexually explicit, of being culturally insensitive, of glorifying gangsterism and violence, and of encouraging copycat behaviour. But the findings of the evaluation suggest a different picture of *YizoYizo's* impact on young viewers. They suggest that young people aged 13 to 20 – the sample mostly consisting of young Africans in township schools – read the series at an intense emotional level and in a far more nuanced and discerning way than their parents or the media, the author says. While the latter found, for example, the verbal and body language offensive and the renditions of sex too explicit, South African youth demonstrated a high level of engagement and identification with *YizoYizo* characters and a sophisticated understanding of the plot and the messages it carries. They were able to interpret the content of the series in an allegorical sense. Ultimately, the over-riding message they took from *YizoYizo 2* was that of redemption and inspiration.

René Smith agrees in her article *YizoYizo: This Is It? A Critical Analysis of a Reality-based Drama Series* that the series can be defined as entertainment-education in that it is constituted by messages, purposively designed to entertain and educate, in order to increase audience members' knowledge of an educational issue, create favourable attitudes, and change overt behaviour. However, her discursive analysis highlights the contradictions of representing the *real* by questioning the imperative of including graphic images in representing real life experiences. The author finds that while the urgent need to acknowledge the presence of violence and HIV/AIDS in the daily lives of all South Africans is commendable, the series' ability to deal with violence against women and HIV/AIDS in a sustained manner is questionable. For example, while the series aims to create dialogue about these very real challenges, it also uses violence for dramatic intent. Moreover, there are many elements that reaffirm gendered stereotypes perpetuated by the dominant patriarchal culture and that do not contribute constructively to the development of the story. The author contends that the series falls short of presenting a sustained approach to dealing with and offering solutions to the very real challenges of living with HIV/AIDS and the threat of harassment as a form of violence against women. The meaning of the title of the series, *YizoYizo* ('This is it') alludes to the programme's relation to 'reality' or real life depictions of, e.g., violence and gender relations. The contradictions of having a dramatic text reflect a gritty reality – of fusing factual and fictional – allows the series to assume an 'authoritative perspective'. *YizoYizo* exists in a very real context of alarming national crime statistics, a HIV/AIDS pandemic and increasing threat of violence against women, amongst others. Within the context of South Africa, more responsibility and specific care are required, and a concerted effort should be made in addressing the realities of HIV/AIDS and gender-based violence, the author says.

In conclusion

As the reader of this introduction can see, the research findings presented by the authors in the book show that the ways young people make meaning from television programmes depend on a complex of factors: the specific programme in question and in which culture it is produced and broadcast, the child's or young person's age, gender, socio-cultural background, previous experiences, personal needs and interests, and the specific reception context. Because the findings emanate from case studies, they must all be interpreted in their respective connected whole. Therefore, the exposition above is a résumé in itself, and it is hardly possible to summarize or generalize the results further.

However, some very general common traits in the findings are:

The studies confirm that many young people in many countries do watch soap operas, *telenovelas*, drama serials and reality TV, often from an early age. Many of these programmes are highly popular both among adolescents and younger children.

Even if everyone makes something different out of the programmes studied, there are, simultaneously, similarities in that the soap operas, *telenovelas* and drama serials have a range of subjectively perceived *entertaining, informative* and *social functions* for children and youths:

Most authors underline the facts that young people get pleasure, excitement, and sometimes laughter from viewing these fictional serials, and that they learn, get ideas and advice about, and insight into, life and people from them, especially with reference to interpersonal relations and interactions that can be useful now and when getting older. Young people identify (and para-socially interact) with certain characters, situations and values, distance themselves from others, check out how characters' behaviour works, or how they themselves would behave in corresponding situations. They also talk about the serials with others. Therefore, young people are, by watching these TV fictions, working with their social identity and how to cope with their own lives, at present and later on. Some children say that the serials also influence them in other ways.

41

In addition, several authors bring out significant age differences in children's and young people's meaning-making, and there are examples of how gender, family integration and social class reflect different needs and play a role in the interpretation processes. Generally, what young people choose to watch are programmes and elements that relate to their own lives, which is why their readings of the programmes often are deeply rooted in the contexts in which they live.

These overall findings support general results of the few previous studies on young people and soap opera. David Buckingham (1987) seems to be a precursor with such research on the then new BBC serial *EastEnders* in the U.K. Other examples are Marie Gillespie's (1995) study on the Australian series *Neighbours*, also in the U.K., Karen Klitgaard Povlsen's (1995) study on the American series *Beverly Hills 90120* as received in Denmark, Graham McKinley's (1997) study on *Beverly Hills 90120* in the U.S.A., and Dominique Pasquier's (1999) research on *Hélène et les garçons* in France.

Recently, the so-called secondary texts of serials, in particular dedicated Internet sites, have increasingly been taken into researchers' consideration. An example is Will Brooker's (2001) ethnographic analysis of U.S. and British young viewers' use of this television 'overflow' or multimedia convergence related to the U.S. teen drama *Dawson's Creek*. The issue is also touched upon in Glyn Davis' and Kay Dickinson's (2004) anthology *Teen TV*. Such instances are found in this Yearbook, as well, e.g., in the article about Korean drama.

Regarding the recent reality TV programmes and young people, there exists even less research. Interesting, however, is that several authors in the Yearbook find that reality TV in many respects has *entertaining, informative* and *social functions* for children and young people similar to those of soap operas, *telenovelas* and drama serials:

Young viewers find reality TV programmes entertaining and exciting. They also say they learn from these serials, and they satisfy some of their curiosity about life and about people, find in the serials a space where they can analyse the behaviour of more ordinary people like themselves, emotions, interpersonal relations, sexuality, mechanisms of inclusion and exclusion for social acceptance, etc. Young viewers identify greatly with some people on the screen (more due to similarity than a wish to be like them), or see them as friends, but condemn others, check out what works and what does not work for being rewarded, something that is important for young viewers' identity building, i.e., how to be and perform oneself. Reality TV is an important subject of conversation, as well.

How young people make sense of reality TV must, naturally, also be understood in relation to the specific programme, the culture in which it is transmitted, and the whole personal and social context in which the young person receives the programme.

However, reality TV has certain dimensions that soap operas, *telenovelas* and drama serials do not embrace. Reality TV presents all 'back stage' behaviour, i.e., basic, 'dirty', 'mediocre', hesitant and anxiety-ridden everyday behaviour among 'ordinary' people – behaviour and people that are usually excluded from television and hidden or more or less invisible in society. This programme feature may satisfy curiosity and identification even more, may reassure especially young viewers of their own capacity, and motivate them to believe in themselves. In addition, reality TV slightly alters the relation of domination between viewers and persons on the screen. Viewers' power is promoted by reality TV, where viewers may vote against contestants. The Internet, among other media, is often an additional tool for interactivity with the programme (and for rendering a feeling of proximity). In this reversed world, where the public and private spheres, and reality and fantasy, are fused more than in previous TV genres, the media-saturated environment of today appears even more authentic than in soap operas, almost transparent, and is, seemingly, opening itself for the viewers – promising access. Some authors also tell about great numbers of applications for becoming contestants in certain reality TV programmes in certain countries.

Conflicting findings appear in the articles about the degree to which young viewers understand that reality TV is not reality. Conflicting findings also appear as regards the out-voting of contestants in these serials – children and young people in some studies show empathy, but in more studies they do not.

As to the questions put to the Clearinghouse mentioned at the beginning of this introduction, one can, thus, preliminary answer: Yes, in their active and partly critical (partly uncritical) search for knowledge about how to be and to live, for the moment and as (young) adults, children and young people do learn about people and life from soap operas, *telenovelas,* drama serials and reality TV programmes.

How much, and in what directions, the serials influence young people's ideas in the long term is, however, impossible to infer from these research examples, as media influences are heavily interwoven with those of family, peers, school and work, with one's own practices, personal needs and interests, and with the cultural and social environment. More and other kinds of research are needed.

Some authors contributing to the book point out the risks associated with the stereotypes, conflicts, mental oppression and lack of ethics in certain serials. Some authors underline, as well, the need for more television programmes that truly tackle social ills.

The youth-oriented South African drama series *Yizo Yizo* with extremely high audience ratings – aiming at reflecting reality, rudely and toughly, at revealing the depth and complexity of social crises, and at raising debate and action in society – both succeeded and can be criticized, two of the authors demonstrate. However, this entertainment series represents an approach to citizenship and communication for social change that seriously challenges the contents of many soap operas and reality TV programmes invented in richer countries.

References (besides the articles in this Yearbook)

Barnett, Clive (2002) " 'More Than Just TV': Educational Broadcasting and Popular Culture in South Africa", in Cecilia von Feilitzen & Ulla Carlsson (eds.) *Children, Young People and Media Globalisation*. Yearbook 2002 from The UNESCO International Clearinghouse on Children, Youth and Media. Göteborg: Göteborg University, Nordicom, pp. 95-110

Boldeman, Marcus (2004) "TV anklagas för cynism (TV Is Accused of Cynicism)", *Dagens Nyheter*, 10 September, p. 2 (in Swedish)

Brooker, Will (2001) "Living on *Dawson's Creek*: Teen Viewers, Cultural Convergence, and Television Overflow", *International Journal of Cultural Studies* 4 (4), pp. 456-72

Buckingham, David (1987) *Public Secrets: EastEnders and Its Audience*. London: British Film Institute

Croneman, Johan (2004) "Blind leder blind i ny dokutragedi (Blind Leading the Blind in New Docu-tragedy)" *Dagens Nyheter*, 5 September, p. 29 (in Swedish)

Davis, Glyn & Kay Dickinson (eds.) (2004) *Teen TV. Genre, Counsumption, Identity*. London: British Film Institute

von Feilitzen, Cecilia, Leni Filipson, Ingegerd Rydin & Ingela Schyller (1989) *Barn och unga i medieåldern. Fakta i ord och siffror* (Children and Young People in the Media Age. Facts in Words and Figures). Stockholm: Rabén & Sjögrens förlag (in Swedish)

Frey-Vor, Gerlinde & Gerlinde Schumacher (2004) "Kinder und Medien 2003", *Media Perspektiven*, No. 9, pp. 426-440

Furhammar, Leif (2004) "Demokrati à la 'Expedition Robinson' (Democracy à la 'Expedition Robinson')", *Dagens Nyheter*, 15 September, p. 21 (in Swedish)

Gillespie, Marie (1995) *Television, Ethnicity and Cultural Change*. London: Routledge

Goonasekera, Anura (2000) "Introduction", in Anura Goonasekera et al. *Growing Up With TV. Asian Children's Experience*. Singapore: Asian Media Information and Communication Centre (AMIC), pp. 1-11

Herzog, Hertha (1941) "On Borrowed Experience: An Analysis of Listening to Daytime Sketches", *Studies in Philosophy and Social Science* 9 (1)

Herzog, Hertha (1944): "What do we really know about daytime serial listeners?", in Paul F. Lazarsfeld & F. N. Stanton (eds.) *Radio Research 1942-1943*. New York, NY: Duell, Sloan & Pearce, pp. 3-33

Klitgaard Povlsen, Karen (1995) *Beverly Hills 90210 i Danmark (Beverly Hills 90210 in Denmark)*. København: Københavns universitet (in Danish)

Lemish, Dafna (1998) "Fighting Against Television Violence. An Israeli Case Study", in Ulla Carlsson & Cecilia von Feilitzen (eds.) *Children and Media Violence*. Yearbook from the UNESCO International Clearinghouse on Children and Violence on the Screen 1998. Göteborg: Göteborg University, Nordicom, pp. 125-138

Low, Jason & Kevin Durkin (in press 1997) "Children's Television Knowledge as a Source of Learning about Law-enforcement" cited in Kevin Durkin & Jason Low (1998) "Children, Media and Aggression. Current Research in Australia and New Zealand", in Ulla Carlsson & Cecilia von Feilitzen (eds.) *Children and Media Violence*. Yearbook from the UNESCO International Clearinghouse on Children and Violence on the Screen 1998. Göteborg: Göteborg University, Nordicom, pp. 107-124

McKinley, E. Graham (1997) *Beverly Hills 90210. Television, Gender, and Identity*. Philadelphia, PA: University of Pennsylvania, Penn Press

Pasquier, Dominique (1999) *La culture des sentiments. L'expérience télévisuelle des adolescents*. Paris: Editions de la Maison de Sciences de l'Homme

Rydin, Ingegerd (1983) *Växa med tv. Om bild, ljud och ord i barns tänkande* (Growing with Television. On Pictures, Sounds and Words in Children's Thinking). Sveriges Radio, Publik- och programforskningsavdelningen (in Swedish)

Rydin, Ingegerd (2000) "Children's TV Programs on the Global Market", *News from ICCVOS*, The UNESCO International Clearinghouse on Children and Violence on the Screen, Göteborg University, Nordicom, Vol. 4 No. 1, pp. 17-23

Sundholm, Magnus (2004) "Kolla in: världens värsta dokusåpor (Check Up: The World's Worst Docu-soaps). *Aftonbladet*, 3 May (http://www.aftonbladet.se)

Tufte, Thomas (2004) "Entertainment-Education in HIV/AIDS Communication – Beyond Marketing, Towards Empowerment", in Cecilia von Feilitzen & Ulla Carlsson (eds.) *Promote or Protect? Perspectives on Media Literacy and Media Regulations.* Yearbook 2003 from The International Clearinghouse on Children, Youth and Media. Göteborg: Göteborg University, Nordicom, pp. 85-98

Television Viewing among 4- to 12-year-olds in Spain

José Ramón Pérez Ornia

Cartoons and fictional series constitute the main television choices among children between 4 and 12 years of age in Spain, along with a growing consumption of "telereality" programs – both conventional "reality shows" and new "reality TV" programs. The latter have come about thanks to the success of Spain's *Gran Hermano* (Big Brother). On the other hand, viewership of conventional *telenovelas* and long-running soap operas (sometimes called "culebrones" in Spain) as well as docu-soaps that recreate everyday stories involving real people – as though they were documentaries about life today, using the style of television series – show lower consumption among the child audience. Supply and broadcast schedules play a role here. Other important fictional television products, such as certain Spanish prime-time series, have a significant child audience because they are conceived as family-oriented series and include children in the cast and storylines. At the same time, almost one-fourth of what a Spanish child watches on television is advertising, sales or promotion of the channel and its programs.

These are hitherto unpublished findings from an investigation carried out by the author and financed by the Spanish Government. Let us look at the results in more detail.

Children as a television audience

With the exception of a few valuable studies conducted by universities and institutions related to children, children's television habits are, generally, not only unknown to television networks, but the main TV channels that operate in Spain also ignore children's tastes with regard to programming. Neither operators or channels nor content producers or control organizations, with the exception of the Consejo del Audiovisual de Cataluña (Catalonia Broadcasting Council), have carried out any research on children's television viewing.

There are two reasons for this: First, children between 4 and 12 years[1] are the least relevant demographic group both in terms of population and television consumption. As time goes by, they lose more clout among the television audience due to the progressive aging of the Spanish population.[2]

Second, channels do not consider children a commercial target. Because of this, programs oriented toward them are marginalized – despite the fact that networks broadcast large amounts of advertising directed at children, as we shall observe later on. Regarding the Spanish population on the opposite extreme of the age pyramid (viewers 64 and older), channels treat this population similarly. The difference concerning this group lies in the fact that, nowadays, elderly people live longer than previously and constitute an increasingly great percentage of the Spanish population and the television audience.[3]

According to various social groups, including academics, a common conception is that children watch a great deal of television. However, our research shows that children up to 12 years of age watch the least amount of television. During the 2002/03 season (September to June), children watched an average of 146 minutes of television daily, including a slight decline throughout the past few years toward watching less television. These 2 hours and 26 minutes contrast sharply with the daily consumption of the average Spaniard: 3 hours and 39 minutes. Among people 64 years and older, viewing is much higher: 5 hours and 16 minutes.

With respect to the way children watch television, one point worth mentioning is that they are least likely to watch television alone. Children watch television by themselves over one-third of the time, especially in the mornings. During prime time, on the other hand, children tend to watch shows with other family members.[4] Furthermore, as an example, more than one-third of children (35.5%) watched television alone on March 11, 2004, the day on which all channels were broadcasting live images that had a great emotional impact throughout the entire nation: the attacks by a group of radical Islamic fundamentalists on different regional trains in Madrid that caused the deaths of 192 people. Children's television viewing in Spain grew that day by 4 percent and the youngest viewers from Madrid (between 4 and 6 years old) watched 40 minutes more television compared to other Spanish children within the same age bracket.

Inadequate relationship between children's demand and program offering

An important fact is that the period of the day when most children are in front of their television sets occurs during the second portion of prime time between 10:00 p.m. and 11:00 p.m. (on average 866,000 children aged 4 to 12 were tuned in during this time throughout the 2002/03 season, seven days a week), followed by 2:00 p.m. to 3:00 p.m. (789,000 children during the time period that coincides with Spain's main meal of the day). Other less important time periods for children's viewing occur between 8:00 a.m. and 9:00 a.m. (just before school begins, with on average 343,000 children) and during the afternoons between 5:00 p.m. and 8:00 p.m. (with more than half a million children on average watching television after returning home from school).

Thus, more children watch television after 10:00 p.m., which falls outside the time slot protected for children's viewing, than at other times. In fact, the following paradox is evident: Puppets in children's programming directed toward the youngest viewers and entitled *Los Lunnis* (The Lunnises) perform a brief sketch shortly before the beginning of the first edition of public channel RTVE's main daily news program *Telediario*. So, between 8:00 p.m. and 9:00 p.m. during the 2003/04 television season, an average of 583,000 4- to 12-year-olds watched television. The volume of the child audience climbed to 764,000 immediately afterwards (between 9:00 p.m. and 10:00 p.m.) and *Los Lunnis* therefore encouraged them to stop watching television; its praiseworthy campaign seems to have produced a boomerang effect.[5] Another point worth mentioning is that during the last important broadcast period called late night (between 00:00 a.m. and 2:30 a.m.), there is a significant number of children – an average of 157,000 – watching television (264,000 children between 00:00 a.m. and 1:00 a.m., 105,000 between 1:00 a.m. and 2:00 a.m., and 49,000 between 2:00 a.m. and 2:30 a.m.).

As a consequence, a strange children's programming "rule of thumb" can be formulated: When more children are in front of the television set, fewer children's programs are broadcast. Children's programming has also been eliminated *par excellence* in the afternoon: Starting after 5:00 p.m., the time when children return home from school, commercial channels and state-run TVE1 never broadcast children's programs. The only networks that do are public autonomous channels (with some exceptions), especially second channels, and the state-run public channel La 2.

In Table 1, this inadequate relationship between demand and supply can be seen when comparing children's television viewing throughout the day and the proportion of children's programs offered on the different channels. Percentages refer to the total amount of channels, including public, commercial, state-run and autonomous channels. The table shows that, Mondays through Fridays, 12 percent of the children's program supply is concentrated between 3:00 a.m. and 7:00 a.m. when fewer children are in front of the television set – however, almost the entire 12 percent is broadcast at 7:00 a.m. sharp and not during the early morning hours. In the evening, from 8:00 p.m. to 11:00 p.m., one of the periods of the day when there are more children watching television, barely any programs exist for them. Children are therefore forced to watch programming oriented toward adults.

It is worth pointing out, and simultaneously disturbing to say, that all three main national channels in Spain that broadcast freely (public channel TVE1 and commercial channels Antena 3 and Telecinco) do not currently offer any chil-

Table 1. **Child audience 4 to 12 years of age** (in thousands) **and distribution** (%) **of children's programming,** by time period/ schedule during the 2003/04 season

look up this chart.

Time period/ schedule	Monday through Friday		Saturday and Sunday	
	Child audience	Children's programming	Child audience	Children's programming
03:00 a.m. - 04:00 a.m.	14		25	
04:00 a.m. - 05:00 a.m.	9		13	
05:00 a.m. - 06:00 a.m.	7	12.00%	8	6.20%
06:00 a.m. - 07:00 a.m.	6		7	
07:00 a.m. - 08:00 a.m.	59		27	
08:00 a.m. - 09:00 a.m.	404	17.40%	188	11.20%
09:00 a.m. - 10:00 a.m.	199		559	
10:00 a.m. - 11:00 a.m.	150	9.10%	817	7.10%
11:00 a.m. - 12:00 p.m.	151		745	
12:00 p.m. - 01:00 p.m.	153		546	
01:00 p.m. - 02:00 p.m.	411	13.10%	504	1.80%
02:00 p.m. - 03:00 p.m.	811		733	
03:00 p.m. - 04:00 p.m.	644		741	
04:00 p.m. - 05:00 p.m.	510	9.50%	727	2.80%
05:00 p.m. - 06:00 p.m.	502		666	
06:00 p.m. - 07:00 p.m.	483	8.80%	532	0.10%
07:00 p.m. - 08:00 p.m.	507		495	
08:00 p.m. - 09:00 p.m.	597	0.70%	549	0.01%
09:00 p.m. - 10:00 p.m.	799		675	
10:00 p.m. - 11:00 p.m.	903	0.30%	774	0.02%
11:00 p.m. - 12:00 a.m.	604		596	
12:00 a.m. - 01:00 a.m.	248		304	
01:00 a.m. - 02:00 a.m.	94	0.03%	133	0.00%
02:00 a.m. - 03:00 a.m.	41		67	
Average	**353**		**443**	

dren's programming during weekdays,[6] but children's programming is concentrated to Saturday and Sunday mornings. However, this is due to the fact that adults barely watch television during this time instead of the channels feeling the need to satisfy the child audience's demand. On the other hand, public channels gear themselves more toward the youngest viewers (between 4 and 9 years old), while the commercial networks orient their children's programming toward kids between 9 and 12 years of age and teenagers. Child viewers of commercial channels are therefore slightly older and commercially more lucrative. Oddly enough, the programming "rule of thumb" can be expressed as an inverse relationship: Children's programs are only broadcast when a significant number of adults are not in front of the television. This means that children's programs are scheduled not in terms of children's needs, or expectations, but in terms of voids left by adults not watching television at certain times.

Genres that children watch most

Accurate statistics do not exist on the distribution of programs by genre in relation to the time children spend watching television. Specifically for this Clearinghouse publication, we have therefore analyzed the distribution by genre during the 2002/03 season by consulting the firm GECA (Gabinete de Estudios de la Comunicación Audiovisual), which specializes in audience research.

In Table 2, information has been compiled about different television genres that children watched throughout the 2002/03 season as a function of hours of viewing time. This is based on their previously mentioned average daily consumption of 2 hours and 26 minutes. Four primary categories of genres or television content tend to stand out. All of them fall above the 10 percent figure. First off, "cartoons" account for 17.7 percent of the time that an average Spanish 4- to 12-year-old watches television. These cartoons are the most important part of the so-called children's programming blocks, whose names in Spain tend to be proceeded by the word "Club" (*Club Megatrix* on Antena 3; *Zon@Disney* on TVE1; *Max Clan* on Telecinco; *Cyberclub* on Telemadrid, *Club Super 3* on Catalonian television; *Xabarin Club* on Galician television; *Betizu* on ETB; *La banda* on Andalusian television; *Babalà* on Valencian television; and *Kosmi Club* on Castilla-La Mancha).

Programming blocks and titles that hint at the commercial interests of channels therefore treat children as just another consumer group instead of as television viewers. Particularly in the case of commercial channels, these networks sometimes do not even conceal their pretext to sell children's products, services and all types of merchandise linked to a given program. These programming blocks therefore become advertising mediums using forms like the sponsoring of sections, contests and abundant product placement. They have very brief narrative segments and are produced by the channel itself (*Club Megatrix*, as an example, consists of on average ten micro-programs that last three minutes and 15 seconds each). These are produced inside a studio with very few technological, linguistic and expressive resources and serve as a way of linking the different cartoons together in a continuous manner and of encouraging participation by children in those programs that contain games and contests. Cartoons primarily nourish the majority of these programming blocks as well as some fictional television series for teenagers. During vacation periods, they also include feature films or television movies.

The second genre in the ranking of most-watched programs by children (Table 2) is "advertising", with 15 percent of children's viewing time, followed by "feature films" (12.4%), and "news programs" (11.9%, which is a fairly high percentage given that this genre is rarely oriented toward children). In fact, only one news program entitled *Info-k* is oriented toward kids; it is broadcast on the second channel of

Table 2. **Time dedicated by children 4 to 12 years of age to main genres during the 2002/03 season,** by hours/minutes and share (%) of total viewing time

Rank	Genre	Hours/minutes	% of total time
1	Cartoons	138h 54m	17.7%
2	Advertising	118h 6m	15.0%
3	Feature films	97h 42m	12.4%
4	News programs	74h 15m	11.9%
5	Drama series	76h 33m	9.7%
6	Self-promotions (by the channel)	67h 18m	8.6%
7	Sports	39h 42m	5.1%
8	Game shows	30h 48m	3.9%
9	Infoshows	26h 10m	3.3%
10	*Novelas* and soap operas	23h 12m	3.0%
11	Informative/educational programs	22h 36m	2.9%
12	Telerealities (reality TV)	14h 18m	1.8%
13	Documentaries	11h 24m	1.5%
14	Reality shows	9h 6m	1.2%
15	Musical progams	8h 40m	1.1%
16	Comedies	7h 2m	0.9%
Total		**785h 15m**	**100%**

Catalonia's autonomous channel K3/El 33 and lasts 18 minutes. The time dedicated by children to "informative/educational programs" is surprising (11th rank, only 2.9% of the time they watch television), not because of the children's lack of interest in this genre, but because such programming does not constitute part of the television offering, with the exception of a few testimonial programs.

"*Telenovelas* and soap operas" constitute 3 percent of the time that children 4 to 12 years dedicate to television. Almost all of these programs are Latin American and are found in TVE1's schedule. With regard to "telerealities" or reality TV (the term that is used here to describe programs such as *Big Brother*, *Survivor*, and shows made using the candid camera technique), these constitute 1.8 percent of children's viewing time, while "reality shows" (a term we reserve for personal testimonies such as a spectacle in a studio, biographical snippets, meetings and misunderstandings between people or prerecorded programs about crime events, etc.) account for 1.2 percent. If we add these two genres, a total of 3 percent is obtained for programs that are related to "telereality" or "reality shows", which is equal of child viewing of the genre "*novelas* and soap operas" ranked in tenth place. Later on, we will observe that even though children dedicate less time to these kinds of programming overall, some of these shows appear on their list of favorites. This is because cartoons are more abundant, but shown during time periods when children view television less, while the fewer "telerealities", "reality shows" and fictional series are broadcast during time slots with greater television consumption, mostly during prime time.

Another paragraph shall be dedicated to interpreting Table 2. If we consider that "self-promotions" (self-referential announcements for the channel that include programming previews and provide continuity to the broadcast time) are a form of advertising that can be added to the "advertising" category (spots and other advertising programs) in the table, these two genres end up being the most-watched category of content by children in Spain. Children therefore dedicate 23.6 percent of their viewing time to this kind of content, a figure that is much higher than that for "cartoons" (17.7%). In other words, almost one-fourth of what a Spanish child watches on television is advertising, sales, or promotion of the channel and its programs.

Reality TV, reality shows and novelas/soap operas

During the 2002/03 season, Spain broadcast 28 programs (i.e., series with several episodes each)[7] within the categories of "telerealities" (reality TV), "reality shows" and "*novelas* and soap operas". As readers can verify in Table 3, all of them (9 telerealities, 10 reality shows, 8 soap operas and 1 docu-soap) have a child audience. Of these 28 programs or series, "telerealities" (reality TV) are the most-watched, especially *Gran Hermano* (Big Brother) and *Operación Triunfo* (Pop Idol), with slightly over 230,000 child viewers on average and market shares between 33.2 percent and 41.3 percent. Both these shows air during the height of prime time and start at 9:37 p.m. and 10:26 p.m., respectively. Therefore, the majority of their broadcast time is found outside the designated time period protected for children, which ends at 10:00 p.m. Children also watched a "telereality" that critics pointed out as one of the main examples of "trash TV": *Hotel Glamour*, which subsequently carried the title *Hotel Glam,* a version of *Gran Hermano* where a group of "celebrities" from tabloid magazines (futurologists and fortune tellers, former *Gran Hermano* contestants, and an extravagant member of a family related to the Franco regime, among other television "fauna" [people who essentially would have a difficult time being recommended as role models for children and teenagers]) lived together in a hotel and participated in a game of nominations and eliminations. Broadcast at 10:00 p.m., this program obtained an average child audience of slightly over 130,000.

The first episode of *Gran Hermano* in Spain inaugurated a new season and subgenre within programs that fall into the category "telerealities" and also altered the scheduling practices for such programs. This program breaks the molds of many approaches and routines used by schedulers. It has reached the point of broadcasting almost 26 times a week between 10:30 a.m. and 11:45 p.m. in Spain: five times from Monday through Thursday, four times on Fridays plus an additional episode during prime time on Saturdays and Sundays. In addition, it has also used the format of live connections with the house (where the contestants live), summaries and gala shows. This omnipresence on a daily and weekly basis

Table 3. Telerealities (reality TV), reality shows, and *telenovelas*/soap operas broadcast by Spanish channels during the 2002/03 season, by child audience 4 to 12 years of age in thousands, ratings and shares

	National Channels			Epi-sodes	Thou-sands	Child audience		
Rank	Channel	Starting time	Title			Rating*	Share**	Genre
25	Telecinco	09:37 PM	*Gran Hermano*	5	235	6.2	33.2	Telereality
26	TVE1	10:26 PM	*Operación Triunfo*	25	233	6.3	41.3	Telereality
47	Telecinco	09:53 PM	*Gran Hermano*	18	197	5.2	24.6	Telereality
74	Telecinco	09:21 PM	*Gran Hermano: el debate*	12	169	4.4	22.3	Telereality
89	Telecinco	09:49 PM	*Popstars, todo por un sueño*	13	153	4.0	23.5	Telereality
101	Telecinco	04:34 PM	*Me gustas tú*	64	143	3.8	28.3	Telereality
123	Telecinco	10:00 PM	*Hotel Glam* (formerly *Hotel Glamour*)	19	130	3.7	18.7	Telereality
159	Telecinco	05:13 PM	*Popstars, todo por un sueño*	15	114	3.0	19.5	Telereality
164	Telecinco	03:42 PM	*Gran Hermano*	75	113	2.9	21.6	Telereality
186	TVE1	05:05 PM	*Secreto de amor*	229	106	2.8	20.5	Soap opera
206	TVE1	05:15 PM	*El manantial*	10	100	2.6	14.7	Soap opera
289	TVE1	05:18 PM	*Gata Salvaje*	170	79	2.3	16.8	Soap opera
294	Telecinco	03:30 PM	*20 tantos*	28	78	2.1	13.3	Soap opera
300	Antena 3	07:53 PM	*Ahora*	62	70	1.9	15.5	Reality show
343	TVE1	04:22 PM	*Géminis, venganza de amor*	376	67	1.9	14.5	Soap opera
373	Antena 3	10:17 PM	*Todo por amor*	12	63	1.6	11.5	Reality show
407	TVE1	11:07 PM	*Ésta es mi historia*	40	57	1.6	14.4	Reality show
438	Antena 3	10:28 PM	*Hay una carta para ti*	57	43	1.2	10.3	Reality show
463	Antena 3	04:50 PM	*Ahora*	55	38	1.0	7.8	Reality show
505	Antena 3	11:44 PM	*El lugar del crimen*	12	31	0.8	10.1	Reality show
516	Antena 3	10:09 PM	*Hay una carta para ti*	15	30	0.9	6.0	Reality show
674	TVE1	12:21 PM	*Así son las cosas*	62	12	0.3	10.0	Reality show
704	Antena 3	0:11 AM	*Sin noticias de...*	12	11	0.3	9.6	Reality show
836	Antena 3	0:45 AM	*Sin noticias de...*	8	4	0.1	5.5	Reality show

	Autonomous Channels			Epi-sodes	Thou-sands	Child audience		
Rank	Channel	Starting time	Title			Rating*	Share**	Genre
55	C.SUR	09:43 PM	*Arrayán*	144	50	6.1	21.3	Soap opera
108	ETB1	09:46 PM	*Goenkale*	186	8	5.1	26.5	Soap opera
75	TV3	10:02 PM	*Veterinaris*	5	33	6.3	21.9	Docu-soap
388	TV3	03:49 PM	*El cor de la ciutat*	188	12	2.3	30.3	Soap opera

* Average percent of 4- to 12-year-old viewers during the program in relation to all 4- to 12-year-olds

** Proportion (%) of children 4 to 12 years of age viewing this program in relation to all 4- to 12-year-olds watching anything on any channel during this time period

causes all audiences, including children, to come into contact with the program. In addition to being a "killer format" by trade as it systematically crushes all of its competitors, especially during the first year of its run in Spain, it acts as what we call a "nourishing program" because it supplies other programs with content, especially morning magazines and evening talk shows on Telecinco (*Día a Día* [Day to Day] and *Crónicas marcianas* [Chronicles by Martians], respectively) and even tabloid programs (*Salsa Rosa* [Hot Sauce]). All of them stock up on this content, broadcast live, and connect with everything that happens in the *Big Brother* house. They benefit by gaining new viewers who tune into these shows in order to follow the course of the "telereality" within other programs.

The first season of *Gran Hermano* (1999/00) also became a noteworthy audience success among children between 4 and 12 years. It was the 5th most-watched show of the season among them (520,000 children and a 55.9% share). This means that more than half of the children watching television overall during this time period chose *Gran Hermano*, which is why it was one of their preferred programs after cartoons like *The Simpsons* (564,000 viewers and a 63.2% share), which occupied first place even though it is not a children's program, followed by the Spanish series *Médico de familia*, which dealt with the professional work carried out by a medical doctor and his family life at home with his children, and two other cartoon series: *Rugrats: Adventures in Diapers* and *Digimon*, in 3rd and 4th place, respectively.

During the 1999/00 season, a "reality show" was also broadcast about accidents (traffic and others), police chases, and various types of crimes that were captured generally by surveillance or security cameras. Occasionally, hidden cameras were used. This was called *Impacto TV* (TV Impact, Antena 3) and occupied 14th place among children with 416,000 viewers and a 46.2 percent share. These types of programs were abundant during the second half of the 1990s and the first years of the current century. Considered to be the most important Spanish "reality show" during the first part of the television "realism" trend was *¿Quién sabe dónde?* (Who Knows Where?), previously broadcast on TVE1; its seasons with highest audience numbers were 1992/93 and 1993/94. This program's objective was to find missing persons searched for by family and friends, in some cases over the course of many years. A considerable number of children were also following these programs at the time: *¿Quién sabe dónde?* had an audience of 306,000 children (a 28.2% share among 4- to-12-year-olds) during the 1993/94 season and 82,000 (13.6% share) during the last season 1996/97. Another pioneer program from the "reality show" genre (which began being broadcast in 1990) was *Videos de primera* (the Spanish equivalent to *America's Funniest Home Videos* in the U.S.), a home video contest with images about curious facts, extravagant content, falls, etc., where children were also involved, especially while they carried out risky, dangerous activities that the audience (at least that recorded on laugh tracks) found hilarious. Audience figures from the first years of this reality show are not available.

Returning to the 2002/03 season (in Table 3), two Latin American "*novelas*" occupied the main positions in terms of audience numbers after "telerealities": *Secreto de amor* (Secret of Love), which dealt with the life of Maria Clara, a woman who is cheated on by her boyfriend Carlos Raúl, and *El manantial* (The Spring), which chronicled the rivalry between two families that wanted to own land where there was a natural spring. Both of them were broadcast on TVE1 and had a child audience of 106,000 and 100,000, respectively. The first "reality show" that appears in the ranking during the 2002/03 season is Antena 3's *Ahora* (Now), which offers news from the tabloid world. It featured an average audience of 70,000 children. The remaining content found in "reality shows" was stories about relationships or events and had a smaller audience. In fact, only 2 of the 10 "reality shows" have more than 60,000 children as television viewers.

Something similar happens with "soap operas" on autonomous (not national) channels (see the last rows in Table 3). These have widespread success among the adult audience and achieve a children's share that exceeds 20 percent: Andalusia's *Arrayán* (Myrtle), whose plot revolves around hotel staff and guests (50,000 children and a 21.3% share); the Basque Country's *Goenkale* (name of a street), which chronicles the lives of neighbors who live on a street in a fictitious Basque town (8,000 children and a 26.5% share); Catalonia's *Veterinaris* (Veterinarians), a docu-soap on TV3, an important type of programming on this network, which is recorded in a veterinary clinic and focuses on the life of these professionals and their relationships with customers and animals, plus *El cor de la ciutat* (The Heart of the City), which tells the story of residents in the Sant Andreu neighborhood of Barcelona; these two lastmentioned *novelas* (a "docu-soap" and a "soap opera") have 33,000 and 12,000 children's viewers with shares of 21.9 and 30.3 percent, respectively.

The first column in Table 3 shows the ranking position these programs occupy in terms of child viewership: Only three programs are found among the Top 50 and five are found among the Top 100 on national channels. (However, all these five programs are "telerealities".)

Programs most watched by children

Table 4 reflects more adequately the behavior of children when faced with the programming broadcast on Spanish channels. This table informs readers about the 50 programs most watched by children aged 4 to 12 during the 2002/03 season. Information is arranged according to rating and the thousands of children who have watched the series.

By grouping everything together in terms of television genres and macro genres, the following results are obtained: Of the 50 most-watched programs,[8] 56 percent (28 programs) belong to the category of "cartoons". "Drama series" follow with 16 percent (8 programs), "telerealities" with 6 percent (3 programs) and the rest are made up of a group of genres that fluctuate between sports programs, comedy shows, informative and educational shows (programs of a cultural nature), children's programs, etc., with percentages that oscillate between 0 and 4 percent (0 to 2 programs).

Various results are quite striking: As mentioned, "cartoons" completely dominate the results. This is not a novelty in Spain or any other country and is true of

Table 4. Most-watched programs among children 4 to 12 years of age during the 2002/03 season, in thousands, ratings and shares

					Child audience			
Rank	Channel	Starting time	Title	Epi-sodes	Thou-sands	Rating*	Share**	Genre
1	TVE1	10:12 PM	Ana y los 7	25	521	14.6	57.3	Drama series
2	TVE1	10:12 PM	Cruzyraya.com	26	404	11.0	39.2	Comedy
3	Antena 3	02:15 PM	The Simpsons	172	400	11.0	54.9	Cartoon
4	Antena 3	02:15 PM	The Simpsons	375	370	10.2	45.9	Cartoon
5	TVE1	10:21 PM	Cuéntame cómo pasó	30	345	9.4	43.7	Drama series
6	Telecinco	10:05 PM	Los Serrano	10	315	8.9	41.3	Drama series
7	La 2	02:10 PM	Digimon	51	305	8.0	36.4	Cartoon
8	Telecinco	11:22 AM	Recess	84	301	8.2	40.5	Cartoon
9	TVE1	08:34 PM	Soccer: League of Champions	27	297	8.1	33.6	Sport
10	Antena 3	02:58 PM	Antena 3 News 1	86	282	7.7	37.6	News
11	Telecinco	10:48 AM	Tarzan	84	276	7.6	33.2	Cartoon
12	Telecinco	07:03 PM	Bewitched	27	276	7.2	38.7	Drama series
13	Telecinco	03:35 PM	Disney movie	42	268	7.3	36.5	Movie
14	Telecinco	11:48 AM	Art attack	8	262	7.1	42.0	Informative
15	Telecinco	11:28 AM	Recess	12	251	6.7	37.4	Cartoon
16	Telecinco	10:32 AM	Pepper Ann	10	247	6.5	36.9	Cartoon
17	La 2	01:57 PM	Jumanji	40	245	6.9	36.7	Cartoon
18	Telecinco	11:57 AM	Art attack	45	245	7.0	41.1	Informative
19	TVE1	10:15 PM	El retorno de Omaíta	12	243	6.9	30.6	Comedy
20	Telecinco	9:48 AM	House of Mouse	80	239	6.5	31.7	Cartoon
21	Telecinco	9:38 AM	Zona Disney	84	238	6.5	30.6	Children's
22	Antena 3	10:27 AM	Adventures of Jimmy Neutron: Boy Genius	29	238	6.5	29.1	Cartoon
23	La 2	01:28 PM	The Triplets	67	237	6.3	44.8	Cartoon
24	La 2	8:36 AM	Nicolás	26	236	6.7	50.2	Cartoon
25	Telecinco	09:37 PM	Gran Hermano	5	235	6.2	33.2	Telereality
26	TVE1	10:26 PM	Operación Triunfo	25	233	6.3	41.3	Telereality
27	Antena 3	11:02 AM	The Return of Spiderman	11	227	6.0	34.5	Cartoon
28	TVE1	10:36 AM	Power Puff Girls	9	226	5.9	26.4	Cartoon
29	Telecinco	10:06 PM	Cine 5 estrellas	43	226	6.2	30.1	Movie
30	Telecinco	10:05 PM	Hospital Central	23	226	6.1	30.4	Drama series
31	La 2	03:50 PM	The New Adventures of Winnie the Pooh	41	225	5.9	33.3	Cartoon
32	La 2	01:58 PM	Momias	9	223	5.8	23.6	Cartoon
33	Antena 3	10:52 AM	Spiderman	55	219	5.8	25.9	Cartoon
34	TVE1	09:46 PM	Fútbol: amistoso	4	217	5.9	27.6	Sport
35	Antena 3	9:48 AM	Titeuf	40	216	6.1	30.5	Cartoon
36	TVE1	10:24 PM	Smallville	3	215	6.1	35.2	Drama series
37	Antena 3	10:18 AM	The Wild Thornberrys	25	213	5.8	37.8	Cartoon
38	Antena 3	10:16 AM	The Wild Thornberrys	48	213	6.0	27.5	Cartoon
39	Antena 3	9:53 AM	Marsupilami	26	212	5.7	28.7	Cartoon
40	Telecinco	10:00 PM	Javier ya no vive solo	3	210	5.6	28.4	Drama series
41	Telecinco	11:12 AM	Tarzan	7	209	5.7	29.7	Cartoon
42	Antena 3	9:36 AM	Yugi-oh	30	205	5.4	28.7	Cartoon
43	La 2	8:20 AM	The New Adventures of Winnie the Pooh	9	204	5.4	39.1	Cartoon
44	Telecinco	10:23 AM	Zona Disney	5	203	5.4	27.2	Children's
45	Antena 3	10:02 AM	Detective Conan	11	203	5.3	24.4	Cartoon
46	Antena 3	10:29 AM	Monster Rancher	8	202	5.3	35.5	Cartoon
47	Telecinco	09:53 PM	Gran Hermano	18	197	5.2	24.6	Telereality
48	Antena 3	01:28 PM	Sabrina, The Teenaged Witch	73	196	5.4	37.5	Drama series
49	La 2	01:38 PM	Pajarería Transilvania	19	194	5.3	29.1	Cartoon
50	La 2	01:43 PM	Memé y el señor Bobo	27	193	5.5	36.6	Cartoon

* Average percent of 4- to 12-year-old viewers during the program in relation to all 4- to 12-year-olds

** Proportion (%) of children 4 to 12 years old viewing this program in relation to 4- to 12-year-olds watching anything on any channel during this time period

both the present and the past throughout the history of television. However, these facts are relevant to the second position occupied by "drama series" that are practically all Spanish productions and that deal with professional and family plots. These normally broadcast during prime time (9:00 p.m. to 00:00 a.m.). Starting after the mid-90s, the majority of these Spanish series were removed from the channel's schedule and American series became more favored by the audience. The Spanish "drama series" most-watched by children according to Table 4 tend to include children within the cast who play characters in the plots and tend to be dramas or comedies. Most of the time, these shows are a mixture of both genres and are classified as "dramedies".

"Telerealities" constitute the third genre with the greatest child viewership, even though these programs are not oriented toward young viewers.

Equally striking is the fact that "children's programs" (programming blocks or segments made by the channel that are recorded in the studio with actual or fictitious hosts that constitute the pretext to, generally, cartoons and children's television series), show a low representation among children's preferences. A paradox therefore is created: With the exception of "cartoons", children watch more adult programs than programs oriented specifically toward kids.

The fact that no "soap operas" appear in the list of the programs most watched by children is also important. However, this does not mean they do not watch these programs. "Soap operas" are relatively scarce on Spanish channels, except for the first, state-run channel TVE. Since the 80s, this network has scheduled *novelas* during time slots that immediately follow lunch during the middle of the day after *Telediario* (the news).

Most-watched programs among boys and girls

By breaking down the information in Table 4 by sex and age, we can verify important differences within the child audience. "Cartoons" are most-watched by boys (35 out of 50 programs, or 70%), as compared to 21 programs (42%) in the case of girls. If we combine these data with one of our recent studies carried out for the Universidad Complutense de Madrid (see further on in the text), "cartoons" end up featuring a greater percentage of male characters than females in leading and supporting roles, something that may be one of the explanations for the different gender preferences. Along the same lines, studies seem to prove that boys prefer action cartoons while girls lean toward dramatic shows. Boys are inclined toward action cartoons like *Spiderman* and *Digimon* while girls tend to favor adventure cartoons like *Tarzán* and *Las tres mellizas* (The Triplets).

Girls also tend to watch more "drama series" than do boys (22% of the most-watched programs among girls as compared to 10% among boys).

The gender difference is even greater with regard to "telerealities": Girls watch more "telerealities" than do boys (5 different programs or 10% of all most-watched programs consumed by girls as compared to 1 program or 2% of the Top 50 in the case of boys). This is not only a quantitative question but also hierarchal: The only "telereality" that boys watch is Telecinco's *Gran Hermano*, which occupies 39th place out of the 50 (129,000 boys, with a rating of 6% and a 31.2% share), while girls prefer *Operación Triunfo* (broadcast on TVE1), a contest that uses the "television isolation" system wherein a promising young musician is awarded with the opportunity to represent Spain in the Eurovision Festival competition. This program occupies 11th place among girls (128,000 girls, with a 7.6 rating and a 46.2% share). Almost half of Spanish girls between 4 and 12 years old who watched television at this time therefore chose to watch the 25 episodes of this program that were broadcast during the season. *Operación Triunfo's* time slot is worth pointing out. This show began airing on the state-run public channel at a time late for the child audience: 10:26 p.m., also considering the fact that it lasted 152 minutes.

All five episodes of *Gran Hermano* found themselves in 23rd place among girls (39th in the case of boys) with 107,000 viewers and a 36% share. Three "telerealities" that do not appear within the Top 50 programs preferred by children overall also appear in the ranking for girls. One is *Popstars, todo por un sueño* (Telecinco), a musical competition, which comes in 33rd place (96,000 viewers and a 32.5% share), a program where a group of young, teenage women closed themselves off inside an "academy" and competed against each other to form a musical group. This fact contributed to this show experiencing more success among girls than among boys.

The other two "telerealities" that came up on the girls' list are two additional *Gran Hermano* series: The episode shown on the weekend finished in 34th place for girls (96,000 girl viewers and a 26.1% share) and *Gran Hermano: El debate* ranked last (50th), with 82,000 girl viewers and a 24 percent share. Despite occupying the last place within the Top 50 among girls, this version of *Gran Hermano* constitutes an important result because practically one-fourth of all children viewing television during this time chose this telereality on the day it broadcast (see the preceding Table 3).

Most-watched programs among different age groups

By observing children's consumption of television programs in terms of age, other factors that are equally significant can also be verified: "Cartoons" prevail among the youngest viewers while "drama series" and "telerealities" are watched more by older children among the 4- to 12-year-olds. As regards "cartoons", 35 programs out of the 50 most-watched shows (70%) are seen by children between 4 and 8 years of age. Consequently, the percentage of "children's programming" blocks among the youngest viewers between 4 and 6 years old (3 programs, which equals 6%) increases with this result.

On the other hand, consumption of "drama series" is lower among children between 4 and 6 years (5 programs that equal 10%) and viewers between 7 and

8 years (4 programs or 8%). The youngest viewers also watch fewer "telerealities": 1 program (2%) when they are between 4 and 6 years and 2 programs (4%) when they are between 7 and 8 years. With age, viewing of "drama series" and "telerealities" grows rapidly and practically exponentially in some cases: "Drama series" end up accounting for 18 percent (9 programs) among 9- to 10-year-olds and 34 percent (17 programs) among 11- to 12-year-olds. Something similar happens with "telerealities": 3 programs (6%) among 9- to 10-year-olds and 6 programs (12%) among 11- to 12-year-olds.[9]

Although the "*novela*/soap opera" genre does not appear among the 50 programs most watched by children across the entire country, an analysis of these data in terms of regional markets indicates that Andalusia – the Spanish region or Autonomous Community with the largest population in Spain and, therefore, with the greatest number of children – is the only place where children watch three *novelas* (within the Top 50 programs). All of them were broadcast on state-run, public channel TVE1 during the 2002/03 season. There are the previously mentioned *El manantial* (22nd place, 5 episodes, 63,000 children and a 30.7% share), *Secreto de amor* (27th place, 121 episodes, 60,000 viewers and a 37.1% share) and *Géminis: venganza de amor*, whose plot revolved around the life of a young entrepreneur named Daniel who walked out on his wife Elena after meeting Clara. However, both of them suffer Elena's revenge (47th place, 188 episodes, 51,000 viewers, and a 27.1% share).

The other Autonomous Community in which "*telenovelas*/soap operas" appear is the Canary Islands, where the genre represents 10% (five programs) of the 50 programs most watched by children. Regional channel TV Canaria chose to broadcast Latin American *novelas* starring children during their afternoon schedule. These were *Vivan los niños* (May Children Live), which chronicled the mishaps of Lupita Gómez, a teacher at a Mexico City school and her students (3rd place, 158 episodes, 25,000 children, and a 62.7% share), *De pocas, pocas pulgas* (A Few, Few Fleas), which revolved around the life of Mr. Julián, a formerly prominent musician who found happiness along with Danilo, a 12-year-old orphan (7th place, 30 episodes, 22,000 children, and a 65.4% share) and *María Belén*, which tells the story of a 6-year-old girl who loses her adoptive parents in a traffic accident (39th place, 46 episodes, 14,000 children, and a 41.5% share). Two *novelas* broadcast by TVE also appeared on this list: *El manantial* (32nd place) and *Secreto de amor* (40th place).

Some characteristics of children's programming

In sum, we have seen that children's interest in "drama series" and "telerealities" (reality TV) increases with age among 4- to 12-year-olds. Several such programs are included in their list of the 50 most-watched programs, especially from the age of 9.

"Cartoons" are, however, the genre that children in Spain view most of all. A few findings about "children's programming" will therefore conclude this article. A content analysis – carried out by the present author at the Universidad Complutense de Madrid (UCM)[10] and about to be published – provides keys to interpreting the nature of children's programs in Spain:

- The Spanish television diet specifically directed at children is unvaried in terms of genres. 71.9 percent of "children's programming" is "cartoons" and the rest corresponds to "drama series" and some "feature films". Almost no programs deserve to be classified as "educational/informative".[11]

- Television homogenizes the child audience between 4 and 12 years of age (sometimes including even teenagers). Channels do not distinguish programs in terms of age or orient their content toward specific age groups corresponding to the child's different stages of development.

- The United States is the main provider of children's television content. 57.9% of the analyzed time excluding commercial breaks comes from the U.S. and only 12.6% is produced in Spain. France is the third producer of children's content (9.5%) followed by Japan (8.5%). The general disinterest on part of Spanish channels in creating locally oriented children's shows means that children in Spain are offered programs very different from their cultural and social environment.

- Children's programs have a quick narrative pace fostered by high frequency of shot changes, a resource that serves to capture the "passive and involuntary" attention of the child[12] and leaves little time for viewers to process the information.[13] Shot changes in "cartoons" can even occur every 1.6 seconds. In some cases, these rates rival those of advertisements (one shot is used per second in an advertising spot).

- Of protagonists in children's programs, 81.8 percent are males and 59 percent Caucasian (while 36% are not assigned any specific race). Another outstanding trait is that few seasonal and geographical references exist in the stories, which helps them achieve greater penetration in all markets.

- Scenes with violence[14] exist in 47 percent of the analyzed episodes. On average, 1.59 sequences with violence are therefore produced per program and 3.38 violent scenes appear in each program that contains violent scenes. Mostly, acts of violence and aggressive behavior are shown, but not their effects. Scenes that contain "happy violence" or "comedic violence" are abundant.[15]

- Gender, ethnic, religious or work discrimination are depicted in 14.4 percent of the programs. These scenes are mostly sexual in nature.

- In terms of advertising, commercial channels press the authorized time limit of 20 percent with this content (which equals 12 minutes of advertising per broadcast hour). And we have already seen that when self-promotion by channels is added, the volume of these two "genres" combined is so immense that children end up watching such material the most.

Notes

1. The child audience in Spain refers to the population segment between 4 and 12 years of age. However, according to parents, 55 percent of children begin to watch television starting after their second birthday. This has been demonstrated by a survey conducted by the Sociological Research Center (CIS), the main public opinion organization that relies on support from the Spanish government, entitled *La televisión y los niños*, estudio n° 2.391, mayo, 2000 (Television and Children, project # 2,391, May 2000).

2. The percentage of children in Spain has progressively declined during the period 1994 (when they represented 12.4% of the overall population and 9.4% of the television audience) to 2003 (when they represented 8.9% of the population and 6.1% of television viewers). The total number of children between 4 and 12 years in Spain in 2003 was 3,521,131.

3. Persons 64+ constituted 20.1% of the television audience and 14.0% of the Spanish population in 1993. In 2003, they accounted for 25% of the audience and 17% of the population.

4. We have taken a sample of children's television consumption during October 2003 from Monday through Sunday. The results are the following: On average, children watched television for 136 minutes, of which ca. 46 minutes were spent watching television alone; ca. 35 minutes were spent accompanied by one other person; and ca. 52 minutes were spent watching television in a group setting with three or more people.

5. On the public channel TVE1, where the campaign is broadcast, 128,000 children between 4 and 12 watch it (a 16.9% share among the child audience). Afterwards, the number of children watching *Telediario* increases to 152,000 (18.2%), according to average data for the 2003/04 season (September through June).

6. We refer to the 2004/05 season in this case, which began on September 1, 2004. This has been a general rule throughout the 2003/04 season, with the exception of Antena 3, which broadcast children's programs throughout the morning during the work week. However, these were only shown during school vacations.

7. We interpret the term program as the overall number of episodes, editions (in the case of news programs) and installments of the same program or title. This is different from episode, which refers to one section or installment of a program. Statistics commented upon here take a program as the unit of analysis and not just a given episode. This means that the total sample of those programs broadcast by a channel provides a more precise figure than that provided by other entities like the French company Médiametrie, for example.

8. See note 7.

9. As regards the importance of differentiating the child audience in terms of ages, see Doubleday, Catherine N. and Droege, Kristin L. "Cognitive Developmental Influences on Children's Understanding of Television", in Berry, G. L. & Asamen, J. K.: *Children and Television. Images in a Changing Sociocultural World*, Sage Publications, London, 1993, pp. 23-37.

10. The study consists of a sample of 132 children's programs (115 different titles), amounting to 70 hours and 45 minutes broadcast during 2000 and 2001 by five Spanish channels: both public channels TVE1 and La 2, both commercial networks Telecinco and Antena 3 (all four of them have national coverage) and the public, autonomous channel Telemadrid (which operates in the Community or region of Madrid).

11. The classic report by Himmelweit et al. about children and television indicates that during the 1950s, the BBC broadcast the same number of news programs (including documentaries with a cultural, educational nature) as television series specifically for children. See Himmelweit,

Hilde T., Oppenheim, A. N. and Vince, Pamela: *Television and the Child. An empirical study of the effect of television on the young*, Oxford University Press, London, 1958, pp. 171-172.

12. See Anderson, D. R. and Burns, J.: "Paying Attention to Television", in Bryan, J. Y. and Zillmann, D. (eds.): *Responding to the Screen. Reception and Reaction Processes*, LEA, Hillsdale, NJ, 1991, pp. 199-216. This issue has been studied in Spain among others by Pablo del Río in his *Psicología de los medios de comunicación*.

13. See Greenfield, P. and Beagles-Roos, J.: "Radio vs. Television: their cognitive impact on children of different socioeconomic and ethnic groups", *Journal of Communication*, 38 (2), 1988, pp. 71-72.

14. As the UCLA report maintains, we define violence broadly as "anything that involves physical harm of any sort, intentional or unintentional, self-inflicted or inflicted by someone or something else" (UCLA Center for Communication Policy: *The UCLA Television Violence Monitoring Report*, University of California Los Angeles, 1995, p. 22).

15. Our study differs in this case from another carried out by the University of Pennsylvania cited by Murray, which showed that one hour during prime time contains five violent acts while one hour of children's programming includes 20 to 25 violent situations. (Murray, John P.: "The Developing Child in a Multimedia Society", in Berry, G.L. & Asamen, J.K.: *Children and Television. Images in a Changing Sociocultural World*, Sage Publications, London, 1993, p. 14). However, our findings coincide with many of the results presented in the annual reports published by The Annenburg Public Policy Center at the University of Pennsylvania.

"Soaps Want to Explain Reality"

Daily Soaps and Big Brother in the Everyday Life of German Children and Adolescents

Maya Götz

Six to 8 p.m. is soap opera time in Germany. Millions of people sit in front of their television sets every evening watching the soaps. People of all age groups, especially women, enjoy watching the endless series of love, suffering, intrigues and strokes of fate. For example, *Good Times, Bad Times* (Gute Zeiten, schlechte Zeiten)[1] has a marketing share of over 50 per cent for 10- to 15-year-old girls. This means that every second young female adolescent viewing television at this time is watching *Good Times, Bad Times*, often five times a week for many years. Far fewer boys than girls watch soaps. However, *Big Brother*[2] – a programme that began being aired in Germany in 2000 – seems to be nearly as attractive to the 10- to 15-year-old boys as is the daily soap opera to the girls. These programmes have some interesting similarities, as the hybrid format of *Big Brother* is a mixture of game and documentary filmed in special locations and edited according to the soap dramaturgy (Mikos et al., 2000: 25).

While for non-viewers it may be rather difficult to understand the success of either format (as the programmes seem to be, for the most part, boring, banal and exaggerated), what cannot be denied is that they do attract children and adolescents in massive numbers.

Why do people watch soap operas? The current state of research

In a 1944 study, entertainment, emotional stimulation and realism were found to be the principal motives for regular listening to soaps on the radio (Herzog, 1944). Uses-and-gratification studies conducted since the 1980s have added the motives of avoidance/escape, social status gains, and the search for information (cf., Carveth & Alexander, 1985; Lemish, 1985; Rubin, 1985).

To understand the enthusiasm for soaps, it is very important to understand that it is a women's genre. In soaps, women characters appear much more frequently and in roles that carry more weight in terms of the plot than they do in other television programmes (Liebes & Livingstone, 1998: 167; Brown, 1994: 49). The contents of soaps revolve around themes that, due to socialization, occupy women's thoughts – themes such as relationships and personal and social problems. The central strategy for solving problems in this genre is person-centred conversation (Brown, 1994). This is the form of women's communication that developed historically in a civilization dominated by men. For centuries women have maintained their potential for resistance through gossip and social networks used to organize social life (e.g., Ong, 1982; Presnell, 1989). It is in such networks that members of dominated groups (e.g., women, homosexually orientated men, adolescents, people with a handicap) act and are taken seriously in relation to their particular concerns.

Further, it may well be the case that certain elements of the construction of soap texts appeal to women. The special attraction to the tragic emotional structure seems plausible, as well. Overall, it seems that it is impossible to remain in a state of happiness in a soap opera. External circumstances and the acts of others constantly prevent the state of happiness from being maintained for any length of time. Harmony only exists as an unachievable ideal. This, too, may reflect the fundamental experience of women (Ang, 1986). In addition, the male figures in soaps act through the frame of sensitive, relationship-oriented men (Brown, 1994: 54).

All in all, it is likely that the soaps' appeal to women involves interplay between very different elements, with pleasure being the central motivation for reception. Thus, for soap fans, reception is above all something that is fun: "Having fun is fun" (Harrington & Bielby, 1995: 131). This interpretation is supported by findings of a study conducted at Oxford University that applied a personality inventory for recording happiness and discovered a correlation between being happy and watching soaps. Researchers found that "while people who watch a lot of TV in general are less happy, those who watch a lot of soap opera are more happy than other people" (Luo & Argyle, 1993: 506). So regular soap watching by adults goes hand in hand with a feeling of happiness and contentment in everyday life. However, while the meaning of soaps in the everyday life of women is well researched, very little is known about girls' enthusiasm for daily soaps.

The research study

In order to advance an initial study of children's and adolescents' interest in soaps, a research study was conducted in 2000/2001, entitled "The significance of daily soaps in the everyday life of children and adolescents", by the International Central Institute for Youth and Educational Television (IZI), Germany. At its core, the study examined why 6- to 19-year-olds are fascinated by the genre of daily soap operas and the *Big Brother* format. We sought to ascertain the significance of these formats in their everyday life, as well as for their developing worldview and conception of themselves.

Interviews were conducted with 401 children and adolescents (80% of them girls) who admitted that a daily soap or the soap-like format of *Big Brother* is their favourite series.[3] In addition to the 308 fans of the four daily adult German soaps, 51 children (16 girls, 35 boys) identified themselves as regular viewers of *Big Brother*, while 40 were fans of the children's soap *Schloss Einstein* (The Castle of Einstein).[4] In order to estimate the position of those who do not watch any of these series regularly, 23 group discussions (divided by sex) took place with a total of 273 primary school children. The focus in these discussions was on daily viewing of soaps and of *Big Brother*. The study applied an action-oriented approach of qualitative reception research. Here media appropriation is understood as an active and subjectively meaningful process that enables the researcher to understand individual's formation of meaning (cf., Bachmair, 1996).

Main findings: The functions of the daily soap

During the research process, it quickly became clear that the daily viewing of soaps is an important function in shaping interviewees' everyday life. Three different kinds of functions were identified: situational, interactive and subjective-thematic functions.

The situational function:
Soaps structure everyday life and create a specific situation

Soap opera viewing assumes a *situational* function due to its repetitive nature, i.e., soaps are viewed at the same time every weekday. Thus, daily viewing serves to structure the course of the viewer's day and creates a specific situation in which she or he sits in front of the television alone or with others. Previous research studies have indicated that, for example, women working in the household use soap opera viewing as "time for themselves" and in order to break up the endless nature of household work (Warth, 1987). For primary school children an added appeal is that this is a situation in which they can watch a television show together with their parents. For instance, children are not the target audience of the daily soap *Good Times, Bad Times*. Nonetheless, in Germany, 540,000 3- to 13-year-olds (28% market share) watch the programme every evening.[5] We found that, in the case of older children, it is girlfriends who introduced them to the soap opera, whereas in the case of younger viewers it was the parents who did so. For example, this is what happened to 9-year-old Vivian who has been watching *Good Times, Bad Times* with her parents every evening for two years:

Interviewer: How did you come to *Good Times, Bad Times*? How did it all begin?

Vivian: Actually it was really my parents, because they watch it every day and I always wanted to see the Children's Channel or something else, and then they said: "No, Vivian, either you go to bed or you watch *Good Times, Bad Times* with us."

Based on her own account, Vivian has been quasi-socialized to regular viewing of soaps. In the research process that included an opportunity to make a drawing, she paints a picture of the "typical reception situation": She along with her father and mother are portrayed sitting on the sofa and laughing; their dog sits at their feet, the cat is lying on the table next to a bowl of delicious sweets. The television is drawn as a very small object on one side of the picture. Without going deeply into interpretations of children's drawings, it becomes clear that although the soap opera programme is not unimportant, the main attraction is the ritual event of the family watching television together.

As soap fans become older, the number of children who deliberately arrange reception without the family rises. And at the same time, they often consciously avoid contact with all others. Their soap opera time frequently includes viewing several soaps. It is a period when these girls demand be solely for themselves. It is "a space for oneself" that is deliberately arranged and that includes things to eat, such as sweets or crisps. Some of the adolescent girls have to work hard to maintain this free space for themselves against the wishes of their family, as in the case of 15-year-old Christel. For five years, Christel has been watching *Marienhof* (Marienhof),[6] *Unter uns* (Among Us)[7] and *Good Times, Bad Times*. Her parents are certain that her passion for soaps is well over-the-top and have no understanding of her fascination with them. For her part, Christel refuses to be talked out of her daily viewing. She says:

> I cannot live without them, and when I don't see them, I'm always thinking about what might happen.

Every evening the soap time becomes a space for her alone:

> I sit down on the sofa in my room and switch on the television. If the soap is on I have no time for anybody. Then it's just me and the soap.

The interactive function: A new subject of conversation every day

A lot of talking takes place during the viewing and/or during commercial breaks, when the latest events of the show may be discussed, even on the telephone with one's best girlfriend. Here the soap takes on *interactive* functions. In addition, girls often discuss the latest developments in the daily soaps during recess or (boring) lessons. In reply to the questions "Do you have anyone you can talk to about your favourite soap?" and "What do you talk about then?" Yvonne (18 years) replies:

I talk with my best girlfriend and with my (girl) cousins. I talk to my girlfriend at school, but at every opportunity with my cousins. Usually we watch it together. We talk about: "How will it develop? Will they stay together? Will something terrible happen? How are other people reacting to it?"

Friendships are begun, cultivated and defined with the help of soap connections. Similarly, values are (symbolically) negotiated and group identity is established. The latter may also be linked with distinct mechanisms, e.g., towards fans of the other soaps or those who reject them. This function of the soap conversation – that is, to draw a clear dividing line – occurs more frequently in families, for example, between children and their mother who enthusiastically supports viewing soaps in contrast to their father who dislikes them. Altogether it can be seen that, as a soap "expert", it is relatively easy to establish and develop communication.

The subjective-thematic function:
Everyone makes something different out of the soap opera

Children and adolescents, however, do not just talk about the soap opera or make use of television reception, they also assimilate and interpret the contents, and in doing so develop their *own thematic* understandings. The diversity of the appropriation patterns that children and adolescents develop here is astounding. Analysis of the 308 individual cases of viewing of the four daily soaps revealed typical forms of meaning making that, among other things, enabled soap fans to integrate their enthusiasm for the show into their everyday life as well as into their self-conception. The forms of meaning making can be arranged in three groupings: entertainment and information; reflecting one's own ideas; and completing or concealing what is missing in one's own life-world by means of the media (see Table 1).

I. The daily soap as entertainment, information and counsellor

Many children and adolescents who regularly watch daily soaps use this genre as a form of light entertainment and for information. This does not mean, however, that they do not incorporate the individually interpreted contents into their construction of reality or use it as a counsellor.

"There's something new every day":
Watching over-dramatized strands of the plot, love and harmony

One primary characteristic of the soap opera genre is the use of over-dramatized plots. For example, it is never "just a cold, but at least cancer"[8] that soap characters contract; the figures come up against the most extreme types of problems,

Table 1. Typical types of making meaning with the daily soap

I. Entertainment and information

    1 Watching
       a) strands of the plot
       b) love and relationship
       c) harmony
    2 Themes and problems are used as a learning programme
    3 Deconstruction as a pleasure

II. Reflecting one's own ideas

    4 Recognizing oneself in a special figure
    5 Finding oneself (aesthetically) in one's experience of life
    6 Recognizing ideals

III. Completing or concealing what is missing in one's own life-world by means of the media

    7 Soap as an emotional sounding board
    8 Developing (unachievable) ideals based on a figure
    9 Para-social relationships with the soap figures
       a) being in love
       b) being a part of the soap friendship group
    10 Stars and being a fan of them

and they are surprised by development of the most spectacular events in relationships – adultery, murder, divorce, etc. Intense, parallel plots develop in each individual broadcast, creating suspense laced with surprising twists that are intensified by use of dramatic cliff-hanger tactics, so that viewers feel continued viewing of the next instalment is necessary. We found that these aspects of the soaps are important for all the children and adolescents in our sample. For 78 of them, the special attraction to the soaps, while depending on their individual interests, tends to be oriented towards the over-dramatized strands of the plot, the love relationships or watching beauty and harmony. While even the youngest of fans realizes that the soap opera is not reality, they do think that the actors are trying to depict something close to reality.

"You can get a lot of advice": Themes and problems are used for learning

For 29 children and adolescents in the sample, daily viewing of soaps is appealing and interesting because of the feeling that they can learn something about important subjects and obtain information about, e.g., illnesses, problems of fringe groups and social connections. For these respondents, the shows are a window into a world that they assume could potentially also be their own future. Ten- to 13-year-olds, in particular, frequently demonstrate these appropriation patterns. For example, 13-year-old Lisa thinks that:

[...] these soaps want to explain reality to children. Everything there is and how to sort it all out.

"When there are inconsistencies in the script everyone laughs out loud": Deconstruction as a pleasure

Thirteen adolescents (primarily 14+ years old) who regularly watch the soaps deliberately dissociate themselves from the series by pointing out mistakes in the production and the actors' lack of talent. In doing so, they clearly position themselves as critical recipients. This enables them to look at problems from a certain distance, to understand connections while, in spite of their intellectual disengagement, still being fascinated by the genre.

II. Reflecting their own ideas

Many children and adolescents have the feeling that they recognize themselves in the characters, lifestyle and basic values presented in the daily soaps. Having an everyday life that tends to be more positive, they turn to the genre every evening and are self-affirmed by what is presented.

"She's like me": Recognizing oneself and being reinforced by a special character

In the case of 39 participants in the research, what is most important about the soap opera is its mirroring function. These children and adolescents (mainly girls from 11 to 16 years of age) have the feeling that they recognize themselves in a specific character. Given that they feel they have a positive attitude to their own existence, they recognize themselves and feel reinforced.

"That's just like me": Finding one's experience of life being presented

The lifestyle presented by the soap is what is most essential to 38 of the older children and adolescents. Here it is not so much the case that certain characters or specific strands of the plot are important, but rather the atmosphere, the presentation of youth themes and the casting. This cluster contains mainly fans of *Good Times, Bad Times* (for the most part the 12- to 14-year-olds) who identify with the lifestyle in the programme and adopt the soap's trends, music, fashion and hairstyles.

"That's the right idea": Recognizing ideals

For 28 adolescents, the central importance of the viewing is that they develop values and ideals in the soap's narrative. Thus, they see the programme presenting options for behaviour towards one another, for example, as possible ways of behaving when faced with a problem. Here we should note that the German soaps display a basically liberal attitude to such subjects as homosexuality or HIV, an attitude based on political correctness. The children (primarily 9- to 13-year-old *Good Times, Bad Times* viewers) and adolescents (14- to 19-year-old viewers of *Marienhof*) in this cluster identify with the values presented in the soap opera. They have the feeling that what is being shown is what they wish for themselves or miss in their environment, and receive confirmation for what they try to con- sciously put into practice or demand for themselves.

III. Complete or conceal what is lacking in one's own life

What is most important for some children, and especially adolescents, is the compensatory or surrogate function of daily viewing of a soap. Doing so may be an unproblematic way to complement an otherwise busy everyday life-world, so that soap viewing becomes an outlet for expression of feelings, para-social rela- tionships and daydreaming. The soap reception, however, is also used to fill time or gloss over a period of emotional emptiness, deficiencies or problematic social situations they are experiencing in their daily lives.

"I completely share their thoughts and feelings": Soap as an emotional sounding board

The emotional aspect of the soap opera is important for many regular recipients. The tension in the over-dramatized plot developments, the great catastrophes and dramas that take place in the lives of the protagonists, provide grounds for emo- tional involvement. Weeping and laughing in front of the television are part of the normal soap experience.[9] Indeed, for 19 girls (primarily 14-15 years of age) the opportunity to become emotionally involved as well as to laugh and to cry while watching the soap were the main motives for their passionate viewing. Here soap viewing serves as an outlet for expression of feelings that may not be per- mitted or given expression in the rest of their everyday life.

"That's how I'd like to be": Developing (unachievable) ideals based on a character

The enthusiasm of 17 adolescents (primarily 16- to 17-year-olds) focuses on the idealization of one or two characters. When we compare the children's and adole- scents' descriptions about themselves to the characterization of the character, it is clearly understood that in these cases the soap figure embodies everything that they themselves are not, but would like to be. Here, however, the admiration does not stem from a positive self-image, but rather it leads to a self-perspective focussed on deficits.

"To be on cloud nine with him" and "They're all my friends":
Para-social relationships with the soap characters

Another typical way of meaning making through viewing the daily soap opera is the para-social relationship with the characters. That is, in their fantasies, adolescents enter into a relationship with them. So in their minds they are involved in a friendly or erotic relationship with characters in the soap. For 19 girls and one boy, all older than the age of 10, their main enthusiasm for soaps is that every day a clique of 10 to 20 friends "come to my place". The group of soap friends become part of the viewers' autobiography and with their "help" the viewers manage to get through their daily routine. For 13 girls (aged 13 to 16) the fact that they are "in love" with one of the soap characters is the primary motivation for their enthusiasm for soaps. The para-social, erotic relationship is usually of a heterosexual kind, but in our sample it also occurs three times as a homoerotic variant.

"I'd do anything for them": Stars

In the case of 15 adolescents (aged 13-17), it is not what is viewed on the screen that is the focal point of their enthusiasm, but rather the actors and actresses involved. The stars are admired and even exalted. The girls write letters to them, visit them at the set, try to call them and to obtain autographs, for example, during the fan club events. Their entire, subsequent reception is influenced by gaining more, intimate knowledge about "their" star's personality and, moreover, taking part in a live event with them. Sometimes these girls even feel superior to 'normal' fans, because they think they are more sophisticated.

Age-typical development of soap enthusiasm

In the enthusiasm for soaps age-specific tendencies emerge. For the youngest of the primary school children, aged 6 to 9, regular reception of a daily soap is integrated into the family routine. The series is watched with parents and probably siblings as a kind of "bedtime story". It turns into an opportunity to exchange views on the connections with the "more adult" world and its ideals. Here the children accept the parents' interests and views in regard to choice of format and ideas developed. However, as the children become older, from about the age of 10, the media experiences are discussed with friends of both sexes.

Increasingly, with pre-teens aged 10 to 13, the daily soap becomes an information resource, a kind of "window on the world". Although viewing is no longer necessarily related to being together with parents, they are tacitly connected. Further, as they watch soap operas, pre-teen girls and boys learn about problems, contemporary issues and options for acting as an adult man or woman. Girls are exposed to interesting, exemplary female characters who influence the plot, and who are hardly found in other programmes. For boys, who are searching for stable points of orientation to the "modernized male", the soaps offer an alternative to the conventional, relationship-oriented state of being a man.

In the case of the older pre-teens and younger adolescents, aged about 12 to 15, daily viewing of the soaps has additional aesthetic implications. These young people recognize in the characters parts of themselves as well as their newly developing philosophy of life, while distancing themselves from other philosophies or personality characteristics portrayed. Often they express their identification with and enthusiasm for a particular character by adopting his or her clothing or hairstyle, taste in music, etc., when presenting themselves to the world.

It is primarily 14- to 15-year-old girls who develop a particular emotional involvement with soaps. This is also the age when most admit to being "addicted to soaps". In such cases, daily viewing of the soap opera becomes a vehemently demanded, zealously guarded retreat. Further, the soaps come to play a considerable role in their fantasies. These findings are all the more important when related to research on female adolescence. In doing so, we understand that such habitual, intensive viewing is involved in the "climax" of the "loss of voice" (Brown & Gilligan, 1994), that is, the period in which girls withdraw their knowledge and feelings from the public domain, re-locate them in the "underground" and only entrust sharing them with their best girlfriends or their diaries. Accordingly, daily viewing of the soap becomes a space that young adolescent girls create for themselves in order to remain in contact with their own feelings and their knowledge about relationships. They symbolically recognize in the melodramatic material their own everyday crises and experience them intensely.

In the older adolescents, aged 16 to 19, there is a "lighter" appropriation of the genre together with a more distant attitude that again emerges to an increasing extent. The family tends to be reintegrated into sharing of enthusiasm for the soap, though the fantasies and emotional participation are remembered and continued.

Thus, the development of enthusiasm for soaps, insofar as it can be reconstructed based upon this data, can be defined (in an idealized form) as follows: often embedded in a ritual of daily viewing by the entire family, the soap serves, too, as an information resource about the world and how to solve problems. Further, through viewing, girls re-discover and determine their own orientation, which, in some cases, can result in a particularly intense period of "soap addiction", from which parents are excluded. Later, often when enthusiasm abates and an aloof attitude towards the contents of soap operas returns, the daily ritual is again shared with the whole family.

Problematic aspects of enthusiasm for soap operas

Soaps have become a regular and significant part of children's and adolescents' lives. Young people do not mistake them for reality and quite early on see through many of the strategies used in their production. Nevertheless, it is precisely pre-teens who have the feeling that they learn much about reality from them. The danger here is the distorted, stereotypic view of the world presented, one that is dominated by inter-personal problems and catastrophes. Because children often look upon soaps as a learning resource and a "window on the world", producers need to consider how to most carefully apply their responsibility in control of a public forum. Further, there is an urgent need for careful research that will expose inappropriate female stereotypes and clichéd situations. Further consideration of the gender roles portrayed is also needed, as it is especially the young girls who seek "guidance" from the soaps for themselves and perceive the female characters to be role models. For example, a reconsideration of the female body image portrayed is necessary so that it matches the diversity that exists in real life, and not the current, nearly exclusive use of the underweight figure.

Equally important is the need to confront the fact that soaps also relate stories containing violence. In particular, it is sexual violence against the characters with whom the young viewers have the most identification that is recalled years later as a reason for shedding bitter tears. Findings regarding this point are extremely revealing: Several children answered the question "What has changed in your life since you have been watching *Good Times, Bad Times*?" by stating:

I now have more nightmares.

While more research in internalization of violence from viewing is needed, this feedback alone should cause producers and parents to develop much greater sensitivity to the role of soap operas in children's lives.

In short, the results of the study provide interesting insights into what viewing daily soaps really means to children and young people – especially to girls. A new format that seems to be similarly meaningful and attractive to boys is the programme *Big Brother*.

Meaning making of Big Brother

From an analytical point of view, *Big Brother* presumes to be a documentary format, but it is clearly dramatized according to the characteristics of a soap opera. While there is a virtual flood of studies in Germany that focus on the reasons why adults watch *Big Brother* (summarized by Götz, 2002), there are very few studies that seek to understand what children find interesting in this show. Our initial study takes into account that a comparison between the two formats is quite difficult, especially because in most cases enthusiasm for viewing the daily soaps develops over and endures for years, while at the time when this study was conducted *Big Brother* had only been on the air for six weeks. This having been noted, we were able to find many aspects that were similar to the *situational* and *interactive* functions of soap operas and even a few points related to the *subjective-thematic* ones.

Situational and interactive functions: "Let's watch Big Brother" and "Everybody is talking about it all the time"

As in the case of the soap opera, it is important to be aware of the integration of the phenomenon of *Big Brother* into the viewers' everyday life. That it is broadcast every evening at a reliable time makes it a suitable candidate for becoming integrated ritualistically into people's everyday life. For primary school children, regular reception of *Big Brother* was further aided by a positive attitude on the part of parents towards this format. All children in the study said they watched the programme with their parents and/or their siblings. 9-year-old Jana relates:

> And then my mother always used to say: "Come on, it's time for us to watch *Big Brother*."

Eight-year-old Lina always watches the first part of the programme together with her brother and reports that she goes over to her mother in the living room so that she can snuggle up to her for a while. From the perspective of the primary school children, in addition to viewing with their parents it also has the positive effect that they are allowed to stay up later.

In some families, viewing *Big Brother* takes place immediately after *Good Times, Bad Times*. Often, the regular ritual surrounding the daily soap is simply extended by one hour into the evening. As a result, the beautiful young characters of *Good Times, Bad Times* as well as ten other (para-social) friends of *Big Brother* come into the home.

In the case of the older primary school children, there is an additional decisive factor: *Big Brother* is something you have to know about if you want to join in conversations in the school playground. The pressure to follow the trend is, accordingly, high. Twelve-year-old Josi says:

> In school everybody is always talking about it.

Thus, *Big Brother* reception offers the chance of togetherness and of being informed through schoolyard talks the next day.

As for the contents, primary school children find it problematic that the show is "filmed everywhere". They especially find unpleasant the scenes in the shower or "when someone picks his nose". All those who took part in the study displayed a naive reception attitude, i.e., the children and adolescents (like many adults as well probably) assume that reality is actually being shown. In other words, none of the respondents in the sample (except for one adolescent) seemed to understand that what they are viewing has been consciously produced and edited.

"They have fun together": Watching togetherness

For many children and pre-teens who watch *Big Brother* regularly, it is the "to-getherness" of the participants that plays the primary role. They focus on the fact that these adults have time to talk things out and on the games in which teams have to prove that they can work together. Primary school children compare *Big Brother* to a holiday period. Some children imagine fantasies of ideal parents or elder siblings. Older children watch *Big Brother* because of the funny and entertaining moments of the format. They enjoy watching the participants joke and play tricks on one another.

"There you can watch it": Modelling skills of everyday life

For some older children and pre-teens the documentary format that exposes "real life" experiences is the most interesting aspect of the format. Watching daily routines such as

how they eat, clean or have a shower, says 12-year-old Nicholas, is very informative.

They use it as an idea or strategy resource for their own everyday lives. For example, 13-year-old Fritz tells us that he often argues with his parents. When he watches *Big Brother* he is most interested in learning

how they can live together without quarrelling.

"It is the real thing": The aesthetic style of the cool and authentic

For a few older children and pre-teens, *Big Brother* exemplifies the style of the cool and the authentic. For them, it is not a children's programme, but rather something for "youth". There "they show how real life is", 10-year-old Olaf tells us. And, Matthias, 10 years of age, says:

It's a great show because it's not following a script, it is reality.

These respondents, most of whom are boys, search for shows in which humour is a little bit more aggressive and comes to the "real" point.

"I have a new role model": Male characters as orientation

For some 9- to 13-year-old boys, *Big Brother* became the chance to grapple with being a man and to reflect on and discuss certain life situations. In particular, these boys focus on the male characters and their behaviours. They often dream they are part of the *Big Brother* team and share good times with their male mates. Thirteen-year-old Arne dreamt he was helping the male characters feed the chickens, and 9-year-old Janek imagined cutting one of the male character's hair. Thus, it seems that the boys pick out for themselves various factors of being a man in everyday life and adopt some of the characteristics of various male participants. So 13-year-old Peter tells us he wants to be exactly like one of the characters, "but I would also cook – that's what Zlatko didn't do". Fourteen-year-old Mario tells us that this is the most exciting show he has ever seen and that he wants to be one of the male characters. To the question: "What has changed in your life since you have seen the show for the first time?" he answers as follows:

More entertainment, more fun in life, and I have a new role model: Jürgen.

Problematic aspects of enthusiasm for Big Brother

There are quite a few problematic aspects in regard to the enthusiasm for *Big Brother*. Only in the group discussion with the girls was the ethical problem of "imprisoning" people in an experimental situation for a couple of months, filming them and publishing everything the TV station is interested in mentioned. The lack of viewers' awareness of the limited representation of different ethnic backgrounds and genders can be cited as problematic. Further, their naive understanding of *Big Brother* as a documentary programme, too, is problematic.

The most complicated point for me is the basic dualistic structure that presents the "right and accepted" way, to the exclusion of options that are not "in". Even primary school children understand that *Big Brother* is a game in which "behaving properly" is of considerable importance. For some, especially for older boys, the important thing is to discuss the participants' behaviours, as well as who and why one or another of the participants should be "voted out" of the house. As a behaviour- and personality-orientated game show, the basic concept of the programme is presentation according to the dramaturgy of soaps (cf., Mikos et al., 2000: 205). Participants are not nominated and selected on the basis of certain specific abilities, for example, athleticism or expertise in a specific field of knowledge. They are generally "voted off the show" because of their (edited) deportment, their opinions or other factors. This is, in principle, a personality-oriented exclusion.

Children and adolescents adopt this interpretation pattern when they grapple with the issue of whether it is possible to not be excluded. Some of the adolescent boys, in particular, seem to take great pleasure in condemning other aspects of the non-conformist characters out of hand. They focus especially on these elements when they have the parallel experience in their own lives of seeking to be "in the right group", wearing the "right things" and listening to the "right music". Further, we found that there seems to be no evidence of empathy for the participants voted off the show. For example, 12-year-old Sasha tells us:

Once it was extremely funny, when Manu, she is the one nobody likes, was sad, and that was funny [...] Manu has to go!

Further research

Daily soaps and such formats as *Big Brother* have become – whether we like it or not – an important socialization mechanism and authority for children and adolescents. The passion that young viewers develop for these programmes as well as the pleasure they find in watching and talking about them is certainly not to be begrudged. Nevertheless, a number of problematic factors exist that require further study, criticism as well as discussion in order to apprise producers of these findings and concerns and to assist them in becoming more sensitive to issues raised in this and future research studies.

Notes

1. *Gute Zeiten, schlechte Zeiten* is the German version of the soap *Good Times, Bad Times*. The concept of Grundy/UFA has its origin in Australia. It came to Germany via the Netherlands and is aired in Germany since 1992 on the private channel RTL right before prime time.
2. *Big Brother*, the German version of the worldwide successful format, takes place in Cologne. After the first three seasons, which were to be seen daily on the private channel RTL II, followed an endless variant in 2004. The aim of this latest development was to find out: Who will stay in the *Big Brother* house for one whole year?
3. The younger viewers (6- to 13-year-olds) were interviewed individually during an approximately 45-minute long session. The older ones were asked the same questions (with slight changes in the language) in a questionnaire format filled in on their own. They were asked, as well, a diverse set of open questions that gave them an opportunity to expand on their answers, such as: "How did you actually come across (name of programme)?", "Have you ever dreamt about (name of programme)?", "Do you talk among yourselves about (name of programme)?", etc. The sample was drawn from the whole of Germany and took into account different types of schools. In the analysis, the functions of fascination with soaps in everyday life were reconstructed for each participant in the sample. Following this analysis, the cases were clustered into typical appropriation patterns, and quantification of results was conducted by applying a coding system.
4. *Schloss Einstein* is a weekly soap, produced by the German public broadcasting system especially for 8- to 14-year-old children. Schloss Einstein is a boarding school and the protagonists of the programme are students of the 5th and 6th grades.
5. During the first half of 2002 (source: AGF-GfK PC#TV).
6. *Marienhof* is a daily soap produced by the German public broadcaster ARD. It is developed for the early evening programme and deals, above all, with social problems of people living in a neighbourhood.
7. *Unter uns* is a German daily soap aired by a private channel in the late afternoon. It focuses on the everyday life of teenagers and young adults living in an apartment house.
8. A quotation of a storyliner of the daily soap *Marienhof.*
9. Almost three out of five children and adolescents in the entire sample say that they have laughed heartily once, and over half describe how they have wept at the especially dramatic scenes, for example, the death of a principal figure.

References

Ang, I. (1986): *Das Gefühl Dallas. Zur Produktion des Trivialen*. Bielefeld: Daedalus. 172 p. (Watching Dallas: Soap opera and the melodramatic imagination)

Bachmair, B. (1996): *Fernsehkultur. Subjektivität in einer Welt bewegter Bilder*. Opladen: Westdeutscher Verlag. 356 p. (Subjectivity in a world of moving pictures)

Brown, M. E. (1994): *Soap opera and women's talk. The pleasure of resistance*. Thousand Oaks, CA: Sage. 213 p.

Brown, L. M.; Gilligan, Carol (1994): *Die verlorene Stimme. Wendepunkte in der Entwicklung von Mädchen und Frauen*. Frankfurt, Main: Campus. 280 p. (Meeting at the crossroads: Women's psychology and girls' development)

Carveth, R.; Alexander, A (1985): Soap opera viewing motivations and cultivation process. *Journal of Broadcasting and Electronic Media*, 29/1985/3, pp. 259-273.

Götz, M. (2002): *Alles Seifenblasen? Die Bedeutung von Daily Soaps im Alltag von Kindern und Jugendlichen*. München: KoPäd. 395 p. (Only soap bubbles? The significance of daily soaps for children and adolescents)

Harrington, L. C.; Bielby, D. D. (1995): *Soap Fans. Pursuing pleasure and making meaning in everyday life*. Philadelphia: Temple University Press. 224 p.

Herzog, H. (1944): What do we really know about daytime serial listeners? In: Lazarsfeld, P. F.; Stanton, F. N. (Eds.): *Radio Research 1942-1943*. New York, NY: Duell, Sloan and Pearce, pp. 3-33.

Lemish, D. (1985): Soap opera viewing in college: A naturalistic inquiry. *Journal of Broadcasting and Electronic Media*, 29/1985/3, pp. 275-293.

Liebes, T.; Livingstone, S. (1998): European soap opera. The diversification of a genre. *European Journal of Communication*, 13/1998/2, pp. 147-180.

Lu, L.; Argyle, M. (1993): TV watching, soap opera and happiness. *Kaohsiung Journal of Medical Sciences*, 10/1993/9, pp. 501-507.

Mikos, L.; Feise, P.; Herzog, K.; Prommer, E.; Veihl, V. (2000): *Im Auge der Kamera. Das Fernsehereignis Big Brother*. Berlin: Vistas. 223 p. (In the eye of the camera. The TV-event Big Brother)

Ong, W. J. (1982): *Orality and literacy: The technologizing of the word*. London: Methuen. 201 p.

Presnell, M. (1989): Narrative gender differences: Orality and literacy. In: Spitzzack, C.; Carter, K. (Eds.): *Doing research on women's communication: Perspectives on theory and method*. Norwood, NJ: Ablex, pp. 118-136.

Rubin, A. M. (1985): Uses of daytime television soap operas by college students. *Journal of Broadcasting and Electronic Media*, 29/1985/3, pp. 241-258.

Warth, E.-M. (1987): 'And that's my time': soap operas and the temporal organisation of women's everyday lifes. In: H. Borchers, G. Kreutzner, E.-M. Warth (Ed.): *Never-Ending Stories. American soap operas and the cultural production of meaning*. Trier: Wissenschaftlicher Verlag 1994, pp. 216-226.

Reception of TV Series among Children and Teenagers in Germany

Helga Theunert & Christa Gebel[1]

Television series are very popular among children and teenagers, mainly because these programmes are a source of entertainment and suspense, but also because they – as one 14-year-old states about the U.S. series *The Cosby Show* (Die Bill Cosby Show)[2] – contain "wisdoms for life". This quote inspired the authors to call their book, on which this article is based, *Wisdoms for Life to be Continued – Series Reception between Childhood and Adolescence.*[3]

The research project presented in the book focuses on German 9- to 15-year-olds' use and judgements of television series, as well as on what kinds of orientations girls and boys search for in these series.

The multiple study design combined qualitative and quantitative research methods, which comprised several stages:

- representative semi-structured personal interviews with 514 male and female recipients aged 9 to 15 from different regions in Bavaria in Germany and with different social backgrounds

- twenty in-depth interviews with girls and boys from the sample

- programme structure analysis of the output of eight public and commercial broadcasters regarding relevant series.

An overview of the research process is given in Figure 1.

In this article, the authors focus on three main findings:

1. the television series preferred by the girls and boys in the sample

2. the meaning of violence for the reception of the series

3. the series as a source of social orientation.

Figure 1. The research process

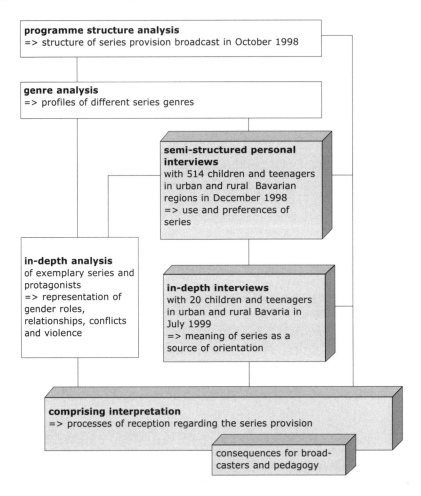

Which series do the 9- to 15-year-olds prefer?

One hundred and fourteen different series were running while the programme structure of the output of eight broadcasting stations was analysed in October 1998. Four fifths of these series were provided by commercial television, which, it turned out, the surveyed age group also prefers to watch. However, 9- to 15-year-olds use the whole supply of series to a rather limited extent. Their favourites are definitely situation comedies and soap operas. Seventy-seven per cent of the girls and boys in the sample prefer both of these predominantly daily broadcast formats.

Soap operas are the girls' domain. Two thirds of the girls in the sample favour them; among the 12- to 13-year-old girls, the proportion reaches 82 per cent. Three

German soap operas top the girls' hit list: *Gute Zeiten, schlechte Zeiten* (Good Times, Bad times) is on the top rung; it is the favourite series of more than one third of the girls. *Marienhof* (The People of Marienhof) and *Verbotene Liebe* (Forbidden Love) follow immediately after.[4] This quote from one 12-year-old mirrors what girls like about this format:

> You deliberately want to know how it ends. If he gets together with the other girl or if they finally try it again.

Confusions in love life and in the general daily experiences of young people on TV entice the girls to switch on the telly.

All in all, the boys are also interested in social communities, but they like it to be funny, with exaggerations and breaking of taboos. This is what they find in situation comedies. Two thirds of the boys prefer this genre. The greatest fans are the 14- to 15-year-old boys (almost 70 per cent of them have sitcoms as their favourites). Whereas sitcoms become less popular with the girls as they grow older, the pattern is just the opposite for the boys. Two American sitcoms top the boys' hit list of series: *Family Matters* (Alle unter einem Dach)[5] and *Married... with Children* (Eine schrecklich nette Familie).[6]

Moreover, it seems that more boys than girls have fun with programmes rich in action and suspense. Especially action, mystery and crime series are well received by boys.

On average, almost half of the girls and boys like genres that are full of suspense and excitement, and in this context particularly the U.S. mystery series *The X-Files* (Akte X – Die unheimlichen Fälle des FBI)[7] is worth mentioning. This series becomes relevant from the age of 12 and is a favourite among both girls and boys. Reasons for its popularity are not only the thrilling stories, but also the agent duo Dana Scully and Fox Mulder. Both of them are shown as confident personalities and offer differentiated gender roles. A striking part of the girls and boys appreciates this matter of fact with increasing age.

Even boys nominate Dana Scully as their favourite character – preferring a female character is extremely unusual among boys. One 15-year-old boy explains his affection as follows:

> In dangerous situations, Dana always does the right thing.

And one 13-year-old boy attests to "her – at times – intelligent charisma". But above all, girls and boys are deeply impressed by the couple's interpersonal interactions.

Soap operas and situation comedies, on one hand, and series rich in action and suspense, on the other, dominate the reception of television series among 9- to 15- year-olds. These selective preferences show what the age group in question has in mind: funny and exciting entertainment, and curiosity about the forthcoming period of adult life. This latter interest of both girls and boys focuses on relationships and interactions in social communities.

The meaning of violence in the reception of series

The television series preferred by the 9- to 15-year-olds do give a hint as to the meaning of violence in the children's reception: Stories containing physical violence – to which the public debate on media violence is usually reduced – are not favoured by the majority of the girls and boys in this sample. Half of the 514 respondents think that there is hardly any physical violence presented in the series they prefer. The other half recognizes violence mainly in series rich in action and suspense, such as the German *Heliocops – Einsatz über Berlin* (Helicops – Police Operation above Berlin),[8] mysteries like *The X-Files* and crime series like the German *Kommissar Rex* (Inspector Rex).[9] After all, every fifth interviewee feels that violent scenes go too far in some series – they exceed even the oldest girls' and boys' limits. The most often mentioned series in this context is the German *Alarm für Cobra 11 – Die Autobahnpolizei* (Alarm for Cobra 11 – The Motorway Police).[10] One 12-year-old girl expresses what is too much very appropriately:

> There is no other subject than violence.

The majority of children and teenagers in the sample cannot find anything "attractive" in violent scenes – in fact, it is rather the opposite.

Whether child or teenager, girls keep their distance from media representations of physical violence much more so than do the boys. However, also most of the boys dissociate themselves from the idea that the stronger sex must use their fists to manage life: From the age of 10, action series daredevils lose their ability to fascinate.

As regards physical violence, the analysed series supply contains disturbing, frightening, confusing and disorienting contents especially for the younger girls and boys. For the older ones, media violence is less troublesome, and if so then only in single action series. However, this result is confined to the output of television series, because older teenagers mention unanimously that films can also contain disturbing representations of violence. Even adolescents cannot cope with everything.

Apart from physical violence, the television series preferred by the majority of respondents contain other types of violence. Without blood and dead bodies, this non-physical violence focuses more on insults and meanness. Such psychic violence does not have less impact than physical violence. Thus, media representations can entail risks even when blood is not running.

Especially in a certain stage of development, when the majority of children have understood that physical violence is no recipe, other ways of getting one's way attract attention. Stepping on other people, taking advantage of them, bullying them – this is especially the pattern of soap operas. For some teenagers soaps also contain "wisdoms for life". One 14-year-old girl from one of the in-depth interviews explains the behaviour of Sonja from *Gute Zeiten, schlechte Zeiten*, who is wicked and always engaged in intrigues:

> Sometimes she pretends to be their friend, but behind their backs she starts shady dealings. I think it's funny when people act like that because sometimes I do the same... I just say "you are my friend" and then I do something against her.

In a way, this girl is checking to what extent such behaviour works, because she has already experienced that physical actions are nothing but disadvantageous. Now she is studying in soaps whether psychic attacks have a chance of success. And she is not the only one in that situation.

Series as a source of social orientation

The kinds of series children and adolescents are interested in depends very much on their stage of identity development and, therefore, on which issues they have to deal with. What is on the minds of the 9- to 15-year-olds is the formation of their sexual identity and their position within social communities and relationships. To find answers to questions related to these issues, girls and boys "scan" the whole output of series. Hence, series in which stories about social communities and relationships are told have top priority. This is particularly true among girls, who are twice as likely as boys to concentrate on such issues.

The contents of soap operas arouse particular interest in – mainly female – children and teenagers. Why this is a valuable source of learning is explained by one 15-year-old girl using *Marienhof* as an example:

> You can put yourself in that position... Because it's a story that could also happen in real life. He falls in love with a girl but she doesn't want him. Instead she falls for his best friend... and then the third one gets egg on his face. But pretty soon he finds himself another one. And this is like in real life, that you accept the facts.

Among the interviewees, a very grave argument for soap operas is their "realism". That soaps provide authentic insight into the everyday life of the younger generation is believed particularly by adolescents from less intellectually stimulating milieus. Children and teenagers with a more intellectual background mention the attempt at being realistic, but do not take the results at face value.

Series as a source of orientation can be illustrated, for example, with relationships. It is particularly girls, even young girls, who pay attention to relationships. However, boys also become interested in this topic during their transition into adolescence. Especially the older respondents come up with two very contradictory ideas about relationships and the ideal couple.

The first idea is illustrated by the previously mentioned couple Dana Scully and Fox Mulder in *The X-Files*. The description made by one 15-year-old, "well, they are simply a man and woman", is typical of the perception of the relationship between these two popular characters. First of all, Scully and Mulder are seen as competent types, who both achieve something and honour each other. At the same time, they cleverly combine their individual skills, something that makes them a "perfect team" and means they can absolutely rely on each other. And, after all, they are at least friends and probably – so their fans presume – there could be more to it than that. Such a relationship – to summarize the ideas of the interviewees – is based on the emancipated negotiation of the interests of two confident individuals. Mainly adolescents from intellectually stimulating milieus come up with this idea. However, in the preferred series they do not really find appropriate encouragement.

Especially soap opera fans have a completely different idea of relationships. "Holding hands through life" is the motto of a relatively large group of girls and boys from a rather impoverished social milieu. For them, love and harmony are one and the same thing. Once the right man and woman have found each other, they are the perfect counterparts, who unconditionally support each other and forgive each other all misconduct.

> They love each other deeply. They are always considerate of each other. When one doesn't like something, then they don't do it. They always talk before they do something. That's what I like.

This 13-year-old girl describes the relationship of Mascha and Sebastian in *Marienhof* as a profound and harmonic togetherness. Should anything disturb this harmony, everything will soon be "repaired" again. The core of this relationship idea is "harmonic togetherness", which solely depends on the notions of the "perfect" couple and that everything else will sort itself out.

It may be astonishing that this kind of relationship idyll is fed through soap operas. Usually soap characters live on relationship trouble, on rivalry, jealousy and separation. But the viewing girls, in particular, seem to overlook this matter of fact, only to dream their romantic vision of an ideal couple living in perfect harmony. Naturally, soap operas and other similar television series are not the only source of this dream. There are also other audiovisual and print media that have long been blatantly propagating this ideal. Still, television is a very important source of orientation for adolescents.

Consequently, television also has a responsibility in this regard. The minimum demand is: Do not send girls and boys, who are searching for a social and sexual identity, into a "dead end".

Two more aspects

Television series are a source of social orientation and therefore contribute to the ideas young people have about their future: about their position in a social community, their own role in a relationship, their dealing with conflicts, and so on.

In this context, two aspects should be considered: The first has to do with age. The majority of the children 10 years old and upward already understand that life takes place in a social context. The teenagers who still believe in the myth that fighting is the only solution are first of all those who really have to "fight" in their lives, either with a violent environment or with their own aggressiveness. The idea that life is a struggle is encouraged through watching series full of action and suspense – and by other TV formats and media.

The second aspect, which is a distinctive feature in our results, is connected with intellectually stimulating milieus. It is mainly young people growing up with the possibility to gain a differentiated picture of the world and their own future who express realistic and self-confident life plans. Their educationally deprived peers, on the other hand, come up with rather irrational ideas in which private happiness is the exclusive guarantee for a pleasant life. These teenagers prefer soap operas. Whatever they pick out from them, and at the same time understand as realistic, is nothing but an imagined modern and juvenile version of the ancient cliché of an ideal world.

Notes

1. The article was translated by Nadine Kloos, JFF (Institut für Medienpädagogik in Forschung und Praxis/Institute for Media Research and Media Education, München).

2. In this series, Dr. Cliff Huxtable, his wife, their many children and other family members cheerfully and self-confidently manage all the hurdles of daily life.

3. Helga Theunert & Christa Gebel (Hrsg.), 2000: *Lehrstücke für Leben in Fortsetzung. Serienrezeption zwischen Kindheit und Jugend.* BLM-Schriftenreihe Band 63, Verlag Reinhard Fischer, München: KoPäd. (in German) The book presents a research project conducted by the authors between 1998 and 2000 and funded by the BLM (Bayerische Landeszentrale für neue Medien), which licences and controls commercial broadcasting services in Bavaria, Germany. Interested readers are referred to the book for more detailed analyses and results, and for the implications for educational policymakers, programme makers and pedagogy.

4. All three German soap operas – soap fans may excuse this simplification – follow the same pattern: mainly young people experience all the complications and pleasures life can entail and try to find their own ways, using all kinds of measures.

5. In this sitcom, next-door neighbour Steve's actions cause nothing but chaos in the Winslow's home, especially when he pulls out all the stops to impress the Winslow's daughter Laura.

6. In this sitcom, Al Bundy and his chaotic lot try to manage – more or less successfully – the ups and downs of everyday live.

7. Two FBI agents try to solve supernatural and unexplainable phenomena.

8. In this series, a special unit of "helicopter cops" face crime using all sorts of high-tech gimmicks.

9. Various inspectors solve cases with the help of "Inspector Rex" – a German shepherd dog. This series is so popular that is it running in about 100 countries all over the world.

10. A detective inspector duo imposes law and order on German motorways.

From Beverly Hills to Big Brother
How Australian Teenage Girls Respond

Robyn Quin

This article discusses the sorts of meanings and pleasures that young audiences take from soap opera, of both the dramatic and the "real" forms. In the first category is the once popular American television soap opera, *Beverly Hills 90210*. This was a teen soapie, which followed the lives of a group of middle class, high school students living in Beverly Hills, U.S.A. Like all soap operas it had a core ensemble, here of ten characters, and regular guest appearances. It was structured around extended narratives but each episode also included a sub-plot, which was resolved within the episode. The extended narratives explored the making and breaking of friendships and romantic relationships, while the sub-plots tended to be issues based – drinking, shoplifting, cheating, sexually transmitted diseases, domestic violence, date rape, substance abuse, and the like. The discussion of audiences' interaction with *Beverly Hills 90210* is based on research undertaken during the 90s with female teenage fans of the drama.

In the second category of programs are the more recent so-called reality series, such as *Big Brother*. The latter part of the article makes comparisons between the sorts of pleasures offered to teenage girls by teen soap operas such as *Beverly Hills* and those offered by the reality television series *Big Brother*, drawing on the research of Jane Roscoe, Catherine Lumby and Elspeth Probyn.[1]

Audience research

The underlying premise of the discussion is that audiences are active in the production of meaning and that their interpretations and understandings will be variable and contingent. Since the mid-eighties, research into media audiences has fundamentally changed the way we view textual[2] meaning and the audience itself. In 1980 Stuart Hall said: "there seems some ground for thinking that a new and exciting phase in so-called audience research, of a quite new kind, may be opening up" (Hall, 1980, p. 131). This audience research was convincing in its argument that there is "more to watching TV than what's on the screen" (Morley, 1986, p. 47). The (then) new audience research offered a radical reconceptualisation of the audience. The work done by Hobson (1980, 1982), Brunsdon (1981) and Morley (1986) revealed how the social conditions of television viewing affect how and what television means. From the work of Katz and Liebes (1985), Ang (1985), and Hodge and Tripp (1986) we gained new insights into the polysemy and ambiguity of media texts. (Polysemy simply means the capacity to produce multiple meanings.) The new audience research shared a view of the audience member as a socially constructed subject. In this understanding the social subject has a history, lives in a particular social formation (a mix of class, gender, age, religion, language, etc.) and is constituted by a complex cultural history that is both social and textual. Briefly, the research found that audiences exerted substantial control of the mass communication process. The polysemic character of media texts allows audiences to construct a wide variety of decodings.

The problem for the researcher is to find out what meanings the audience is actually constructing from the media texts they consume. Most of what happens "when the text is 'realized' as a 'live' discourse, when it is read by the consumer is a mystery" (Hartley, 1982, p. 138). In order to unravel this mystery it is necessary to look at actual audiences and the ways audiences understand texts. It is only by understanding the meanings constructed by audiences, in this particular case, study the meanings of *Beverly Hills 90210* and *Big Brother*, that we can know "how that cultural form functions within the larger culture" (Radway, 1984, p. 99). But as Lewis says: "doing audience research is a messy and slippery business" (1991, p. 73), and working with teenage girls proved to be a messier and slipperier task than most. Teenage girls are not ideal subjects – they rarely finish a sentence, talk over each other and frequently dissolve into giggles. They speak a lot of the time in a code intelligible only to themselves: "yeah – but no way", "hot, real, real hot", "its like so magic", and so on.

Methodology

The approach used in the study of girls' responses to the soap opera *Beverly Hills 90210* – and Lumby's and Probyn's research into teenage girls' reactions to *Big Brother* – was modelled on the work of ethnographic researchers like Hobson (1982), Ang (1985), Radway (1984), Morley (1986), Tulloch (1989), and Livingstone and Lunt (1994). The best ethnographic methods require the researchers to immerse themselves in the culture of the viewer. For example, Morley and a team of researchers spent weeks living in households watching television with family members and subsequently published *Family Television* (1986). In the research into the young viewers of *Beverly Hills 90210* the researcher restricted herself to interviews, observations, group discussions and the analysis of fan letters, publicity materials and questionnaires. Group discussions, one-on-one interviews and written accounts of responses are all methods, which reveal the participants' own understandings of what they see and the pleasures they take from the viewing.

This research method has its own strengths and weaknesses. One major problem is that it relies on people telling us what they think. The fact that there is often, maybe always, a gap between what people think, and what they say they think, is to state the obvious. A second shortcoming (and it is one shared by all audience research methodologies) is that the method does not tell us why people think the way they do. We can collect evidence about their backgrounds, tastes, and experiences depending upon what they are willing to tell us, but in the end we can only guess at the relationship between their social history and what they say they think.

A strength of the method is that interviews and focus groups enable the researcher to have access to the opinions, viewpoints, attitudes and experiences of others. Of course, interviews are constructed situations involving differential power relations between researcher and subject and, in most cases, an unspoken but implicit agreement about what can be said, who can be spoken of and in what terms. Focus groups have proved useful to researchers who wish to minimise the distance between themselves and their research participants. In support of the use of focus groups is that the group situation may reduce the influence and power of the interviewer and shift the balance of power towards the group (Madriz, 2000, p. 838). Because focus groups emphasise the collective, rather than the individual, they are seen to foster the free expression of ideas (Denzin, 1986; Frey & Fontana, 1993). Furthermore, the literature suggests that potentially insightful communications occur in focus groups as a result of participant interaction. It argues that participants will often expand on experiences recounted earlier, add new information, and/or give the experience a new and sometimes different interpretation (Williams, Rice and Rogers, 1988, p. 38). An analysis of the interaction in a focus group can reveal the shared language on the topic, the taken-for-granted beliefs and attitudes, and the sources of information people call upon to justify their views and the types of information that stimulated changes of opinion or reinterpretation of experiences.

In the case of this study the focus groups for the soap opera *Bevery Hills 90210* were in fact affinity groups – groups of friends or classmates. Affinity groups offer certain advantages over focus groups that employ strangers. In an affinity group the participants do not spend most of the research time trying to get to know each other, establishing some sort of pecking order or laying claim to a specific role. The participants share ideas and concerns, compare experiences and sometimes debate with each other. On the other hand, in practice, the use of affinity groups raises other problems. Often participants already know, or pretend to know, the views of some of the other members and are not receptive to hearing them again. Although the influence of the power relations between the researcher and the participants may diminish, other power hierarchies are reproduced or quickly established within the group.

91

In the case under discussion the researcher watched ten episodes of *Beverly Hills 90210* with ten different groups of girls aged between 12 and 14 years – a total of 114 girls. During the screening she observed their interactions and recorded their comments. Immediately after the screening she encouraged a discussion of the episode, which was recorded on audiotape and later transcribed. In some, but not all, instances the focus group discussions were followed up with one-on-one interviews.

The process used was an iterative one. First, there was developed a tentative set of categories (or topics) from an analysis of the literature on television and audiences. These topics were used to generate discussion in the first three focus groups. The initial set of topics – characters both liked and disliked, the story line, the locations, the life styles, the conflicts, romances, peer and generational interactions in the series – were the conversation starters. If the topic held no interest for the participants in the focus groups it was not pursued and the girls determined the direction of the conversation. In this manner the first three focus groups were used as a tool to verify the categories previously constructed and find new topics, which seemed to be germane to the girls' interests. New issues, such as the importance of clothing, sex, physical appearance, or popularity, which had not figured in the initial set of categories, were raised again and again by participants. Thus, as the data collection progressed, new categories were added based on the participants' responses.

Using the categories generated from the literature and the focus groups, the transcripts were marked up and coded, which allowed for the complete range of responses to the issue to be called up. Transcripts were employed because:

> Actual words people use can be of considerable analytic importance. The situated vocabularies employed provide us with valuable information about the way in which members of a particular culture organise their perceptions of the world, and so engage in the social construction of the reality. (Hammersley & Atkinson, 1983, p. 153)

Findings

The pleasurable returns on the girls' investment of their time in viewing *Beverly Hills 90210* were multiple and various – but some pleasures were common to the group. The first point to be made about the results is the importance of genre in generating pleasure and meaning. Without exception the girls were familiar with the evening soap genre and delighted in exhibiting their knowledge. This took the form of second guessing what might happen next in the narrative, predicting characters' responses to situations, predicting (usually accurately) the resolution to a conflict. Some of the viewers could even accurately predict the location shifts in the narrative from one scene to the next. If the text is one they know, or from a genre with which they are familiar, then it is reasonable to assume that textual (and generic) competencies will be influential in the readings (Corner, 1991, p. 276).

Genre functions "like a code of behaviour established between the author and his reader" (Dubrow, 1982, p. 2). It raises audience expectations, its conventions make possible and impossible some events and actions and frames the viewer's approach to the text. In the case of *Beverly Hills 90210*, the genre and the girls' familiarity and expertise in the genre was a major source of their pleasure in the text. Even those respondents who purported to dislike the program and ridiculed the characters and narrative engaged in the same second-guessing and exhibition of knowledge of the genre as their fan friends:

> *Kylie:* Watch, watch Brenda will overhear and she'll get it wrong. She'll think Kelly is on with Dylan.

The second recurring theme in the responses related to respect. The level of deference the program showed for the intelligence and maturity of its audience was a strong source of pleasure for the young female viewers. The respondents made frequent and appreciative mention of the fact that the program tackled "big issues", "important issues" or "serious issues". When pressed to name these issues they were able to give detailed accounts of episodes dealing with AIDS and having an AIDS test, binge drinking, parental extra marital affairs, breast cancer, cheating and shoplifting. The interminable love affairs, petty jealousies and infidelities of the genre they dismissed as "part of the fun", "typical", "boring" or "American", but they spoke highly of the manner in which the program treated what they considered to be the important issues. The following interaction relates to an episode about Dylan's (a major character) alcohol abuse:

> *Sue:* He's had a problem with alcohol all along. He's tried to give up.
>
> *Jan*: He did. He's only drinking again because of his mother. It's the stress.
>
> *Ros:* Why did his mother come back? Where was she?
>
> *Sue*: It's like a disease – always waiting to come back.

The girls believed that the program "presented real problems" in "realistic ways", avoided "preaching" about behaviour and did not always "pretend that every problem got solved like most American TV shows". The presentation of open-ended, unresolved problems in the narrative they saw as a mark of respect for the viewer – "they don't treat us like dummies".

A third common theme in the participants' responses had to do with projection of themselves into situations and, most especially, relationships. The girl viewers invested most of their interest (and subsequent discussions) in the evolution and dissolution of relationships, sexual and platonic, same sex and opposite sex. Much of the discussion during the viewing sessions was about how the girls themselves would deal with the issues raised in the narrative representation of characters' relationships. These sorts of discussions were peppered with phrases such as "If I were her… If he did that to me I would… I would never… If it were me I would feel…". Their discussion of their own probable or possible behaviours did not always fit with the generic expectations raised by the program. For example, in response to the issue of alcohol abuse nearly half the girls in the study insisted that they would end the relationship rather than helping (as do the characters in the episode) the abuser with his problem:

> *Ann*: If it were me I would get out quick smart.
>
> *Julie*: Me too. Here he will get over it in a month or so but in real life I know it takes a lot longer.
>
> *Ros*: My uncle was an alchy… he always went back to it.

The issue of projection and the ways in which the girls in this study used the soap opera to air and test their 'solutions' to virtual but potential problems in their own lives has a corollary in teenage girls' responses to reality television.

Reality TV and teenage girls

Teenage soaps such as *Beverly Hills 90210* may be a thing of the past but reality television now seems to be used in a similar way by girls in their early teens. Following *The Truman Show* (USA, 1998, Peter Weir)[3] surveillance has become a key narrative device of television and teenagers are some of its keenest fans. Following an original concept developed by Dutch producer John de Mol, programs under the title *Big Brother* have been produced in several countries. *Big Brother* and its various offspring present surveillance as spectacle. The shows follow the same format – a group of people lives for a set number of weeks in a purpose-built house complete with hidden cameras and microphones. Each week one of the participants is evicted after a secret ballot within the group (or more lately by the viewers) until the last remaining participant is left to collect the cash prize at the end of the series.

Despite the fact that *Big Brother* does not use a script or professional actors these sorts of programs bear no more resemblance to any meaningful definition of the real than does *Beverly Hills 90210*. *Big Brother* does not present a real home inhabited by real people but a location riddled with cameras and microphones just like a television set. While the participants do not have a script to follow they must play a role – a role which requires them to change their behaviour in order to be a winner and avoid eviction from the set for as long as possible. This is not life seen through the lens of a television camera but, like *The Truman Show*, life within television (Tiso, undated).

Jane Roscoe, Head of Screen Studies at the Australian Film, Television and Radio School, found that the females in the 10-17 year-old demographic were not only a significant fan group for *Big Brother* but very high users of the web sites supporting the program. She found the ratio of male to female viewers accessing the website to be 20:80. She argues that reality programs like *Big Brother* create a space in which emotions, interpersonal relations and sexuality are scrutinised and examined (Roscoe, 2003). Roscoe contends that the first *Big Brother* series was transformative in its reversal of public and private life in that they allowed traditional expectations and assumptions to be questioned and problematised (2003).

Lumby and Probyn have reported on their initial findings from focus group data gathered as part of a large research project into "GirlCultures". They questioned hundreds of girls about what they found engaging in *Big Brother*. The girls repeatedly said that they were searching for ways to be themselves and still be acceptable to their group. Lumby says: "when you look at Big Brother through that lens, it's all about how do you perform yourself" (quoted by Tuohy, 2003). This, she says, explains the huge popularity of Sarah-Marie, one of the participants from the first *Big Brother* series. An overweight girl, she said in one episode: "I woke up this morning in love with my tummy again. I love my tummy sometimes, it's so big and soft…" In another episode she is congratulated by the host for having the courage to lie in a bikini alongside one of the very glamorous stick-thin contestants. Sarah-Marie replied: "Well we've all got the same bits, mine are just bigger." According to Lumby and Probyn, teenage girls feel themselves to be under constant surveillance from their peers, males, the popular media, parents, teachers and other "experts" and Sarah-Marie was seen by them as someone who was sufficiently brave and tough to return the gaze and not feel compelled to conform to other people's expectations (Lumby, 2004).

Lumby and Probyn found that girls used the *Big Brother* series in a similar manner to the viewers of *Beverly Hills 90210*, that is, to observe and analyse the behaviour of others, to check out what worked and what did not, and to try to ascertain what sorts of behaviours brought the rewards they were seeking. The program offers viewers a sort of "relationship laboratory" where friendships, passions and feuds can be observed and contemplated, judged and criticised without any threat to the self. *Big Brother* makes it socially and ethically acceptable to sit and stare at others.

In conclusion

In conclusion, the key to understanding teenage girls' pleasure in reality programs seems to revolve around their interest in "relationship-watching" and here their pleasures are similar to those delivered by the soap opera *Beverly Hills 90210*. Girls too old for Barbie and Ken, but too young for full-on real life relationships, get some visceral satisfaction from reality TV shows. For early teenage girls "relationship-watching" is as important a preoccupation as latest MPG (music) downloads from the Internet, mobile phone attachments, text-messaging, eating disorders and fickle fashion fetishes in denim and plastic.

Notes

1. Catherine Lumby and Elspeth Probyn have a large scale Australian research Council grant to investigate the culture of teenage girls. Their work is articulated in the online article by Lumby – see the list of references.
2. 'Text' here is used to refer a signifying structure that has a physical existence independent of its sender or receiver. A text consists of a network of codes working on a number of levels and is thus capable of producing a variety of meanings according to the socio-cultural experience of the reader. In this way a book, a film, a television show, a CR music recording, and a transcript of a speech are all texts.
3. *The Truman Show* presents us with an insurance assessor, the Truman of the title, who unbeknownst to him is living inside a 24 hour a day comedy melodrama in which he is the star. Hidden cameras and microphones capture his every deed and word while the television director calls the shots from a studio high in the sky.

References

Ang, I. (1985). *Watching Dallas*. London: Methuen.

Brunsdon, C. (1981). Crossroads: Notes on a soap opera. *Screen, 22*(4), 31-37.

Corner, J. (1991). Meaning, genre and context: The problematics of 'public knowledge' in the new audience studies. In J. Curran & M. Gurevitch (Eds.), *Mass media and society* (pp. 267-284). London: Edward Arnold.

Denzin, N. (1986). A postmodern social theory. *Sociological Theory, 4*, 194-204.

Department of Employment, Education and Training. (1991). *Retention and participation in Australian schools 1967 to 1990*. Canberra: Australian Government Publishing Service.

Dubrow, H. (1982). *Genre*. London: Methuen.

Frey, J. H. & Fontana, A. (1993). The group interview in social research. In D. L. Morgan (Ed.), *Successful focus groups: Advancing the state of the art* (pp. 20-34). Newbury Park, CA: Sage.

Hall, S. (1980). Encoding/decoding. In S. Hall, D. Hobson, A. Lowe & P. Willis (Eds.), *Culture media language* (pp. 128-139). London: Hutchinson.

Hartley, J. (1982). *Understanding news*. London: Methuen.

Hobson, D. (1980). Housewives and the mass media. In S. Hall, D. Hobson, A. Lowe & P. Willis (Eds.), *Culture media language* (pp. 105-114). London: Hutchinson.

Hobson, D. (1982). *Crossroads: The drama of a soap opera*. London: Methuen.

Hodge, B. & Tripp, D. (1986). *Children and television: A semiotic approach*. Oxford: Polity Press.

Katz, E. & Liebes, T. (1985). Mutual aid in the decoding of Dallas: Preliminary notes from a cross-cultural study. In P. Drummond and R. Paterson (Eds.), *Television in transition* (pp.187-198). London: British Film Institute.

Lewis. J. (1991). *The ideological octopus: An exploration of television and its audiences*. New York: Routledge.

Livingstone, S. & Lunt, P. (1994). *Talk on television: Audience participation and public debate*. London: Routledge.

Lumby, C. (2004). Out of the slipstream: The creation of celebrities. *On line opinion: e-journal of social and political debate*. Retrieved 18 September 2004, from http://www.onlineopinion.com.au/print.asp?article=2541

Madriz, E. (2000). Focus groups in feminist research. In N. K. Denzin & Y. S. Lincoln (Eds.), *Handbook of qualitative research* (2nd Ed., pp. 835-850). Thousand Oaks, CA: Sage.

Morgan, R. (1996). Pan textualism, everyday life and media education. *Continuum: The Australian journal of media and culture, 9*(2), 14-34.

Morley, D. (1986). *Family television: Cultural power and domestic leisure.* London: Comedia.

Radway, J. (1984). *Reading the romance: women, patriarchy, and popular literature.* Chapel Hill: University of North Carolina Press.

Roscoe, J. (2003). Reality Television. Radio interview on *Perspective*, Radio National, presented by Sandy McCutcheon. Retrieved 17 September 2004, from http://abc.net.au/rn/talks/perspective/stories/s873795.htm

Tiso, G. The spectacle of surveillance: Images of the panopticon in science-fiction cinema. Retrieved 19 August 2004, from http://homepages.paradise.net.nz/gtiso/filmessay

Tulloch, J. (1989). Afterword: Approaching audiences – a note on method. In J. Tulloch & G. Turner (Eds.), *Australian television: programs, pleasures and politics* (pp. 187-201). Sydney: Allen and Unwin.

Tuohy, C. (2003). Hooked on watching others do the ordinary? *The Age,* 18 July. Retrieved 17 September 2004, from http://www.theage.com.au/articles/2003/07/18/1058035202821.html

Williams, F., Rice, R. E. & Rogers, E. M. (1988). *Research methods and the new media.* New York: The Free Press.

Children Interacting between Values at School and in Media

Reflections from a Norwegian Project

Asbjørn Simonnes & Gudmund Gjelsten

Our research project constitutes an attempt to discover how a group of children aged 11-12 and 15-16 years experience the dual value influence from school and media. At school they are taught normative, "intentional" values. In media productions they encounter value profiles ranging from values close to those they are taught at school to values that are, quite obviously, the contrary. We have chosen to label the informal "functional" values as values from the "parallel school" of the media. As researchers we have, just as many other adults do, several assumptions about what this value dualism does to children. Our research, however, had as its main goal to enter into a dialogue with children, and to elicit their reflections on how they experience being in an interaction between the values of school and media.

This four-year research project, "The Child in the Interaction between Intentional and Functional Education", in Western Norway was endorsed and financed by The Research Council of Norway.[1] We are not able to give a comprehensive presentation of our research project here, but will concentrate on only a few aspects of children's attitudes toward soap operas.

The context and approach

The about 500 children participating in this study come from seven municipalities in the county of Møre and Romsdal in Norway. The municipalities were not chosen randomly – we aimed at getting a varied representation of municipalities with regard to population density (rural-urban), source of income, etc. As a consequence, our investigation does not allow statistical generalization, a problem shared with most social research. However, there is no reason to consider the investigation as a mere narrative about some pupils in some places at a given point of time. Most issues regarding generalization must be discussed on a rational basis, considering different factors that weigh for or against the transferring of results to other contexts. The trends in our findings are very similar in the different municipalities, which supports the assumption that they are reasonably valid for the whole county of Møre and Romsdal.

Seeing the media world from a child perspective is a difficult task for several reasons. Some questions may have been misunderstood by the children. Some children may have paid lip service to adult expectations, or may have tried to provoke adults. Further, children (as well as adults) have a limited ability to express their real attitudes, not being fully conscious of how they are influenced by the media. In addition, we should keep in mind that there is more than one child perspective, as different children live in different media environments.

In the research project as a whole, we have chosen to focus on three main problem areas:

- What dominating values do we find in the "parallel school" of the media? Are these values similar to or different from the set of values in the latest governmental planning document for the Norwegian public school (grades 1-10), called L-97? We focus especially on values and norms regarding relationships, attitudes, tolerance and problem solving.

- How do children and young people react to what they see and hear in the "parallel school"? How do they consider the relationship between the values and attitudes existing in the established upbringing/education passed on to them in home and school, and the values and attitudes they encounter in the products of the "parallel school"?

- To what degree do children and young people experience being in a "crossfire" between the intentional school/upbringing and the "parallel school"? What challenges do the "parallel school" represent for pedagogical research and practice today and in the future? And how do these challenges affect family life?

Definitions of some key terms

The public school curriculum in Norway includes both legal directives and a syllabus that make it an intentional teaching document. By "intentional" we mean that the objectives of L97 by law are to be implemented in the Norwegian public school system, implying both the value profile and the factual knowledge in each subject. With "functional" education we mean non-formal education outside the classroom – in the home, in the local environment and through the media. We have focused on the role of the media, considering the media to be the major "parallel school" of functional education today.

The term "intentional values" has been studied in the context of L97, which has a value universe similar to that found in the UN Universal Declaration of Human Rights. We have compared these values with the value profiles of mass media products, primarily visual media, including computer and Internet presentations.

The term "child" we understand, as defined by the UN, as a person up to the age of 18. In practice, we deal with children up to the age of 16, which marks the end of the Norwegian primary public school education. By the term "interaction" we maintain that children have competencies to interpret media messages and also assess the teaching in the classroom.

Method

As a normative document, L97 does not inform about the real teaching practice, or how values are practiced and taught in classrooms. However, the status of L97 as a legally binding directive suggests a reasonably high degree of correspondence between values in L97 and values emphasized in real school life.

The "parallel school" of the media has no legally binding directives, often not even common guidelines. Therefore, to have an idea about values in the "parallel school", we must study the media products themselves. It is, naturally, impossible to analyze the enormous universe of media products.

As concerns television, we therefore decided to analyze episodes from TV series that in our questionnaires turned out to be the most popular among the age groups in question. For this article, we will focus on the two most popular TV programs, which were *Hotel Cæsar* among the 11- to 12-year-olds and *Friends* among the 15- to 16-year-olds. *Hotel Cæsar* is a Norwegian produced soap opera that has been broadcast for five years. The market share of this action drama is especially high among children and young teenagers. *Friends* is an American, ten-year running, internationally popular comedy series. Both programs are comical in character. Two episodes of these series were analyzed both by the researchers and, after being shown to the pupils, by the pupils.

As emphasized, we do not claim that the values appearing in these episodes of *Hotel Cæsar* and *Friends* are representative of all values in the "parallel school". However, focusing on children, our aim was to make a selection as representative as possible of *their* "parallel school" experience. Ideally, we would have analyzed more than one episode of each of the series, and more than two series. Practical reasons made it necessary to limit the analysis. Nevertheless, considering some of the results in this article, there is reason to believe that the two episodes lay a fairly good foundation for comparing values in the Norwegian school and the "parallel school", as comedies, soap operas and action series are generally the most popular types of TV programs in the age groups studied. To the degree that differences are found between the values in the selected episodes and the dominating values in the Norwegian public school, there should be no reason to believe that we would have found more significant differences if we had been able to analyze a larger sample of the pupils' favorite programs. It should once again be noted, however, that we compare *prescriptions* for the school, not the concrete values taught in the classroom, with actual TV episodes.

In our research project, we used both quantitative and qualitative methods, as well as literary and literacy analysis. In Table 1, we give an overview of all data collection procedures.

Table 1.   Overview of data collection procedures

	Questionnaire, Sept-Dec 2000	Interview, Feb-April 2001	Literacy analysis form, Feb-April 2001
6th graders,11-12 years and10th graders,15-16 years	Information about yourself Media equipment and use of the media in the home Use of media outside the home and school School and visual media use Favorite TV programs The visual media and their influence Attitudes to the visual media Values in the media and values in school	Media and leisure activities The content of media programs Values in school and values in the media Media and advertising	The goal of the program, and the target age group Experiences of the persons in the program Emotional reactions to the program Values in the program and values in school Wish for changes in the program
Parents	Information about your family Media equipment and the use of the media in the home Your own information/ knowledge and experience of the media Values in the home and values in the media The home in a media society	Media in the family's daily life The content of the media programs Values in the media and values in the home Media and advertising The school and media	
Teachers	Personal information Thoughts regarding the relation between school and the visual media Values in school and values in the media The role of the teacher in a media society	Values in school, in homes and in the media The content of media programs	

The children's program preferences

The pupils were asked why they use various media. The alternatives given were for "excitement", "learning", "entertainment", "nothing special" and "other". It turned out that "excitement" and "entertainment" are the most common reasons for using most types of media. However, when it comes to the use of a PC, with or without Internet, a wish to "learn" seems to be an important reason. "Learning" is also mentioned as one of the reasons for watching TV by 22 percent of the 6th graders and close to one third of the 10th graders. Generally, we see that it seems easier for the older children to choose the alternative "entertainment", while the younger children prefer "excitement".

Table 2 shows that "comedies/comedy series" are the television genre most preferred by both age groups and both genders. Among the 6th graders, 65 percent of the boys and 74 percent of the girls have this type of program among the three they like best, and the same is the case for as many as 83 percent of the boys and 90 percent of the girls in 10th grade. Among the girls, "soap operas" is a clear number two; 70-80 percent of them in both grades have marked this type of program. Sixth grade boys show a preference for "action", but in 10th grade the difference between boys and girls in relation to action has almost disappeared.

"Cartoons" is popular among half of the 6th graders, while just below 15 percent of the 10th graders have marked this category. Among the boys, 40-50 percent have marked "sports programs", compared to about 20 percent among the girls. Sports programs seem to have slightly higher popularity in 10th grade than in 6th grade. "Science fiction" is also a more popular genre among boys than among girls.

About one quarter of the 10th graders have marked "news/information" among the three types of programs they like best. In both these age groups, just a few persons take an interest in "debate programs".

Table 2. **Which TV programs do you usually prefer to watch?** Percent having mentioned each type of program among the three types they like best. N = 291 (6th grade), 212 (10th grade)

	6th grade			10th grade		
	Boys	**Girls**	**Total**	**Boys**	**Girls**	**Total**
News/information	18.5	23.1	20.6	26.9	24.0	25.5
Cartoons	55.4	44.0	50.2	13.9	14.4	14.2
Sport	43.9	17.2	31.6	49.1	24.0	36.8
Quiz shows	23.6	26.9	25.1	14.8	17.3	16.0
Debate programs	8.9	6.7	7.9	4.6	8.7	6.6
Action	57.3	32.1	45.7	43.5	39.4	41.5
Documentaries/nature programs	22.9	20.1	21.6	13.0	12.5	12.7
Comedies/comedy series	65.0	73.9	69.1	83.3	90.4	86.8
Science fiction	31.2	12.7	22.7	25.0	11.5	18.4
Soaps	45.9	71.6	57.7	38.9	79.8	59.0

The children were also asked to write down the names of three TV programs, series or individual programs they personally had liked or like best. The 6th graders spread their first choices over close to 100 different programs and the 10th graders over more than 50 programs. Nevertheless, there are two clear favorites, *Hotel Cæsar* and *Friends. Hotel Cæsar* received 20 percent of the first votes in 6th grade and *Friends* 7 percent, and these two series also received most second votes among these younger children. In 10th grade the sequence is reversed – *Friends* received nearly half of the first votes, while *Hotel Cæsar* received 8 percent and *Ally McBeal* 4 percent, programs that received most second choices, too, among the 15- to 16-year-olds.

The main reason for liking *Friends* is "entertainment". Besides, some say they like the program because of the actors. "Entertainment" is the most commonly mentioned reason for liking *Hotel Cæsar*, as well, among the older children. Most 6th graders say they like it because it provides "excitement". It is worth noting that about 10 percent of those who chose *Hotel Cæsar*, in both age groups, mentioned "to gain insight into adult life" as a reason.

Naturally, the kind of program a child wants to see may depend on her/his mood at the moment. The questionnaire does not capture such variations, but they are reflected in the interviews. One 10th grader reflected on his choice:

> It depends on the mood I'm in. If I'm sort of depressed, then I prefer killings and actions. If I'm in a good mood, then I want conflicts to be solved peacefully.

As a reply to our question of whether a positive program would be uplifting when one is depressed, he answered:

> Yes, maybe, but actually I think I might have turned off such a program, because when I'm in a bad mood, I don't like looking at scenes showing friendliness and goodwill.

Another question asked the pupils which type of media they personally feel is most beneficial to them. As expected, television wins. In both age groups, 75-80 percent give TV programs (among the three types of media preferred in this respect) the highest ranking. Two thirds of the 10th graders mentioned PC with Internet (among the three types giving them most benefit), compared to close to half of the 6th graders. Computer and video games are mentioned by somewhat more than 60 percent of the 6th graders, and 35 percent of the 10th graders. Other media are mentioned by less than half of the children.

Hotel Cæsar and Friends

In our comparison of values in L97 with values in the "parallel school", we focused, as mentioned, on the values of "relationships", "attitudes", "tolerance" and "problem solving". We find differences between the two analyzed episodes of *Hotel Cæsar* and *Friends* in these regards. While "problem solving" through dialogue seems to be absent in the episode of *Hotel Cæsar*, it is clearly present in *Friends* – but more as an entertainment detail than as a serious attempt to solve the problems. The "relationships" portrayed in the episode of *Hotel Cæsar* may be characterized by an "I don't care" attitude and an absence of "tolerance".

Nevertheless, even if the two TV episodes are different in style, they show some similarities in their treatment of value issues: Because the programs aim to entertain, value issues are not treated seriously. To the extent that the children use the programs to learn about adult life, there is an obvious value conflict between the values in the programs and the values in L97 in the school.

The researchers' analysis of the two episodes

The dramaturgical profile of *Hotel Cæsar* is dominated by interpersonal conflicts of all kinds and levels. The episode shown to the 6th graders is filled with conflicts. Smiles seem to be ironical and condescending except for in one incident: A young father returns from the hospital with his baby son. He is warmly received by a couple of members of the staff.

The episode starts with two female staff members giving a young non-white foreigner, the boyfriend of another staff member, a drink mixed with pills, which causes him to lose consciousness. The foreigner is subsequently undressed and put naked in a wheelchair. The wheelchair is set moving down the reception floor, hits a lady and the naked man falls upon her, causing the laughing reaction of the two female staff members.

The grand old lady in the plot is furious because she is not selected as a guardian. She declares the person preferred as inferior in character and useless. Other members of her family are afraid that the choice of guardian may have serious economic consequences. A young member of the family has been kidnapped. The police seem unable to do much. Secret negotiations are under way with one of the kidnappers. Two lovers in the staff have a confrontation, which leads to hard words and a break off of relations.

What is the purpose of this production? It is produced by a commercial television company and must be financed and yield a profit through advertising. This purpose seemed to have been met, as the series has long been broadcast daily. But what is the purpose of this particular format filled with all kinds of conflicts and mistrust in staff and ownership relations at this very special hotel? We find that this episode presents an adult world full of intrigues and questionable behavior and wonder whether the more or less normal real-life tensions between adults and young teenagers may increase through this highly geared conflict profile. Data also show that a large part of the actual viewers are not only between 11 and 16, but also below eleven years of age.[2] As mentioned, some of the 6th graders in our study watched *Hotel Cæsar* to "learn about adult life", and many children in general often watch adult programs. Adult behavior in programs is then considered to be a source of information about what it means to be an adult.

Letting a non-white be exposed to abuse and ridicule sends a very negative signal to young people. Likewise, the mixture of tablets and alcohol is irresponsibly and superficially treated.

The manifest messages in this episode are easy to describe. But are the children able to detect the *latent* messages? Mixing alcohol and pills is dangerous and in certain circumstances lethal. The fact that there is no reaction to this on the part of the hotel administration is more than strange. In real life settings, incidents such as this would have led to severe reactions, and the staff members involved might have lost their jobs.

How do the values in this episode of *Hotel Cæsar* compare to the key values we give special attention to in our research? The term "relationship" in our context indicates contact that may be of a high or inferior quality. The Jewish philosopher Martin Buber contends that normal life is dialogic. In his view, persons are knowable only in I-Thou (Ich-Du) relationships.[3] This implies that genuine human communication requires an interaction of mutual interest and respect. The *relationships* portrayed in this episode of *Hotel Cæsar* are characterized by mutual distrust and an "I don't care" attitude. The quality of relationships depends on the *attitudes* of the persons involved. The attitudes displayed in this TV episode appear to be cold and tactical. *Problem solving* through honest dialogue seems to be absent. The absence of *tolerance* of a person of a different race is, implicitly and explicitly, revealed in action and conversation. We observe, therefore, a collision between the values in *Hotel Cæsar* and those in L97.

The actors in *Friends* are able professionals. They are a mixture of older teenagers and young adults in appearance. Their backgrounds indicate more the young adult situation than that of teenagers. Nevertheless, the plots expose young persons attempting to find partners and jobs – interesting issues for both teenagers and young adults. Insecurity, clumsiness, self-irony and good humor give the series an enjoyable and relaxing atmosphere. The nervousness of Ross meeting his possible future father-in-law, and the teasing comments of his friends, create a natural and inviting opening sequence. The dialogue between Ross and his prospective father-in-law is portrayed in a humorous and quite entertaining way. The same is the case with the problems facing another member of the group, trying to settle down in a new job.

Turning our attention to the value aspects, the issues are less simple. The manifest "messages" are entertaining descriptions of two young men, representing quite normal situations in the life of young people. What are the latent messages? There is little overt discussion about values, but value issues often surface throughout this episode. Ross has been married before, more than once. He also has a six-year-old son from one of his marriages. His former marriages appear more as a back stage decoration than as an issue for serious ethical consideration. The flirting intimacy between the prospective father-in-law and one of Ross' ex-wives makes Ross furious. But Ross calms down when this seems to have been done to help him. The covert messages are that what really matters is to adjust to new situations, and live on without bothering to discuss seriously ethics and morals in inter-human relations. The ethical profile indicates an immoral or amoral attitude despite a friendly and humorous appearance. Is the covert message perhaps a purposeful caricature of modern life regarding man – woman relations, as well as of the situation on the labor market? But is it a sound policy to create 'pure entertainment' of something that has many serious consequences for so many – divorce, misuse of alcohol, problems at work? Mass production of plots that make fun of strongly felt human problems is problematic. There are happy marriages; there are good working situations. There are problems that are being solved. We consider that the value aspects in *Friends* are superficially treated.

Principally, we find a collision between L97 and this episode of *Friends*, as well. But the collision is softer and friendlier than in the episode of *Hotel Cæsar*.

Both *Hotel Cæsar* and *Friends* expose a "value free" attitude vis-à-vis intentional value norms (in our context in L97). If the problems touched upon in these programs are in fact considered as a type of education about adult life, then children are receiving an erroneous picture of the responsibility aspect involved in adult life. Even if we have to take into account that these episodes represent an entertainment genre, there need not be a contradiction between being entertaining and paying more attention to generally accepted ethical norms.

6th graders' analysis of Hotel Cæsar

Immediately after we had shown the episodes of *Hotel Cæsar* (for the 6th graders) and *Friends* (for the 10th graders), our pre-prepared literacy analysis form was distributed to the pupils. After the pupils had completed filling in the forms, an informal discussion followed between the researchers and the pupils on various aspects of the episode. The inputs from the pupils were interesting and thought provoking.

Two questions in the form for *Hotel Cæsar* deal explicitly with the values passed on by the program. As can be seen from Table 3, most pupils 11-12 years of age find that people in *Hotel Cæsar* are "dishonest" and "don't tell the truth" – about three quarters mark these alternatives. Accordingly, close to 70 percent have marked that people "solve conflicts in a bad way". About 60 percent think that "people who are different are made fun of" (while about 30 percent think they are "respected"). These answers may indicate that the pupils are critical of the values in the program – but perhaps this is just what makes them feel that the program is exciting? At the same time, one cannot ignore the possibility that they have learned that they should be critical of *Hotel Cæsar*. We, therefore, do not know to what degree the results are based solely on the children's own reflections.

It is obvious from Table 4 that the 11- to 12-year-olds experience a clear difference between the values they meet in this program and the values they learn

Table 3. **What kind of values do you find in the program?** Percent.
N = 285

People...	tell the truth	don't tell the truth
	15.4	76.8
People are...	honest	dishonest
	13.0	75.8
People solve conflicts...	in a good way	in a bad way
	21.1	69.1
People who are different are...	made fun of	respected
	59.3	29.5
You notice some people because they are...	extra nasty	extra nice
	64.6	24.2

in school. The difference is particularly clear in relation to the use of "alcohol and narcotics". More than 70 percent of the pupils characterize this difference as large. More than 60 percent do the same in relation to "swearing". When it comes to "honesty", "politeness", "obedience", "respect for other people", "stealing", "brutality" and "violence", most pupils think there is a difference between *Hotel Cæsar* and what they learn in school. The only given values for which more than 20 percent of the pupils have marked "no difference" concern "responsibility for the environment" and "equal treatment of boys and girls".

Table 4. **What do you think of the values you meet in this program compared to those you learn at school?** (Check one square on each line below) Percent. N = 285

	No difference	Slight difference	Big difference	Not answered
Be honest	9.1	34.7	54.0	2.1
Show respect/caring	12.6	44.6	40.4	2.5
Obey your parents/guardians	17.5	32.3	46.3	3.9
Speak politely	11.9	29.8	54.4	3.9
Tell the truth	12.6	37.5	46.3	3.5
Respect other people	11.2	45.6	39.3	3.9
Don't be brutal towards others	14.0	31.6	48.1	6.4
Solve problems by talking	14.7	44.2	37.2	3.9
Don't use violence and vandalism	15.4	22.5	56.5	5.6
Show responsibility for the environment	26.7	35.4	33.7	4.2
Avoid alcohol/narcotics	10.9	11.9	71.6	5.7
No backbiting or gossip	14.7	37.2	42.8	5.3
Don't steal/shoplift	12.3	30.5	52.6	4.6
Don't swear	14.7	20.4	61.1	3.9
Treat boys and girls the same (equality)	32.3	36.5	27.4	3.9

The children were also asked "whether there was anything they would like to be different in the program" (and could mark several alternatives). Sixty-eight percent "would have liked more humor in the program", and slightly over 50 percent "more excitement and drama". This result is in good correspondence with the fact that the children give high priority to entertainment and excitement when they watch TV. Of the three other alternatives given, each has been marked by slightly more than one third of the pupils: "the way people talk to each other", "the way they solve problems" and "the use of alcohol". We notice that, even if the children are aware of the differences in values between the program and the school, and some of them even give the program relatively hard criticism because of that, there seems to be a much more widespread wish to have more excitement and humor in the program than there is wish for changing the values.

The 6th graders, as well, were invited to give further comments on the program in their own words. About 200 (of the 285) took this opportunity. There is a clear dominance of critical and negative comments. The program is particularly criticized for sex, swearing and extensive use of alcohol. Another example is:

> It's stupid that they show so much violence. The program is on quite early in the evening. Sometimes it's quite amusing, but I'm not allowed to watch it. It's rubbish-TV most of the time.

However, the entertainment aspect is often mentioned as something positive. One pupil writes:

> It's fun to watch when something exciting happens. This isn't wrong, it's almost exactly what happens almost daily in real life, not all, but most of it.

Some of the comments show that even if the parents do not allow the child to watch the program, the pupil is nevertheless well informed and seems to be able to watch the program in some way or another.

Again, one may wonder whether the critical attitude of the pupils is due to their ability to reflect or whether they have been influenced by parents and teachers. It is striking that so many 6th graders critically comment on *Hotel Cæsar* and the values in the episode, at the same time as the program is clearly the most popular one in this age group.

10th graders' analysis of Friends

The 10th graders were asked to respond on a 7-graded scale concerning the values they found in *Friends*. We see from Table 5 that nearly 30 percent neither agree nor disagree with the statements that characters "are honest" and "tell the truth", but those agreeing with these statements are somewhat greater in number than those disagreeing. When asked whether "the extra unpleasant actors are revealed for what they are", close to half of the 15- to 16-year-olds neither agree nor disagree. A possible reason in this case may be that they do not find any extra unpleasant actors in the program. However, the responses to the statements about "people who are different" may be worth noting. Half of the 10th graders agree, at least to a small degree, that "people who are different are made fun of" in the program. At the same time, 36 percent neither agree nor disagree that "people who are different are shown respect", and those agreeing are greater in number than those disagreeing. The statement that receives most support from the 10th graders is "people solve conflicts in a good way".

Table 5. What kinds of values do you find in the program? Percent. N = 204

	Disagree completely	Disagree a lot	Disagree a little	Neither agree nor disagree	Agree a little	Agree a lot	Agree completely
People tell the truth	1.5	5.4	24.5	29.4	27.5	8.8	2.9
People are honest	1.5	3.4	25.0	27.0	27.9	13.2	2.0
People solve conflicts in a good way	1.0	4.9	22.1	15.2	28.9	20.6	7.4
People who are different are made fun of	6.9	10.3	10.8	22.1	27.5	13.7	8.8
People who are different are shown respect	2.9	5.4	21.6	35.8	23.5	8.8	2.0
The extra unpleasant actors are revealed for what they are	2.9	2.0	6.9	48.0	22.1	13.2	3.9

From Table 6 it becomes evident that the 15- to 16-year-olds experience a clear difference between the values in the *Friends* episode and the values taught in school concerning most aspects included in the question. More than 60 percent think the program places less emphasis on "avoiding alcohol/narcotics", and more than half think this in relation to values such as "honesty", "obedience", "polite-ness", "avoiding backbiting and gossip" and "swearing". Just a few pupils think the program places more emphasis on such values than school does. When it comes to "respecting other people", "avoiding stealing" and "violence and van-dalism", many pupils (between 40 and 50%) think these values are as much emphasized in the program as in school. About one tenth think these values are more emphasized in the program than in school, while very many think they are less emphasized in the program. Most pupils experience the issue of "equality between boys and girls" as being as much emphasized in the program as in school, and those maintaining a different view are almost equally distributed on both sides. The only value mentioned that quite a few (about 30%) find more empha-sized in the program than in school is "solving problems by talking". Worth mentioning is also that the questions "regarding respecting other religions and cultures" and "showing responsibility for the environment" have received about 30 percent "don't know". However, the majority of the answers show that this group feels these values are less emphasized in the program than in school.

Table 6. **What do you think of the values you meet in this program compared to those you learn at school?** (Check one square on each line below). Percent. N = 204

	Emphasized less in the program than at school	Emphasized as much in the program as at school	Emphasized more in the program than at school	Don't know
Be honest	54.9	24.0	5.4	15.2
Obey your parents/ guardians	52.5	23.0	7.4	16.7
Speak politely	56.4	27.9	5.4	9.3
Respect other people	33.8	48.0	9.3	7.8
Solve problems by talking	19.6	41.7	29.9	8.3
Don't use violence and vandalism	22.5	41.7	10.8	23.5
Show responsibility for the environment	42.6	17.2	5.4	32.4
Avoid alcohol/narcotics	61.3	11.8	4.4	20.1
No backbiting or gossip	52.9	23.5	9.3	12.7
Don't steal/shoplift	31.4	42.2	8.3	17.6
Don't swear	55.4	25.0	5.9	12.3
Treat boys and girls the same (equality)	13.7	57.4	15.7	11.3
Respect other religions and cultures	28.4	39.2	4.4	27.5

In light of these facts, it is interesting to note that relatively few 10th graders mention anything they want to be different in the program. Of four alternative answers to this question, slightly more than a quarter of the 10th graders say they "would have liked more humor in the program".

The 10th graders were also asked to write a few words on how they evaluate the morals in the program in comparison with what they have learned at school. One hundred and seventy-five of the 204 participating pupils gave comments. Most of the comments are mainly positive with respect to the program as such as well as its moral content. Just a few comments are critical, while some pupils seem to think it is irrelevant to ask about morals, as the program emphasizes humor and entertainment. One writes:

All *Friends* episodes actually conclude with a moral message, but they communi-cate this message in an amusing way. They manage to present the message in a humorous way.

Another one says:

> All characters in this series are impulsive, and often do things without deep reflection. At school we have to argue our views when conflicts arise. The morals in this series are fine, and there's humor. It's not wrong to watch this program.

Some 15- to 16-year-olds show that they find the morals somewhat different from the morals they learn at school, but seem to find this an advantage of the program rather than a drawback. One says:

> I like this program. In this program the morals are more like the morals of young people. The school has "adult morals".

Another comment is as follows:

> The way the people in this TV series live is not completely in line with what we have learned at school, for example when it comes to using alcohol, etc. But sometimes alcohol has to be used to create funny situations.

One pupil writes:

> The participants in *Friends* don't always have the ability to see what's right and what's wrong and to be polite. However, it's not the purpose of this program that we should learn anything. We should just be entertained, and this they can do in an excellent way.

As an example of a comment that rejects the question as irrelevant, one pupil simply writes:

> What does this have to do with morals?

Another 10th grader gives voice to this reaction in a somewhat more considered way:

> I think it's totally impossible to compare a TV program with school education. The TV program is produced mainly for entertainment, while the teaching at school is intended to give both general knowledge and ethical reflection. I watch TV when I want to relax.

Finally we present a few quotations from pupils whose reflections on the moral issue have made them somewhat more critical to the program:

> This program has a lower level of morals than what we have at school. The actors have more relaxed attitudes toward how to relate to and treat other people. At school,

for example, we're not allowed to ridicule others, but in this program they're always making fools of each other.

The morals aren't so very different from what we learn in school, but a little different. The plot is about six young people trying to find the meaning of life and their moral attitudes aren't highly profiled, but it is fun. It's OK that the program is sent that late in the evening.

A general assessment of tendencies

The 11- to 12- and 15- to 16-year-olds in our study seem to be aware of the different emphases on values between their favorite program and the school. However, the two age groups differ in how they react to this difference. The 6th graders give many critical comments on *Hotel Cæsar*, while the 10th graders seem to be quite satisfied with *Friends* as it is. They find the program entertaining, and that is what they want it to be. To the degree they want any changes in the program, they want even more humor. So do the 6th graders in relation to *Hotel Cæsar*, but in addition, they express wishes that would bring about more conformity with the values in school. There is reason to believe that the 6th graders do not control their own use of television as much as the 10th graders do, and the younger children's spontaneous comments may indicate that at least some of them would like changes in the series that would facilitate permission to see the program at home. On the other hand, some 10th graders may perhaps want to oppose the adult values of school through exaggerating their satisfaction with the program. The comments in their own words indicate that a few of the pupils have felt somewhat provoked by being asked to particularly evaluate the morals of a program like this.

In this article, we have touched upon and discussed only a few findings in our research project. We would like to conclude with some general reflections and other findings.

There is a difference between the values in school and the values in the "parallel school" of the media. Our research project as a whole shows that this difference is observed not only by the children, but also by parents and teachers. Most children, and especially the 10th graders, remain comfortable with this situation, and do not feel they are in a "crossfire" between the intentional school/upbringing and the media. Teachers and parents are more apt to think there is a "crossfire" situation for children today. The data indicate that this may be because adults are more concerned than are children about the subtle influence of latent media messages.

When we asked the children to indicate which persons were their main source for learning about what is right and wrong in attitudes and behavior, parents received the top score. Next on the list was the school. One 10th grade pupil said:

> If I want to listen to wisdom, I don't want to listen to the media. Then I should listen to the people who've taken care of me, and who've taught me things about the world.

However, 10th graders who express "traditional" values concerning issues like sex and living together, family life, and violence, think they have been mainly influenced by their homes and the school, while those maintaining more "liberal" views refer to influence from friends and visual media. The pupils emphasize influence from friends more than from media, while their teachers tend to emphasize influence from visual media more than from the peer group.

At the same time, most teachers find that the pupils' use of visual media gives inspiration and positive impulses to school work, even if some pupils may be sleepy at school because of too much media use. Most parents experience some degree of conflict between the values and norms for behavior they are trying to establish in the home and the values they feel the media communicate.

Why, then, are the parents so popular as a point of reference at a time in a child's development when strong opposition to parental authority is a normal trend? Might it be that they do not trust the adult behavior and maxims they see on the TV screen? Despite all the criticism they might voice toward their parents, children seem to find that parents are generally trustworthy. Parents do not just talk, but they try in practice to do their best for their children. Parents may be old-fashioned and irritating, but they are among the adults children can have confidence in. Here we are reminded of the two-step hypothesis.[4] This maintains that when you receive information from the media and do not know whether it can be trusted, you seek the advice of knowledgeable persons you trust, before you accept or reject the given information. The main sources for teaching about right and wrong – parents and, following them, teachers – indicate the role of intentional teaching in the ethical and moral development of children. Is this something that is unique to the seven municipalities in Western Norway, or might it indicate a tendency that can be found in other contexts, as well? This question poses a challenge for further research.

While some children often declare very strongly that they certainly are not influenced by media exposure, others admit quite openly that they are. One says, after some discussion:

> I guess I've been a little influenced by advertising after all.

One 10th grade girl admits more explicitly to being influenced by commercials:

> It certainly affects my everyday life. Because when you see advertising for soft drinks on TV, you want to buy a bottle. If you see biscuits, you'd like to find out how they taste. Yes, I'm truly affected by advertising.

When asked about brands the same pupil continues:

Up to now I haven't been so concerned about having clothes of a special brand. I dress the way I want to, but I've been influenced by others. Some friends ask me directly if I really don't wear clothes of a particular brand. They make me aware that when I start junior high school, I have to wear clothes of that particular brand, if I want to be accepted by my classmates. I'm basically against being dressed like everybody else and I never bully anyone who chooses other types of clothes. I feel it's a positive thing to be self-conscious, and it would be quite boring if everybody wore the same types of trousers and sweaters.

In these quotations we again find this subtle duality in the way things are being said. We sense a struggle for the individual young person to be independent and individualistic, yet she nevertheless decides to adapt to her peer group. This is said reluctantly and indirectly.

We also find in our data indications of negative influence from media exposure. About 10 percent of the 10th graders say that the media have a negative influence on their self-esteem. At least some of them connect this influence to the feeling that the media show an abundance of perfect bodies, while they consider their own bodies imperfect. This is a serious issue both for the media and for pedagogy.[5]

Notes

1. The research design was prepared by Asbjørn Simonnes, Volda University College, and Gudmund Gjelsten, Bergbo Media, in close consultation with a steering committee and a reference group. Sociologist Tore Hagen, Volda University College, became a member of the research group, but died tragically in an accident in October 2001. In January 2002, Thor Arnfinn Kleven, University of Oslo, accepted an invitation to replace him as a member of the research team.
2. During in-depth interviews, some of the pupils reported that some of their younger siblings watched *Hotel Cæsar* with them.
3. Christians, Clifford G. et al.: *Good News. Social Ethics and the Press.* New York and Oxford: Oxford University Press, 1993, pp. 62-64.
4. Griffin, Emory A.: *A First Look at Communication Theory.* Fifth Edition. New York: Wheaton college, McGraw-Hill Higher Education, 2003, pp. 378-379.
5. For further reading about the research project and reference to the bibliography on "The Child in the Interaction between Intentional and Functional Education", see: http://www.hivolda.no/index.php?ID=12575 For those who wish to read the printed version of the research report no. 56 prepared by Asbjørn Simonnes, Gudmund Gjelsten and Thor Arnfinn Kleven, please go to: http://www.hivolda.no/attachments/site/group15/forsk_56.pdf or contact project director Asbjørn Simonnes, e-mail: asbjorn.simonnes@hivolda.no

Critical Appreciation of TV Drama and Reality Shows
Hong Kong Youth in Need of Media Education

Alice Y. L. Lee

The 21st century is the age of the Internet. However, in Hong Kong, young people still spend most of their leisure time watching television (HKFYG, 2003). On average they watch television about three to four hours a day, and television serials are their most favored television programs. Apart from local television serials, young people are also interested in foreign reality TV shows. While the youth continue to enjoy watching television serials every day after school, local media educators try to inform them of the importance of critical appreciation of these programs.

In Hong Kong, a survey conducted by the Breakthrough Youth Organization (1999) showed that 50 percent of young respondents aged between 12 and 16 were heavy viewers of TV drama serials. They watched all of the drama series broadcast in prime time (7-10 p.m.). Research results of the Commission on Youth even indicate that 72 percent of youth aged between 12 and 24 often watch drama serials (Commission on Youth, 1993; Leung, 1999). In fact, studies during the past twenty years clearly show the obvious: Viewing television has been the most popular media activity among young people in Hong Kong (Chan, 2001). Researchers are amazed that young people are so loyal to television serials.

Critical appreciation

Hong Kong is a small place with a very high population density. Compared with youth in other countries, young people in Hong Kong are less engaged in outdoor activities. They generally regard watching television as a convenient way to spend their spare time, and over the years it has become a cultural habit. To many educators and parents, the excessive amount of time spent on television serials by youth is not a major concern. The focus of attention, instead, is on what young

117

people learn from the television serials. The Commission on Youth conducts studies from time to time on the media use of the youth, and its findings indicate that media products including television drama have great influence on youth attitudes and behavior (Commission on Youth, 1993; Leung, 1999; So & Chan, 1992). Schoolteachers also allege that they can observe great effects of some television serials on their students' daily lives. Since media education gained momentum in Hong Kong in the late 1990s, television literacy training focusing on television serials has become very popular (Lee, 2002).

To many local media education practitioners, the fact that the media construct reality is the core concept of media literacy training. It is important to alert the youngsters that what they consume are only media images and not real things. Regardless of whether it is news, advertisements, television drama or radio documentaries, what is represented is different from the objective reality. Young people are not only taught how to distinguish between the two (the constructed and the objective) realities, but also encouraged to think about *how* media reality is constructed and *why*. Young people are guided to uncover underlying values embedded in the media construct. Thus, in television literacy classes and workshops, media reality and the hidden values of television drama naturally become the central focus of discussion. However, media educators have no intention to spoil the youth's enjoyment of television drama. While young people are trained as critical viewers, they are also cultivated to have a good aesthetic sense of appreciation.

Historical and professional serials

In the past few years, two television drama genres, historical and professional serials, have been particularly popular in Hong Kong. They are special kinds of soap opera. Apart from gaining high TV ratings, they also obtain high TV appreciation scores as revealed in the television appreciation index surveys. Historical serials are stories associated with Chinese history. Most of them are woven around politics and the private lives of Chinese emperors and their families.

In contrast, professional serials are contextualized in modern settings, focusing on the works and lives of particular groups of professional people, such as lawyers, doctors, firemen, or policemen. In the last decade, one local television station, TVB, has produced more than 40 professional drama serials.

Compared with general soap operas, the historical and professional serials are capable of constructing media reality that seems to be closer to real life and with more powerful messages. The popularity of both types of serials has raised concern about the need to help young people to understand what the historical and social realities are.

Historical serials

Most of the content of these historical serials are not based on factual history. However, as the stories are situated in specific historical backgrounds and the major characters are based on historical figures, the younger audience will easily mix the fiction with the fact. In Hong Kong, there are constant complaints that these historical serials mislead young people and that they are "obstacles" instead of "facilitators" in history education.

The historical series *Kangxi Empire* is a good example of the blurring between media reality and history reality. The show was very popular in Hong Kong among both adults and young people. In media workshops, young participants were asked why they were so fond of the show. The answer was that they could learn about the Qing Dynasty through the show, and that many of the characters were very capable figures so that the viewers could model themselves after these characters. However, the plot of *Kangxi Empire* was not completely faithful to historical facts. During the period when the TV serial was shown in Hong Kong, there was a review article published in the *Guangzhou Daily* entitled "Kangxi Empire Misplaces Historical Facts" (Song, 2001). The critic pointed out that one of the heroines in the drama, Suma Lagu, was a real historical figure, but she was an old servant and was much older than Emperor Kangxi. Yet, to introduce romantic elements, the serial turned Suma Lagu into a young orphan girl and made up love affairs between her and Emperor Kangxi.

Media educators and parents are not only alert that the young people will learn the wrong history, but also ask whether the values conveyed by the show are suitable for youth to follow (Lee, 2003a). In *Kangxi Empire* there are numerous dark aspects of politics, and it constantly exposes the evil aspects of human nature. Emperor Kangxi ordered his beloved daughter to marry his Mongolian enemy, Ge Erdan, as a trick to gain time for his army. When well prepared, he commanded the military to exterminate the Mongolian troops and chopped off his son-in-law Ge's head as a war trophy. Emperor Kangxi willingly succumbs to inhuman tolerance and compromises during difficult times to stay in power. He uses political tricks and curbs enemies without mercy. The entire serial is, on the one hand, brimming with sighs of inability to control one's own fate, and, on the other hand, the Emperor is complacent for being able to consolidate his power. In the serial, Emperor Kangxi sacrifices the happiness and lives of many people (including his wife's and his daughter's) in exchange for the stability of his rule. He never feels sorry about it and even takes it for granted.

As mentioned above, young people have expressed great admiration for many of the main characters in the serial, particularly the Emperor. They admire them for being so "cool and smart" and say they have "learned something from them". What have they really learnt? The cheating tricks the characters play against one another? The illusion that one has to act indecently when there are few alternatives? If *Kangxi Empire* was not a historical serial and Kangxi not a historical figure, then it would have been easier to convince the young people that the evil tricks were just products of the scriptwriter's imagination. However, the show was presented as a historical story and the characters as historical figures, why the values embedded in it became extremely persuasive. The interactions between the history reality, media reality and youth's own constructed reality created a scenario that was so complex that the young people might not be able to handle it by themselves.

Therefore, parental guidance or media literacy training in school are regarded as useful for offering some advice to remind young people that they do not have to make the same kind of decision as the characters in the historical serial. The young people are encouraged to weigh different resolutions when facing different challenges, and learn that Kangxi's solution might not be the best.

Professional series

If the media reality of historical serials is rather deceptive, then professional series are even "better" at blurring the media reality and the objective reality. A number of strategies are employed to achieve this goal. Firstly, producers of professional television serials claim that they have done detailed research about the profession in question, implying that their serials reflect the objective reality of the profession. Secondly, the television station seeks support from the industry or profession to strengthen its production. On the one hand, it invites experts in the profession to serve as consultants. On the other hand, it gets approval from the related authority to facilitate the production work. For example, the Hospital Authority was asked to support the production of a doctor's serial, and some scenes of the serial could be shot in hospitals. That placed the story closer to reality. However, professional serials usually "beautify" the professionals. Young people like to watch these shows because they are curious about the lives of professionals and they also want to join the professional ranks in the future.

In Hong Kong, after the release of the professional serial entitled *Up to the Sky*, young people flocked to apply for jobs in airline companies (*Apple Daily*, 2003). The applications for pilot trainee even increased by 70 times (*Sing Pao*, 2003). *Up to the Sky* is a drama about commercial airline pilots. The serial was supported by both Cathay Pacific Airways (Hong Kong) and the Airport Authority and depicted the career development and love affairs of a group of pilots. The romantic love of the pilots and their high-class living style are extremely attractive to youngsters. The series was shot in airports, pilot training centers, and on real planes. Moreover, crewmembers of Cathay Pacific Airways joined the promotion activities of the serial. Many young people then regarded the drama as real reflection of the lives of the pilots and airhostesses.

In fact, findings of the large-scale study on youth consumption conducted by the Breakthrough Youth Organization (1999) indicate that young people in Hong Kong believe what they are shown on television. They perceive that the content of serials truly reflects particular issues in the real world. In particular, they have a strong belief in "deviant content", such as complicated love affairs, undisciplined sexual relationships, human conflicts and weakened marital relationships. To them, these phenomena frequently happen in everyday lives. Almost 70 percent of the 1,384 young respondents aged between 12 and 16 in the study believed in the television depiction that "one will very often run into complicated human conflicts in the work place" and "some people will attack you behind your back". About 55 percent of them think that in the real world, like on TV, "people will hurt or even kill one another for conflict of interest". Drama themes that young people believed in also included: that premarital sex is acceptable if the couple are lovers; that the pub is the place to shop for "one-night-stand" partners; that most successful professionals are single and love to visit pubs after work; that a marriage will break up if the couple's characters are not compatible; and that people will easily fall in love with their colleagues in the workplace. More importantly, heavy serial viewers have a stronger tendency to learn ideas from the stories, particularly those concerning personal relationships.

Findings from the same study also show that young people like to model themselves after the characters in the dramas, and apply the messages they receive from them in their everyday lives, especially in the areas of friendship, love affairs, and other relationships. Over 45 percent of the young respondents expressed that they "learn from the television drama characters and follow their way of handling people and things", while 32 percent revealed that they "take pleasure in the emotional ups and downs of the main characters in the serial, and hope that they themselves can have the same experiences". In addition, 31 percent said that they "think about their own love affairs from the perspective of the main characters in the drama". Others expressed that they "regard the lifestyle of the professionals in the serials as their ideal lifestyle".

In response to these findings, youth workers and educators suggest that local youngsters acutely lack television literacy and more media education training should be provided for them (Chan, 2001).

As professional serials are particularly popular among young people, many media education workshops are held to deconstruct them. The Hong Kong Association of Media Education held a workshop in 2003 to guide young people to deconstruct *Up to the Sky*. Other workshops were also conducted at schools and universities. The evaluation results show that the participants benefited from the training. After receiving media education, the young people were able to employ critical appreciation skills to their television serial viewing.

For example, a group of university students who took the media literacy course were fans of *Up to the Sky*. They followed the show every night and did not miss a single episode. They revealed that even though they were busy with their homework or needed to go out, they would tape the episode for later viewing. They really enjoyed the romance in the show and the charm of the aviation industry. Similar to what the Breakthrough survey found, they put themselves into the role of the main characters and followed their emotional ups and downs. They liked the fantastic job of the pilots who could travel around the world and lead exciting lifestyles. They hoped that they could have the same life experience as the handsome pilots and their girlfriends. Yet, while the well-written plot and the good acting fascinated them, they were able to distinguish the media reality of the serial from the objective reality. In their media reports, the young students pointed out that the profession of pilot was "romanticized". The pilots were stereotyped as professional, cool, handsome and having the opportunity to travel around the world. Their lives were simplified and reduced to just love and work, and the pilots seemed to be very satisfied and proud of their work. In reality, the pilots' union in Hong Kong had a prolonged fight with the management of Cathay Pacific Airways some time ago. Cathay Pacific pilots complained about over-time work, unreasonable work schedules and an unfair pay scale. During the labor dispute, some pilots were laid off.

The students concluded that the middle class scenario in the show obviously greatly contrasted with the objective reality (Hui *et al.*, 2003). Applying their critical thinking to this case, some students even questioned the motives of the involvement of Cathay Pacific Airways in the show. The students pointed out that the support Cathay Pacific Airways offered to the production of *Up to the Sky* was in fact a public relations strategy to promote the company's corporate image (Ip *et al.*, 2003). However, after all this criticism, the students did not dismiss the aesthetic value of the serial and they praised it for stimulating young people's interest in the air industry. They still expressed their deep preference for the serial and said it was reasonable for it to win "the most popular television program award" in 2003 from *Next Magazine*.

Foreign reality TV shows

If historical serials and professional serials are blurring media reality and objective reality, then reality television shows are doing so even more intensely. Since the end of the 1990s, reality television shows have been the hottest television genre in the Western television industry. In Hong Kong, only recently did the genre gain a foothold in the local English television channels. In the past, Hong Kong youth were not enthusiastic about watching foreign television programs because of the language barrier. Now, however, the NICAM TV system (which enables simultaneous bilingual broadcasting) and Chinese subtitles greatly help young people in their watching of foreign television programs.

Foreign reality shows are quite popular among the youth in Hong Kong, particularly among the middle-class youth. These shows are popular because they are so different in format from the local television programs – they are "real". Therefore, in Hong Kong, reality shows are called "true man shows". Local television stations tried to copy the genre and produced local reality television shows, such as *The Great Run in the Rain Forest*, *Outward Bound Competition of the University Elite*, *Slimming up Quickly* and *Green Tourist Guide Competition* (*TVB*

Weekly, 2004). However, the attempts were not particularly successful because the local Chinese participants were shy of presenting themselves naturally in front of the camera and the effect was not "real" enough. Therefore, foreign reality television shows are much more popular.

Of course, having ordinary people instead of actors in front of the camera does not mean that these programs reflect reality, but it is undeniable that they look much closer to objective reality when compared with other television genres. In reality television shows, ordinary people seem to run their "real" lives, reveal their "real" thinking, and express their "real" emotions. Their real identities, jobs, ages, personalities and other personal information are all revealed. Young people are particularly interested in reality television programs because they are in an age full of curiosity. They are curious about how normal people like themselves will act under real special circumstances. Moreover, many reality shows are packaged as game shows or competitions, stimulating excitement. Young people like new things and they appreciate the innovative presentation skills of the reality television programs.

Also, in the eyes of some local young people, foreign reality television shows are great because they integrate different types of genres. The "reality-based" content of the show is like that in a documentary, while the plot and the flow created by the producers make the story line develop dramatically like a soap opera. The way that it presents prizes or money to the winners mirrors game shows (Cheung *et al.*, 2003). Reality shows are not in rigid format, and have much variety. In some shows, the participants know that there are cameras shooting them, but in others they are not aware of the hidden cameras. Programs such as *Survivor* and *Temptation Island* create a new environment and put people in it. Some shows, such as *Queer Eye for the Straight Guy*, are situated in the "real society". For instance, in *Temptation Island* couples are separated geographically and some beautiful ladies and handsome guys are sent to "provoke" them. But in *Queer Eye for the Straight Guy*, the gay people are helping the straight guys to transform themselves in terms of outlook and lifestyle in their own homes.

All the above-mentioned programs are American products. Currently, the big three Hong Kong television stations, TVB, ATV and Cable TV, are importing more and more foreign reality television shows. They also launch intensive promotion campaigns for these shows. *Queer Eye for the Straight Guy* is an outstanding example as TVB not only invests a lot of advertising money in promoting the show, but also invites local famous actors and actresses to dub it in Cantonese. The lively and funny dubbing makes the show more appealing to local youngsters.

Some students in the School of Communication at the Hong Kong Baptist University wanted to find out why the local audience is interested in reality television programs. They conducted a (non-representative) questionnaire survey among their peers and their friends' family members (Cheung *et al.*, 2004). They asked the respondents how many reality television programs they watched, their reasons for watching them, and their views on how "real" the shows were. The survey found that 90 percent of the respondents watched reality television shows and that the average number of shows watched was 2.4. *America's Next Top Model*, *Queer Eye for the Straight Guy* and *Survivor* were the most popular shows. *America's Next Top Model* is basically a model competition which records the transformation of everyday young women into potentially outstanding supermodels, while *Survivor* depicts how groups of people are left in the wild and compete with one another to see who can finally survive in the game of gradual elimination.

The respondents in the survey mentioned no local reality television programs, which indicated that local shows were not as attractive as foreign shows. The younger people, who were between 16 and 25 years old, tended to watch more reality television shows than the people aged 26 or over, but there was no significant difference between genders. Sixty-eight percent of heavy viewers were youngsters (16-25), and they were more willing to accept new ideas in reality television shows than older people.

For the young audience, the top five reasons for watching reality television shows were "excitement of competition", "freshness", "good word-of-mouth" (meaning good reputation and of high opinion), "charming scenes and characters", and "strong sense of reality". Youngsters particularly valued the "strong sense of reality". Girls valued the "strong sense of reality" more, and boys were keen on "seeing how people get rich or famous quickly". In general, the young audience under 26 took the "reality" in the show for granted. They were not critical about how "real" the reality show was. In fact, they did not seriously think about this issue. Many of them just casually believed that these shows, such as *America's Next Top Model*, reflected the dark side of human beings and demonstrated how common people struggle for success. For example, young respondents said after watching the show, they believed that there are no friends in a competition and that models have no privacy and need to show their bodies. In another study (Leung *et al.*, 2004), young fans of the show said it made them learn more about the life of a model and how one could become a top model. They thought that models should have good body figures and be sexy. They also believed that it is difficult to make friends in the workplace. Again, they did not question whether the show truly reflected the reality of the modeling profession.

Yet, students who have received media education training seem to be more critical about the "reality" of these shows than the general young audience (Leung *et al.*, 2003). They can point out that these shows put people in "unusual situations" that deviate from their everyday experiences. Therefore, the shows do not necessarily reflect the objective reality. Moreover, the contestants may voluntarily act in front of the camera and pretend that they are friendly and kind. In the shows, winners are determined by elimination and all the participants are enemies. However, in everyday life, people can become friends in competitions. The media literate students raised their concern about the promotion of the worst aspects of human behavior in reality shows, such as *Survivor* and *America's Next Top Model*. They also warned against romanticizing the modeling industry. Modeling in the show is glorious but in the real world many models lead a hard life. Some other students in the media literacy workshop pointed out that materialism and consumerism are the underlying values of the show, in which the only way a girl can be regarded as beautiful is that she must wear makeup and dress with famous brand names.

Many young students in the media education workshops liked to watch *Queer Eye for the Straight Guy*. As mentioned, the show is about five gay professionals transforming a style-deficient and culture-deprived straight guy. While the students enjoyed the charming clothing and stylish food on the screen, they could identify the unrealistic social "realities" presented by the program hosts as follows: change is easy and fast; change is beautiful and essential; change is high-class and prestigious; change is about throwing old things away; and change is about appearance and social status (Li, *et al.*, 2003).

These students were able to distinguish between the media reality in the show and the actual social reality in their daily lives. More importantly, they learned how to unveil the hidden ideologies of the show. They said the show strongly promoted a kind of materialistic living style and that consumerism plays a very important role in it. A nice straight guy cannot necessarily transform himself into a man who dresses well and looks handsome. The media literate young students also raised the following questions: Is improvement in personal appearance essential in helping a person to boost self-esteem? Will one become more fashionable if one follows the Fab 5's (the five gay professionals') guidelines? Is homosexuality acceptable? Is the show a package of TV commercials by advertisers and sponsors?

This kind of reflective thinking is badly needed for the young people who live in a modern, media-saturated world. The major selling point of reality television shows is their "real" sense, but media literate students do not easily take the face value of the reality of these shows for granted. They challenge it by asking what the reality is and what ideologies are embedded in the show. Reality television shows reshape moral and ethics standards. *Queer Eye for the Straight Guy* and *Temptation Island* are outstanding examples, with the former promoting gay culture and the latter challenging marital relationships. These shows have important influences on young people's value judgments. Media literacy can help youngsters to be reflective and become active television viewers who know how to "negotiate meaning" (Ontario Ministry of Education, 1989).

The joy of watching television serials

As mentioned, in Hong Kong television serials are young people's favorites. Thus, teaching them to become wise TV viewers is an important task for media education practitioners. There are four steps to achieve that goal:

- Observation: observing the characteristics of a television drama, and distinguishing the media reality from the objective reality.

125

- Analysis: analyzing the values and ideologies behind the visual images of a show.

- Reflection: reflecting on one's mode of consuming television drama.

- Action: deciding whether one should keep on watching the show or stop spending time on it, or whether one should recommend the program to one's peers or send a complaint letter to an authority (Lee, 2003b).

In following these steps, young television viewers are able to achieve what media education expert Len Masterman (1985) described as "maintaining critical autonomy". However, training young people to be critical should not deprive them of the joy they gain from watching soap operas, reality television shows and drama programs. Roger Silverstone (1999) suggests that pleasure and play are central aspects of young people's relationships with the media. David Buckingham (2003) echoes the idea and proposes that a more open-ended, playful approach to media literacy training should be adopted. As Davies (1997) emphasizes that children and young people need to be aware of the significance of television programs realistically representing reality, he also highlights the importance of pleasure.

In fact, when we closely examine how Hong Kong young people watch television serials and reality television shows, it is not difficult to discover that they take true pleasure in watching them. Regardless of whether the realities of the shows are fake, distorted, or not realistically represented, young people enjoy watching the programs and appreciate the aesthetic sensation that the shows bring to them. Yet, media literate youngsters can better decode the shows and see through the hidden messages in them. "Being critical" and "appreciation" are not mutually exclusive. Thus, a critical appreciation approach to television serial viewing is highly recommended for youngsters who need to properly handle their close relationships with television.

References

Apple Daily (2003, December 14). Aviation training becomes popular due to Up to the Sky. *Apple Daily*, p. A12.

Breakthrough (1999). *Media and youth study (television)*. Hong Kong: Breakthrough.

Buckingham, D. (2003). *Media education: Literacy, learning and contemporary culture*. Cambridge: Polity Press.

Chan, T. C. F. (2001). Television literacy of Hong Kong youngsters. *Journal of Youth Studies*, 4(1), 119-124.

Cheung, W. Y., et al. (2003) Audience attitude towards reality TV in Hong Kong. Unpublished paper, School of Communication, Hong Kong Baptist University.

Commission on Youth (1993). *Report on the study on the influence of mass media on youth*. Hong Kong: Commission on Youth.

Davies, M. M. (1997). *Fake, fact, and fantasy: Children's interpretations of television reality*. Mahwah, NJ: Lawrence Erlbaum Associates.

HKFYG (2003). *Cultural lives of the youth in Hong Kong*. Hong Kong: Hong Kong Federation of Youth Groups.

Hui, K. P., et al. (2003). The flight of love and dream. Unpublished paper, School of Communication, Hong Kong Baptist University.

Ip, C., et al. (2003). Decoding "Up to the Sky". Unpublished paper, School of Communication, Hong Kong Baptist University.

Lee, A. Y. L. (2002). Media education movement in Hong Kong: A networking model. *Mass Communication Research, 71*, 107-131.

Lee, A. Y. L. (2003a). Children, television and family media education. *House of Tomorrow, 11*(1), 1-14.

Lee, A. Y. L. (2003b). Media education and civic consciousness. In P. S. N. Lee (Ed.), *New Perspectives on Hong Kong Media* (pp. 231-250). Hong Kong: Chinese University Press.

Leung, G. L. (1999). *Study on the influence of media on youth*. Hong Kong: Commission on Youth.

Leung, P. K., et al. (2003). Examining America's Next Top Model. Unpublished paper, School of Communication, Hong Kong Baptist University.

Li, P. L., et al. (2003). Decoding the Queer Eye for the Straight Guy. Unpublished paper, School of Communication, Hong Kong Baptist University.

Masterman, L. (1985). *Teaching the media*. London: Comedia/MK Media Press.

Ontario Ministry of Education (1989). *Media literacy: Intermediate and senior division*. Toronto: Ministry of Education.

Silverstone, R. (1999). *Why study the media?* London: Sage.

Sing Pao (2003, December 13). The TV drama effect: Pilot application increased by 70 times. *Sing Pao*, p. A8.

So, C. Y. K., & Chan, J. M. (1992). *Mass media and youth in Hong Kong*. Hong Kong: Commission on Youth.

Song, C. (2001, December 15). Kangxi Empire misplaces historical facts. *Guangzhou Daily*, p. B1.

TVB Weekly (2004, July 27). TV Guide. *TVB Weekly*, p. 221.

127

Everyday People, Everyday Life
British Teenagers, Soap Opera and Reality TV

Dorothy Hobson

The popularity of television programmes, which are watched by young people although not particularly targeted at them, is a cause of many debates and some concern in public and academic circles. Conflicting pictures of the way that television is provided for children and young people relies on two different perspectives – programmes which are made for young people, and programmes which they watch from choice and which are made for the general audience. One of the areas of programmes which children and young people in Britain consume with avid interest is soap opera and, to a lesser extent, reality TV. The latest Ofcom report[1] states that although children now have access to more dedicated programmes, including several dedicated channels as well as an 8 per cent increase in hours on terrestrial analogue networks, nevertheless, the spend on children's programming on the five main terrestrial channels has fallen by 8 per cent in total. Further it states that 'there is little programming catering for children over the age of 12' (Ofcom 2004:37). Coupled with this is the evidence that there is concern about the programmes which children watch which are intended for the general audience and are transmitted before the 'watershed' at 21.00 hours.[2] Ofcom reported that parents felt they did not have control over pre-watershed content, particularly in soap operas, which they felt might be unsuitable for children. However the research also revealed the widespread view that soaps can bring important social benefits.

The dichotomy of protecting young people or giving them information which would be of benefit to them (Ofcom 2004:58) is worth considering in relation to the views of the young audiences who watch television programmes. Whatever regulators think about the programmes which young people chose, they will continue to watch programmes which they like and they will make their own readings (interpretations) of those programmes. This article considers the way that young people in Britain watch the genres of soap opera and reality TV and reports their own views on the programmes. Additionally, the article reviews some of the earlier research which has been conducted specifically on soap opera and young people, and presents new research by the author on this genre and the newly emerged genre of reality TV. The research uses the ethnographic method and presents the words of the interviewees to construct the narrative of their own views of soap opera and of reality TV. It also examines the genres and considers the storylines or themes which are included in the programmes and suggests why these are of interest to young people or why they are rejected by them.

Soap opera and the new genres

The genres of soap opera and reality TV, also known as docu-soaps, have become linked in recent years for reasons that are not always clearly defined but the delineation between the genres is important. While television genres do have global similarities there are also national characteristics which determine the distinctiveness and specificity between cultural representations from different countries. While there are many forms of series and serials which have elements of the soap opera, if we are to maintain the purist form of the genre, my own definition of soap opera on British television is as follows:

> Soap opera is a radio or television drama in series form, which has a core set of characters and locations. It is transmitted at least three times a week, for fifty-two weeks of a year. The drama creates the illusion that life continues in the fictional world even when viewers are not watching. The narrative progresses in a linear form through peaks and troughs of action and emotion. It is a continuous form with recurring catastasis as its dominant narrative structure. It is based on fictional realism and explores and celebrates the domestic, personal and everyday in all its guises. It works because the audience has intimate familiarity with the characters and their lives. Through its characters the soap opera must connect with the experience of its audience, and its content must be stories of the ordinary. (Hobson 2003:35)

While this definition relates to the relationship between all viewers and the genre, it is important to consider the sentences 'It works because the audience has intimate familiarity with the characters and their lives' and 'Through its characters the soap opera must connect with the experiences of its audience...'. For it is through these two specific means that we must consider how the young audience read the soap opera and relate to the characters and their stories. The other important feature to register is that the soap opera is a work of fiction, created by writers while based on reality which is seen as ordinary. This concentration on the ordinary is important and relates to the relationship of the two genres.

The relatively new genre of reality TV like the soap opera has many different forms subsumed beneath the blanket name. Developed through the early use of

130

small video camera by which the audience told their own story, the widespread use of surveillance cameras by the police gave rise to the 'police chase' programmes with ordinary police and ordinary people starring in the programmes. Cheap and popular with audiences, the broadcasters developed new forms by using ordinary people in supposedly ordinary settings but they also developed a theme whereby ordinary people are tested in relation to their own lives and norms. There are many versions of these programmes but I have only concentrated on the two programmes which the young girls in my study identified as being of interest to them.

Academic studies on soap opera and young people

Two important academic studies which specifically examined the way that young people watched soap opera in Great Britain, are David Buckingham's (1987) *Public Secrets*, a study of the then new BBC soap opera *EastEnders* as perceived by young people, and Marie Gillespie's (1995) *Television, Ethnicity and Cultural Change* that examined the role of television in the transformation and creation of identity among young Punjabi Londoners.

Buckingham was following the research conducted by Hodge & Tripp (1986) with Australian young people which revealed that children are extremely media literate and that this was a strength which should be encouraged by parents and educators. Buckingham's study of the opinions of young people on *EastEnders* also revealed that the children made complex readings of the series and while they recognised the importance of some of the storylines they also knew that this was a fictional work and they joked and mimicked the more extreme elements of the drama.

The study made of young Punjabi Londoners and their perception and use of soap opera formed the main thesis of Gillespie. She reveals how the young people related to and use the Australian series *Neighbours* to fulfil functions in their own lives. They used incidents which happened in the series to negotiate their own roles within the family and to discuss matters which might have been taboo if they tried to talk about them in relation to their own lives. Again these young people found the soap opera useful and they worked with the dramas for their own needs.

Young men and soap opera – a changing story

While my own research has not concentrated specifically on the views of young people and soap opera, nevertheless there have been occasions when young men have been the subjects of my research projects and these have included their views

131

on soap opera. The two projects which I cite here provide two differing views on the genre which are separated by about ten years and show the way that developments in the genre attracted young male audiences to watch soap operas.

In the mid-1980s, I was conducting research about Channel 4 Television and its audience. As part of this study, I interviewed some young men who were subject to the terrible youth unemployment which was prevalent at the time. Out of work and out of school, one of the few places where these 16-year-olds could meet was at a youth 'drop-in' centre funded by the leisure services department of the local authority. This was a location where research was conducted with more of a talk and catch their answers than anything resembling a formal interview. While they played pool[3] in the tiny wooden hut, I sat on the side of the room while they stalked the table and played their game. What came out from the talk about television was their considerable expertise on the schedules right across all channels, with knowledge of every programme, its time of transmission and duration and what was the programme which enabled them to stay up the latest in order to fill their endless hours with no money and nowhere to go at night. They selected programmes which would keep them occupied until the early hours of the morning. What was also revealing about their choice of viewing was they either rejected soap operas, or they were selective in their choice by whether there were young men in the series. Most poignant was the comment by Mark, who when I asked if there were any programmes which he would never watch, responded:

Dallas, Coronation Street and *Crossroads* – I don't watch things to do with the family.

As soap operas deal with issues which are all based on aspects of family, it was significant that Mark, who also told me that he did not like to stay in when his family was at home, was adamant that he would not watch the programmes which were about families. It was not the moment for me to pursue his reasons but it could be surmised that he did not want to watch families when he did not have a happy family life of his own.

Another young man, Neil, had a very catholic taste and watched films, drama, and documentaries, particularly about insects and animals. His choice of soap opera was the then newly transmitted Channel 4's *Brookside* about which he commented:

I've been watching from the start. It's funny. It's like real life in it.

He was seeing the representations of the young unemployed in *Brookside* as being nearer his life than other programmes shown on television. During 1983 and 1984 when I conducted these interviews, there were few representations of young people as main characters in soap operas and the programmes were not the first choice of the young men. What they did watch related to their own lives, unless

the themes of happy families were too painful. They also appreciated stories which showed the situation of the young unemployed, as this was their own situation.

By the mid-1990s, the soap opera was sufficiently established as a form to appeal to the apparently toughest of young men, who identified the genre as one of their favourites. In 1996, I conducted a pilot study interviewing young men aged 16 to 20, who were in a young offenders unit, to ask them about the way that they saw various forms of mass media and its effects on them. Some of the questions were about soap opera and the genre was one of their favourite choices of viewing both when they were 'on the out' – not in prison – and while they were in prison. They all watched a wide range of soap operas, including *Neighbours*, *EastEnders*, *Brookside*, and the Australian *Home & Away*.[4] The reasons why they liked the programmes were like those of other young people but their favourite characters in *EastEnders* were characters and stories to which they felt they could relate:

DH: What do you like about *Brookside?*

Wesley: Stories, all what's going on.

DH: What do you think about the way they are into…

Wesley: Drugs.

Steve: It's more closer to life.

DH: What do you think about *EastEnders?*

Many voices: That's better, that's more down to earth, that's more to do with real life.

Unidentified voice: It has things that happens in your life. Proper problems like, they understand our problems.

DH: Who are your favourite characters then in the soaps?

All: Grant, Grant, the Mitchells (all laughing) Grant.

The Grant Mitchell character was one who was deeply troubled. An ex-offender, his problems had begun when he had left army service and had suffered from Posttraumatic Stress Syndrome. He and his brother had many disagreements and fought over a shared lover, Sharon. However, they were not involved in drugs and their conflict and violence was at this time about personal matters. The boys I talked with saw them as realistic characters and admired the programme for its representation of a reality to which they could relate. They lauded Grant who embodies the essence of tough male aggression twinned with vulnerability. However, they also commented that the representations of criminality were not enough to show anyone how to commit a crime.

What was also interesting about their views on television in general was that they did not want to see too much representation of violence and crime because this was the life which they knew and they wanted to see something different.

This fondness for programmes, which did not reflect aggression, was revealed when they told me that *Home & Away* was their favourite programme. I asked them why they liked the programme:

> *Rudy*: There's a lot of humour there, 'cos things like that... it's hard to imagine like what it would be like to be there.
>
> *DH*: ... As you know, *Home & Away* is all about... well, most of the characters there have been in trouble or they...

Steve interrupted my attempt at setting up the programme as he and the others were well ahead of me in knowing what the programme was attempting to represent:

> *Steve*: Yes, but they are all like, it's all like these pretty people, like with the mothers, they try to make out they are like us.

The boys interrupted in unison with a clear analysis of the programme:

> *All*: Yes, stereotyping!
>
> *Rudy*: Everything's all-cushy, like there's no one there to sign on the dole. (Laughter.) They all get jobs like, and everybody's like willing to help everybody else, you know what I mean. (Laughter from all the boys.)
>
> *DH*: So do you think that it's nothing like what life is like here?
>
> *Rudy*: No, it's paradise there, imagination – what, living there, next to the beach, living next to a beach, mm, paradise, paradise.

As one, the young men signified their assent to his proposition. If only they could be there, that would truly be paradise. This brief insight into the reading, which these young men made, reveals how they worked with different opinions on the programmes – selecting tough male characters as their favourites in *EastEnders* but watching the young offenders in *Home & Away* and dreaming of the unattainable paradise of life in the Australian soap.

Young people and television in 2004

While this article has concentrated on the depth of opinion which young men have had about the soap opera genre over a number of years, in order to present up-to-date research on the topic of this Yearbook, I arranged to conduct interviews with three groups of girls who all attended a girls school in the suburbs of Birmingham, U.K. The school is situated in a fairly affluent area of the city with a wide catchment area which incorporates council estates and terrace housing, as well as expensive and medium range privately owned properties. The pupils are from a wide range of different races and religions.

I conducted the interviews during early September 2004, when the girls had just returned from their summer holiday. I initially gave them brief questionnaires to complete which gave details of their age, family, number of television sets, number of hours viewed and then specific questions about their favourite channels and programmes before moving onto the questions about soap operas and reality TV. I then conducted informal interviews with them which often resulted in them having a discussion between themselves. They certainly were completely open in their opinions and this article can only give a glimpse of the views which they held.

Young teenage girls

The first group of 23 girls was the youngest (about 13 years of age) and was in an English class. They were heavy viewers and while two said that they watched for 1 or 2 hours per day, most of them watched for 4 to 6 and three even 10 hours per day. As this research was conducted at the end of the summer holiday, this may have affected the time available for viewing. Their favourite choice of channels was a surprise. Very few of them mentioned terrestrial channels – some did include BBC1, ITV and Channels 4 and 5 but by far the most popular channels were satellite channels (particularly Nickelodeon, Trouble, Zee TV, Cartoon Network and Sky 1). This is a serious situation for terrestrial broadcasters.

However, this did not mean that the girls did not watch soap operas and other programmes on terrestrial channels. They were avid soap opera viewers and the words which they used most to describe what was the appeal of the genre were: 'interesting', 'funny', 'good', 'exciting', 'good acting', 'good storylines'. The most used adjective was 'funny' and this was the highest praise in contrast with the harshest criticism, which was for a programme to be 'boring'. *EastEnders* was their favourite soap opera and favourite characters were the young ones aged between 18 and 30 (Kat, Alfie, Spencer, Ronnie, Zoe, Dennis, Sharon, Vicki, Mickey and Tariq). All these young characters have had dramatic storylines which are family orientated. The interviewed girls' reasons for liking them revealed the way that they perceived the characters and their personalities. They liked Dennis because he was shy – and they giggled through their shyness when they suggested that he was good-looking. Kat was liked because she was feisty, but the storyline when it was revealed that she was Zoe's mother and had had her when she was 13 was chosen as a serious storyline which they liked. Their views on teenage pregnancies handled in storylines showed an engagement with both the fiction and the reality of such situations. They mentioned a new family and talked of the 13-year-old who had moved into the Square who was pregnant. One commented:

> If you had stories like the teenage pregnancy it could be dangerous because you
> could end up like them because you thought it was acceptable.

Other girls disagreed and offered a different view:

> But it could give you information which you might not know.

The group then decided that a programme would not influence *them* – but *others* might be influenced. They continued the discussion and decided that information included in a programme was a good thing:

> It gives you a lesson on something. It's a good way of getting information across.

But they did not think that they would be influenced by negative suggestions in the programmes:

> They can show anything they like on soaps, it will not make you go out and do it.
> We're not stupid.

While they appreciated young characters and their storylines, they also mentioned older characters which were judged for their acting ability. Den Watts, a character in his 50s who returned to the programme in 2003 and who had been involved in a number of extra marital relationships, was appreciated for his acting and his affairs were seen as laughable.

These girls were not particularly enamoured with the genre of reality TV. They did watch some programmes, and *Big Brother* and *Wife Swap*[5] were cited as their favourites. *Big Brother* was seen as funny but of no particular interest. *Wife Swap* did not impress them and they commented that all the families were portrayed as if there was something wrong with them. It was clear that reality TV in its various guises did not have any meaningful connection with their viewing habits. They would not go out of their way to seek out any of these programmes. The positive aspect of reality TV was that it gave an insight into how other people lived and showed different people who would never meet each other, having to live in the same house. One girl referred to the winner of this year's *Big Brother*, Nadia who was a transsexual, saying it was interesting to see the woman who had been a man and how everybody liked her. Positive and discerning reactions were the norm as they discussed these programmes.

What was the most interesting feature of the discussions with this young female group was that they are the first group of people I have ever interviewed who used name of the actor and actress when they talked about them. Jessie Wallace, Nigel Harman, Shane Ritchie were mentioned as actors as well as characters. This generation of viewers have celebrity as a concept in their vocabulary of media and the fact that they are referring to actors by their own as well as their character names, belies the often rehearsed argument that viewers believe that soap

Not passive audience

opera are real rather than fiction. The girls know the performers for their appearance outside the soap operas and have no problem distinguishing them.

The second group of girls who were a year older (about 14) held very similar views but they showed a progression to other genres. Heavy viewers who watched a very wide range of programmes which are outside the range of this article, one interesting point was that they selected documentaries which told of the lives of young people as a genre which they watched. The documentaries, which told the lives of music performers, and actors who showed that they have often had a bad childhood and how they had overcome their difficulties, were mentioned as being very moving.

They had an understanding of the need for production values to exaggerate the storylines and the differences in the people who are selected for the reality TV shows. They were not all fans of soap opera but if they were critical it was because the storylines became too boring and they lost interest. One girl said:

They're OK but they drag on about the same thing.

However, reality shows were praised for telling stories that 'you can relate to in real life'. This group of young girls had a critical approach to their viewing and they might watch regularly and widely, but they did retain a detached and active opinion on their choice of viewing.

17- and 18-year-olds – a sophisticated analysis of the genres

After talking with the 13- and 14-year-olds, I returned the next week to meet the 17- and 18-year-olds. These girls were entering the second year of their A level studies and were taking Media Studies as part of their course. This meant that they were well informed about the media and this showed up in the sophisticated views, which they had about issues and values shown on television programmes. The group consisted of eleven girls. They were avid viewers who had a wide knowledge of various television programmes. While some of them watched up to 6 hours of television a day they were discerning and informed in their opinions of what they watched.

Since the purpose of the interview/discussion was to discover what these girls thought at the two genres of soap opera and reality TV I began asking about their opinions of soap opera. Although all but one had said that they liked watching soap opera, they were critical and made thoughtful analysis of the benefits and problems of the genre. Jasmine felt that the storylines had begun to drag and she had stopped watching two years earlier and had not been tempted back. As she said why she did not watch soaps, this naturally led into a discussion between the girls which went into a discussion of the value of the genre. One of them said:

Sometimes they do pick up and when it does it is good because basically the storylines that are in soaps are realistic... Like you can have dramas going on like abortion, relationships, (someone else says 'teenage pregnancies') yes, teenage pregnancies.

Another girl took up the argument and puts a different perspective:

I agree with the fact that they reach out to the young people and that they can help people in their situations but sometimes it seems to me that it could be really dangerous and I don't think you should need to watch a soap to get your advice. I think that first of all there should be more things out there for people. You should not need to switch on BBC1 to find out if you should have an abortion or not.

One of the areas, which provoked a lot of debate, was the question of the 'helpline' at the end of programmes. British soap operas have a tradition of putting a helpline with telephone numbers of official agencies which can give advice to viewers who have been or are affected by the issues which are covered in the programme. These do attract a number of calls from viewers. One example is that when the BBC soap opera *EastEnders* was running the Little Mo story of domestic violence, 5,000 people telephoned the helpline after the programme (Hobson 2003:211). The fine line between showing sensitive issues and maintaining an entertainment show was also discussed in this exchange about the domestic violence story, a story of a stillborn baby, and a miscarriage and illustrates the way that the girls are thinking about the issues, at the same time considering the fact that this is a television production with an aim to educate and to entertain. I include this exchange in full because it illustrates so many of the points which are pertinent to the understanding of soap operas by young people:

Well they put the soaps on to draw more people and that is fair enough and that is why they have those situations, apparently for young people but I just think that you should not have to follow the paths of Little Mo.

Yes, but when they do have the stories, then at the end of the programme they do have the 'Call this helpline' if you need help. So it is helping as well.

But still I do understand that they help young people.

They aren't just bringing everything into the storyline. They are making you think of it after the programme.

Yes but that could be because they know that people are saying that *EastEnders* is really depressing 'cos of what... what's that woman's name who lost her baby? (Someone answers 'Lynn'.) Yes, 'cos that was really depressing so people would watch it who had may be gone through that situation and be sad. Like that girl, what's her name? ('Sarah.') ...yes, in *Coronation Street* who lost her baby and then her boyfriend was gay – yes I'm thinking what about so many women out there who have lost their baby, I think that must be like hitting a nerve at some point and I think that they might be saying that many people have been through this, but to sit there and watch your favourite show, a soap, and see somebody else go through what you have been through must like bring up bad memories.

But it could also help because it shows how somebody else deals with the situation and overcomes it because obviously now she's all right. ('Yes' from some of the girls.)

This exchange of views from the girls is interesting. One thinks that social information should be provided from other sources than from a television programme, while others think that the programme makers are responsible by bringing in other agencies (the helpline) to offer help on matters included in the dramas. The girls appreciate that issues such as losing a baby or a miscarriage can bring painful memories for those who have suffered the same sadness but can see that sharing the experience of the fictional character in their lives can be of help. Finally, they are well aware of the needs of the broadcasters to entertain their audience and they are in no doubt that they are watching fictional forms, which are created for entertainment, education and information. One further exchange occurred during this part of the discussion, which related to the use of helplines. As mentioned, one girl said that helplines were a positive aspect of what is the public service element attached to popular genres:

When they do have stories then at the end of the programme they do have like 'Call this helpline' if you need help. So it is helping as well.

Another girl laughed in a quizzical manner at this comment:

It's just... it's like the soaps, they do deal with real issues and everything but its like, you have watched the soap, now it brings you back to like reality and you have got the helpline. It's – do you know what I mean? (*DH*: 'Yes.') It's not funny like the show, but its different – but to me it doesn't create a sense of realism. It shows that it isn't real. Yes, as soon as the show ends you have got something serious.

This is an interesting and perceptive comment because it shows that the girl has seen beyond the drama and identifies the connection between the subjects of the drama and the situations in real life to which they relate.

Finally, the girls discuss the questions of whether the situations in soap opera are likely to have an adverse influence on their behaviour as viewers. I discuss the concern among people that young people might be encouraged to imitate situations seen in soap operas:

DH: There is a concern that if they show a storyline with a young girl getting pregnant that will make people think that it is acceptable.

The reply not only gives a perceptive answer from one of the girls, but also perhaps puts the responsibility for their behaviour back in the hands of parents:

It depends on the parents. It depends on how strong your head is; do you know what I mean? If you want to get pregnant. If you are not strong willed and you are level-headed and you know what's right and what's wrong then it shouldn't. But if you just do what other people do then they might influence you.

Clearly these girls are engaging with the drama in the soap operas and taking the information from the drama, but bringing their own beliefs and behaviour systems which they see not as being from the soaps but from their own family situations.

Reality TV – interesting/transparent production

As said previously, the phenomenal success of the soap opera as a broadcasting form has resulted in newly developed genres taking some of the main character-istics from the soap opera and including them in the new hybrid genres of reality TV or docu-soaps. While these genres purport to be connected to the soap opera by virtue of the stories of everyday life, in fact they are carefully edited and the story is constructed by the producers in the same way as the drama of soap opera is constructed by the writers. The docu-soaps are not realistic in the sense of watching unmediated everyday life, but where they do relate to the soap opera is through the concentration on the personal and the stories of ordinary people, albeit they have to be extraordinary to be chosen by the production team in the first place. While there are many forms of reality TV on British television, I chose to concentrate on the two programmes which the girls defined as being of inter-est to them. These were *Big Brother* and *Wife Swap*. I asked the group of 17- to 18-year-olds what reality TV they watched. One of them said:

Like chat shows and *Big Brother*, things like that. Life showing everyday people and everyday life.

Another girl gave an insight into how she defined the genre:

They are programmes which are not rehearsed. Programmes without a script. Other programmes are all set out and rehearsed but in reality TV people are just filmed doing what they would normally do. So it's just interesting to see. ('Yes, yes' the others concurred.)

The programme, which they chose to discuss and which was their favourite, was *Wife Swap*, a programme shown on Channel 4, where two families swap wives and they live with each other's family for two weeks. One girl describes the show:

They show you actually two families and they swap the mothers to another family and you actually see their rules without the mother – what they would do in the first week. And then the mother from the other family would change the rules for the family and you see how they would react from what they would normally do. At the end the mothers and fathers would meet and actually put their points across: 'We found this and we found that.' And sometimes there would be arguments.

This is a very fair description of the programme but what is significant is that this girl and others who commented described the main character as 'the mother' and talked about the 'mother and father', showing that she is making a reading of the programme which related to the participants as mothers and fathers, not as husband and wife. She, and others who commented, made it clear that they saw these stories as being about the power of the parents in the family and they way that they behaved. The viewing girls had taken the family rules as put in place by the mother as being the most important part of the programmes. In a further comment, Jasmine stated:

> It made me appreciate my mom. Yes, because I realised that if anybody else had come into my house and they started changing her rules I realised how much I would have missed her. I think it did make a lot of people realise that certain people are essential in the family. ('Exactly', another girl concurred.) And that's just to make things work and make a little routine and I think when they bring somebody else in the house they stick to your rules but it's not the same.

The fact that Jasmine had watched these programmes and witnessed the chaos which resulted in homes when the wives/mothers were removed, had given her an insight into the work which her own mother performed in her own home. Far from being counter to values taught in the home, these girls had seen the value of the role which was performed by the mothers in the programmes and their own lives.

They had also understood and identified the skills of the programme makers in choosing families which were different in order to provide the dramatic content:

> People that set them up they are clever though because if the two families were done like a middle class family and then like a family and a mom that had six children and she was on benefits or whatever, so obviously when they swapped there was a contrast.

They even identified that there could be positive aspects to the change with the other mother brought to a family:

> And sometimes, if the mother from the other family does clean the house and the mother comes back to a house that is clean – if she saw it was clean she would actually do something, 'cos one of them she did say: 'Oh, my God my house is clean.' And after that she did make changes in the house.

What the girls revealed was that they watched the programmes and made their own readings, which were determined by their own position within their own family. They also made informed comment on the professional skills of the broadcasters in choosing families and they way those contrasting types of families contributed to the drama of the programmes.

Big Brother is actually a game show which has elements of reality TV in its make up. It was first transmitted on British television on Channel 4 in July 2000 and it immediately became a success for the channel. The idea behind the programme, which was devised by the Dutch independent production company Endemol put ten contestants into a warehouse, purpose-converted into open-plan living accommodation, where they lived under the constant scrutiny of the cameras. It was not a docu-soap but a game show with a prize of £ 70,000 to the contestant who was voted to stay in the house until the end of the contest. The programme became a summer phenomenon and was heralded as a new form of programming. It imprisoned its participants and their activities were also available for viewing on the Internet twenty-four hours a day. The series transmitted in 2003 was not as popular as the previous years and so the producers decided to make the 2004 version 'more evil'. Although the 17- to 18-year-old girls I talked with watched the programme they did not subscribe to its thesis as entertainment. I asked them what they thought of this year's (2004) *Big Brother*.

> Nasty, I didn't even watch this year but I read somewhere that they purposely got like different people into it, like what was her name… Nadia (someone says 'the transsexual' and someone adds 'one wants to be a glamour model'). And, what's his name… Ahmed didn't like gay people and Marco didn't like immigrants, so they put them in.

> And they made the house smaller 'cos it was like so they could be exploited more and like they were doing more sex and drunken nights and everything and more alcohol brought into the show and because of that it was more entertaining and they said themselves this was the best ever *Big Brother*.

> *DH*: Do you think it was the best?

> No they tried too hard. It was too much, it wasn't reality.

The girls continued with the exposition on the production of reality TV:

> They are carefully selected to make the story. Which is why sometimes on *Wife Swap* they only show the bad things and they don't show the good things and the couple actually get along and the producers have only chosen to show the bad parts.

> What the producers do is find somebody who will make trouble because obviously… because then they know if somebody goes into a house and does everything you would expect – who's gonna watch that? So they go out looking for these kind of people who will make scenes and dramas, so that when they go in the house they will react to everything and they… that way they get more viewers.

At every point of contact these girls (taking Media Studies) were aware of the production which was behind the television programme which was shown. They know that participants are selected for their outrageous behaviour and to provide contrasts with other participants. They appreciate that the purpose of television is to entertain, remember that to be 'funny' is one of the requirements of young people when they are judging any television choices. One final comment was significant in that it revealed that programmes which do achieve almost a cult status, gather more viewers because not to know what is going on is to remove them from the cultural capital which circulates in their social situations:

> Programmes like *Big Brother* I didn't find interesting at all but I was still watching it just for the fact that everyone's talking about it and it was for the social aspect of it. If you weren't watching it you would not know what the conversation was about. 'Cos we come to school and if you did not watch it you wouldn't know what you were talking about. (Laughter from the other girls.) It's true.

The importance of cultural capital in the guise of knowledge of what has happened in a programme is one of the reasons why viewers watch programmes. For broadcasters this is the famous 'water-cooler' programme, meaning that viewers will gather round the water-cooler in an office to talk about their last night's viewing. For young people, too, this is an important part of their cultural capital and social standing in the school situation. But what they have done with these programmes is take their views on appropriate behaviour from their family, and seeing different representations of the family has been of interest but it has also confirmed their appreciation of their own family lives.

Conclusion

Mass media is a major part of the everyday lives of young people. Much of what is produced is of a high quality and gives a commentary on everyday life particularly through the popular genres. All the research, which I have conducted with young people, has confirmed my academic theoretical position that audiences make their own readings of any media form. Not that the message which is inscribed by the producers does not have any effect, but that the reading made by individuals and groups is overdetermined by what they bring to the media form. While the young boys who did not get on with their family chose to reject soap operas precisely because they were about families, the young boys in the remand centre saw the family representations in *Home & Away* as a fantasy which they would never know. While they identified with Phil and Grant Mitchell, the more aggressive characters in *EastEnders* whom they saw as realistic, they also saw Peggy Mitchell only in terms of her position as a mother.

Similarly, the young girls in Birmingham saw the positive elements in *Wife Swap* and appreciated the role of the female participants and saw them as mothers rather than wives as defined by the programmes. They also saw the value of the soap opera in giving information about the issues, which might relate to their lives but they would have preferred information to be available from other sources, as well.

Far from being badly affected by the storylines, these young people revealed that they questioned the representations and were aware that these were media productions which also had a function as entertainment for the broadcasters. Their sophistication as viewers was evident. Their viewing patterns showed that they chose programmes which were related to their youth, their favourite characters were either young, or ordinary, and programmes had primarily to be funny. It is perhaps naïve to worry that young people, at least in their teens, will be badly affected by the values and explicit storylines in soap operas and reality TV. The recent research which I did with the girls in Birmingham revealed that they had a sophisticated understanding of the programmes which they perceived as drama or a version of reality but with no sense that they were being unduly influenced by what they saw. Rather they enjoyed them, valued some of the information which they gave, and thought about them, discussed them and made readings which were positive and perceptive. Indeed, the positive aspects of this research shows that the role of soap opera and the recent reality TV programmes are not genres which should cause concern amongst authorities regarding adolescents, for the series both reflect the reality with which the young people are familiar and enable them to make their own judgements in relation to the portrayals of that reality either in a fictional or pseudo-reality form.

Notes

1. Ofcom (Office of Communications) set up by the British Government is the new regulator, which became operational in December 2003. Its first task was to begin an investigation into the state of public service broadcasting. The report of Phase 1 – *Is Television Special? Ofcom review of public service television broadcasting* – was published in April 2004.

2. The watershed is a legal requirement to which British terrestrial broadcasters have to adhere. It requires them not to show any material which would be deemed unsuitable for children before 21.00 hours.

3. Pool is a game played on a table which is a small version of a snooker table. Played in pubs and youth clubs it was popular during the 1980s as a game which was culturally acceptable by working class youths.

4. Brief notes on soap operas mentioned in the article:
   Brookside, produced by Mersey Television for Channel 4, was broadcast during 1982-2003. Innovative series set on a Liverpool housing estate. Wide range of characters with natural language, strong storylines including drugs and violence. A cult programme which changed British soap opera.
   Coronation Street is a British soap opera from 1960 set in the North of England. Wide range of characters – age, class, some ethnicity. Comedic and serious storylines. Handles issue-based

stories, particularly schoolgirl pregnancy, transsexuality, relationships. Britain's longest running soap opera – top rated with *EastEnders*.

EastEnders that started in 1985 on BBC1, is a British soap opera set in the fictional district of Albert Square in the East End of London. Wide range of characters reflecting class, age, ethnicity, and respectable and criminal elements. Top rated soap opera with *Coronation Street*.

Home & Away is an Australian soap opera transmitted on ITV and now (2004) on Channel 5. Stories revolve around young people who have been in trouble with the authorities or there has been a breakdown within their families. In the series they live in a foster home in the idyllic surroundings of a small community, Summer Bay, near the sea.

Neighbours transmitted on BBC1 is an Australian soap opera set on a small housing development. Stories of neighbours, wide age range and excellent relationships between generations. "Good stories for young people."

5. *Big Brother* is the British version of the format devised by the Dutch independent company Endemol and was first shown on British television in July 2000.

Wife Swap is a reality TV series created and produced by the British independent production company RDF Media. It is transmitted on Channel 4 and has been sold internationally both as the British programme and as a format.

Bibliography

Buckingham, D. 1987: *Public Secrets: EastEnders and Its Audience*. London: British Film Institute
Gillespie, M. 1995: *Television, Ethnicity and Cultural Change*. London: Routledge
Hobson, D. 2003: *Soap Opera*. Cambridge: Polity
Hodge, B. & Tripp, D. 1986: *Children and Television: A Semiotic Approach*. Cambridge: Polity Press
Ofcom 2004: *Is Television Special? Ofcom review of public service television broadcasting*. London: Office of Communications.

Latin American Telenovelas

Interview with Valerio Fuenzalida[1]

conducted by María Dolores Souza

Why all this interest in telenovelas?

Latin American *telenovelas* are a complex genre and therefore very interesting. They have a clear Latin American identity, but also a universal appeal. How is this possible? How can they have this cultural impact on audiences so different from each other? I think this is because the genre stimulates social and family conversation in our region. That is more so than factual, i.e., non-fictional programs do. This might seem like nonsense for scholars with rather rationalistic views of social conversation – for Habermas, for example.

Also, *telenovelas* have introduced the Latin American television industry into the global cultural industry; in this respect, through *telenovelas*, Latin America is doing better than Europe, because Europe is not succeeding in the task of producing a genre with a universal appeal.

What's the definition of a telenovela?

Here there is a difference of opinion among scholars. Some Latin American scholars think there is a difference between soap operas and *telenovelas*, others don't. I would tend toward the first standpoint, in the sense that *telenovela* plots cover *private life and affectivity as lived at home*, and soap operas are more situational, i.e., the scripts have a broader context so you can also see some situations outside the home, outside the family. In *telenovelas* there is always one important love story – maybe two – and the end of the *telenovela* is the accomplishment of love *in marriage, moreover, religious marriage*. The love story in *telenovelas* creates an inner textual tension to an end. Soap operas, on the contrary, can have an endless narrative. Our genre has these particularities and some scholars point them out as specific cultural and identity elements of our Latin American culture.

Are there differences between telenovelas from different Latin American countries?

Yes, in our country and in others, there is a certain coincidence in consumers' appreciation of at least three kinds of *telenovelas*. The more traditional ones – emphasizing drama with more 'black and white' characters – are produced in Mexico and Venezuela, and the quality ones are represented by Brazilian productions. Some countries are in between these extremes – between tradition and innovation – such as Chile, Colombia and, perhaps, Argentina. But at the same time, it is possible to produce and broadcast these three kinds of *telenovelas* in one country.

Are the traditional ones those that focus on emotion, drama, love affairs...?

Yes, every *telenovela* has its basic characteristics, namely a love story. The more innovative ones have more stories, where you also can find some topical questions. That is, observing from home, from within the family, the problems of the country, of the modern world, or life itself. For example, the argument of a *telenovela* can include the new roles of women, how to combine work and family, or the life of entrepreneurial women.

What about young viewers and telenovelas?

There is a growing interest among children and young people in watching some kinds of *telenovelas* and this is associated with different factors. For instance, in Chile the producers make family-oriented *telenovelas*, really aiming at the family as a whole, not only women, which was the traditional target group. As opposed to this, you have the Mexican or the Venezuelan *telenovelas*, which, as I said before, are more traditional and thus targeted to housewives; these more traditional ones are broadcast in the early afternoon hours, around 2 to 3 p.m.

On the other hand, when you choose to air such a program at 8 p.m., before the central newscast at 9 p.m., as in Chile or Brazil, you will have all the family watching, and therefore the genre evolves toward a family target audience where you have to appeal to different age groups, such as young people and adult men, too. The plots involve more people, i.e., more characters, and different stories within one program, so you have a more diverse staff of actors, including women, youngsters and seniors, perhaps children too, and men in different roles. Men acquire more importance in the stories, so there is an adaptation to a family-oriented interest.

Would you say that there is a cultural identity in Latin American telenovelas? Moreover, is there a Latin American identity as such?

Well, I think that academics are trying to find out how to study the subject of identity in *telenovelas*. We know that real people consume *telenovelas* and it is very difficult to find out what elements of recognition and identity they can find in the programs. It is not easy to discover these signs. I think there is some agreement around the identity traits in the scenery, that is, in the natural setting of the production. Identity then has to do with the satisfaction the audience feels when it recognizes these settings. This is, for example, a very important characteristic of Brazilian *telenovelas*, and most recently of Chilean ones.

I think that there are two other identity characteristics represented in *telenovelas*, which are typically Latin American. One is the oral culture – and here we have a great difference from Europe where you have a more written culture. We have an oral culture and tradition, where storytelling through stories and tales, songs, dance – and nowadays the audiovisual language – is very prominent. This is striking in the tropics, for instance in Cuba, where the reading of books out loud was an important practice in factories in the 19th century. In this context of orality, which we also have in *telenovelas*, dialog is very important, the audio track is sometimes more important than the image and visibility.

A second characteristic of our continent is – as Martín-Barbero says[2] – the emotional and affective pattern of our culture, which is less rationalistic than European culture. This is, thus, a dominant feature of *telenovelas*, too.

Moreover, *telenovelas* have another very interesting characteristic, namely the effective capacity to produce social conversation, family conversation in the first place, but peer conversation as well, at school or in the office. There you see that oral culture reproduces itself, not only because of the text of the genre, but because it stimulates oral tradition – conversation.

Telenovelas in countries such as Brazil, Peru, Chile or Colombia have the capacity to produce social conversation – they have a socializing effect. In these stories there is a reference to modern problems, so *telenovelas* bring the outside world and social problems into the family, into domestic conversation.

There is a recent Brazilian research study – conducted by Emile McAnany and Anamaría Fadul – where the initial hypothesis was that family planning was associated with the consumption/conversation of *telenovelas*. They conducted focus groups with families in Sâo Paulo and one of the main results was that *telenovelas* effectively put the problem of family planning on the table. And this was not the intention of the producers, there was no social marketing so to speak, but the fictional topic of the program gave rise to conversations within the family, between youngsters and their mothers. This was possible through remarks made by the audience about the different characters in the program; they liked to watch their story, their aims and goals in life, so they discussed the case of marriage, professional goals, childbirth and family planning with other family members.

In Chile, there was a telenovela that put the subject of homosexuality on the table, something new for a country that is very conservative in that respect...

Yes, that was a *telenovela* called *Machos*, which presented through fiction a different way of looking at homosexuality. In other television programs people tend to make fun of homosexuality – through jokes and stereotyped imitations – but there is audience evidence that in this *telenovela* the subject was presented in such a way that it could be talked about seriously within the family, something that other programs – even very well made documentaries like *Informe Especial* – have not achieved. Documentaries do not elicit the same kind of conversation, because they are more rational as a genre. They discuss very important matters, of course, like the medical or psychological implications of homosexuality, but *telenovelas* stimulate family communication because they show the affective bonds of people involved in such a situation. It is no longer about a social problem, about strange people, it is about a family situation like mine, people who could be my relatives… And that creates proximity, something that strikes people and elicits conversation among the young and old, especially the young.

Is there a special worldview in telenovelas, a 'Weltanschauung'?
I think this genre does not care very much about a Latin American worldview – at least not deliberately. The important element here is affection, the emotional way of looking at real life problems. It is about the value of private relations, of the family, of the status of your family, of religion. Martín-Barbero has pointed out these elements and I think he has had an important role in recognizing the value of this kind of approach in Latin American fiction.

Martín-Barbero says that the appraisal and valuation of the genre is parallel to the appraisal of dance and romantic music produced in our continent, like *boleros*, for example. He says that, in Latin America, we appreciate this emotional view of the world and the self as opposed to a more rational view.

The more traditional *telenovelas* are about social mobility, about rural and urban folks going one step further in the social ladder, something very important in countries like Mexico and Peru. Social mobility is an important problem in our region, and the genre shows the sensibility and conflicts that this gives rise to.

But telenovelas are not only about longing for love and affectionate relationships; we see a lot of conflict, hatred and disloyalty. Does this also reflect our lives?
I think that in countries such as Brazil there is a great ability to introduce social problems in the stories. Some people say that the audience is better informed by watching *telenovelas* than newscasts; of course this is an exaggeration, but some *telenovelas* can fictionalize and stimulate social conversation about real problems. For example, corruption has been fictionalized in Brazilian and Mexican *telenovelas*, not through the representation of real people, but of real situations through fictional characters, and this has had quite an impact on the audience.

With respect to private life, viewers constantly interpret the content of the programs and talk about them making sense – individually and collectively – of the characters. For example, there is an important character in a Chilean *telenovela*,[3] a nasty landlord who treats people very badly, and the reaction of the audience is quite ambivalent. The importance of villains in the stories is great; otherwise there is no action in the story. Audiences react against this character, who at the same time is appreciated as a good actor, so it is not true that viewers identify with and are modeled by villains. In another *telenovela*, about the 60s and the hippies,[4] there is a mother who teaches at university and neglects her relationship with her own son. And many adolescent viewers are upset with this character and do not agree with her, because she is not appreciated as a good mother.

You said earlier that Latin American telenovelas succeed in other countries...

I know that Miami in the U.S.A. is a very important place from which *telenovelas* are exported,[5] and they have opened markets in Asia, in some Arab countries and in Eastern Europe. There is a discussion nowadays about the issue of how global or local *telenovelas* should be. This is a current discussion because you can go global, but then you could miss some local identity characteristics. I have the impression that the reaction of the new markets mentioned is very interesting; it is a new sign that *telenovelas* have a somewhat universal appeal.

Do you think that telenovelas have a positive or negative effect on young audiences?

This is a very difficult question. I think that socialization has to do with many contextual elements. There is interaction between the text of the programs on the screen and family reception of that content. There is a social reception of this genre, as there is a social enjoyment – in the family environment.

There we can see a difference from cinema for example, even with films aired on television, where reception is more individual. *Telenovelas'* landmark is oral culture, as I said before, and orality always has a social setting. When the end chapter of a successful *telenovela* is aired, there is great expectation; you can see that street traffic decreases, because everybody is at home watching it. For instance, the day that *Machos* ended, I was teaching at the university and when I went back home, the city was empty!

The consumption of *telenovelas* is social, so the influence of *telenovelas* always interacts with the family. We talked a while ago about homosexuality; well this *telenovela* brought the subject into the family, allowed all family members to have a say in the matter. So it is no longer about learning a specific attitude or behavior seen on the screen. Some fictional situations or behaviors stimulate family talking – the *telenovela* as a genre has the capacity to elicit communication, not behavior. This is my conclusion from audience research.

You have been studying telenovelas for over 20 years now. Why would a scholar like you want to study this genre?

Because *telenovelas* are the only television production in Latin America that dramatizes some of our characteristics, some of our identity elements, and this cultural characteristic has an amazing universal appeal. So, I think *telenovelas* are a very important cultural product. And they not only reflect somehow the way we are, but they are a very important industrial product, too, for the global television industry. Television cannot be financed only through advertising. You need to have exportable products, and the only product we have been able to export up to now is the *telenovela*. So their importance for our region is at the same time cultural and industrial.

Additionally, I think that fiction will be increasing its importance on the television screen, because it is easier for a fictional genre to be innovative, more so than a live show, for example. Moreover, we also have these hybrid kinds of programs, like 'docu-dramas', where you can see a mix of reality and fiction, in other words, reality has been fictionalized. I think that this is a very interesting development in the television industry, a genre that perhaps could be exported, too. Being a mixture of reality-based problems shown in a fictional way, docu-dramas are perceived by audiences as having a learning value from other experiences in everyday life and they are, thus, conceived as highly educational. I can think of one Chilean docu-drama, *Mujer Rompe el Silencio* (Woman, Break the Silence!), which fictionalizes real problems of women, or the Mexican series *Mirada de Mujer* (Woman's View) – in my opinion, these programs can have ethical standards.

The more sensationalistic programs are produced within the talk show genre – I remember a talk show on Peruvian television conducted by Laura Bozzo, lover of Montesinos (Chief Intelligence and Security Head during Fujimori's dictatorship), where sensationalism was used to attract the audience and to convey propaganda for the government.

Notes

1. Valerio Fuenzalida is a Chilean Senior Researcher, studying television, and Director of the Postgraduate Degree Diploma in Audience Studies at the Catholic University in Chile, Santiago de Chile.
2. Jesús Martín-Barbero is a Colombian-Spanish expert on culture and communications.
3. Called *Los Pincheira*, based on the legend of a family of large estate owners who lived around 1850 (during Chile's independence).
4. Called *Hippie*.
5. Miami (as well as Los Angeles) in the U.S. is an important center of Hispanic popular culture and commercial interchange – an exchange center for Latin America and U.S.A., as well as for Latin America and other regions of the world. Thus, Latin American *telenovelas* are to a great deal exported from companies in Miami.

On Possible and Actual Lives

Young Viewers and the Reception of Brazilian Telenovelas

Thaïs Machado-Borges

Meire and Marina (both 18-year-olds, live-in babysitters) were planning to go to a Sunday market to buy some earrings:

> *Meire*: I prefer the earrings for pierced ears. I think they're more chic.
>
> *Marina*: Yes, but in *novelas* they only use that other kind of earring. Every time they talk on the phone they take them off, like this [makes the gesture of taking something from her ear lob and brushes her hair backwards, as if to make room for the telephone].
>
> *Meire*: All right! But that's in *novelas*, right?!
>
> *Marina*: Always with those earrings. They don't use earrings for pierced ears. No, they don't.

Brazil is a country with one of the most unequal income distributions in the world. The richest 20 percent of the Brazilian population earns 29 times more than the poorest.[1] Roughly 30 percent of Brazilians live in abject poverty, earning less than US$ 100 a month. Forty percent of the population makes less than US$ 300 a month.[2] Brazil is also a country with one of the largest television audiences in the world. Eighty-eight percent of households in the country have at least one television set – in sheer numbers, this means 40 million TV households.[3] One of the most broadcast – and most watched – type of program is the *telenovela*.

Telenovelas are broadcast throughout Brazil six days a week, in the afternoon and during prime time. They attract a daily audience of more than forty million viewers. Individual *telenovelas* are able to capture and maintain the attention of a faithful audience during their duration of six to eight months. Unlike the U.S. or British soap operas that may last for many years, a Brazilian *telenovela* ends after 150 to 200 episodes, and is immediately substituted by a new one. Their plots can conform to real-life seasons and holidays, and often they introduce fashions and products, approach polemical subjects and comment upon (in a realistic or parodic way) contemporary social issues.

What impact do *telenovelas* have on young viewers? Do they shape the way viewers think and act? Do their representations of gender, sexuality, race and class work as guidelines for, or enablers of, particular kinds of subject formation?

The argument

This article argues that viewers' engagement with *telenovelas* should be seen as part of the practices of coping and hoping that make up their lives. Their dialoguing with *telenovelas* is neither duped nor completely subversive, and it does not preclude laughter or pleasure – it is a way for viewers to imbue their lives with fiction, images and fantasy, not only to momentarily escape from reality, but also as a way to hope and act in order to be embedded as a subject, as "someone who counts", in a society where "counting" is anything but self-evident for the majority of the population.

When I proposed to investigate the reception of *telenovelas*, I started from the idea that a subject is, as Donna Haraway puts it, "partial in all its guises, never finished, whole, simply there and original; it is always constructed and stitched imperfectly [...]" (Haraway 1991:193).[4] Numerous social voices impact on subject formation. Media (and in this special case *telenovelas*) are, or may be, some of these voices.

There has been a polarization in the debate on the relationship between readers/viewers and popular culture (Stam 1989; Walkerdine 1997):[5] People are either described as revolutionary and resistant in their readings of popular culture, or as duped, unable or unwilling to make critical readings and concrete demands on the real world. The people who became my informants and their ways of relating to *telenovelas* cannot be easily characterized as resistant; but neither are they duped or uncritical. My informants' engagement with *telenovelas* is part of everyday practices that, together with a range of other activities, come to shape and constitute their positions as subjects within Brazilian society.

Method and sample

Ethnographic material was gathered during longer and shorter periods of fieldwork conducted between 1995 and 2000, in the state of Minas Gerais, in southeastern Brazil. In 1995, I spent three months in the city of Ouro Preto doing preliminary fieldwork. In 1997, I spent six months in the city of Belo Horizonte. After this period of fieldwork, I have returned to Belo Horizonte for shorter periods (generally a month), once a year.[6]

I gathered a total sample consisting of 45 people – 38 women and 7 men. The majority of them, i.e., 32 persons, were aged between 14 and 30 years. Informants occupied different social positions: Thirteen of them had truly low incomes (about 100 *reais* a month, which corresponded to US$ 100), 3 of them had originally low incomes but ascended socially and economically, and the rest of them, i.e., 29 persons, had higher educational levels and higher incomes. I tried to compensate for the predominance of female informants by gathering 183 essays about *telenovelas* written by undergraduate university students at their first year of Communication Studies. Of these 183 people, 107 were women and 76 men, all aged between 17 and 40 years (with a majority aged between 18 and 22), coming from different socio-economic backgrounds.

The research

Most previous studies on the reception of *telenovelas* (Beltrão 1993; Fachel and Oliven 1987; Tufte 1993; Vink 1988)[7] have focused on women's reactions to and interpretations of the plots of *telenovelas*. I chose to move my focus away from the moment of broadcast, the moment when people actually sit and watch television, to the streets, parties, and people's everyday interactions. In other words, I was interested in asking not only "How do viewers interpret what they see?" but also "What do viewers do with what they watch?". I was interested in understanding how and when *telenovelas* intercept everyday life.

During the course of my fieldwork, I realized that outside of the context of immediate reception, when my informants mentioned *telenovelas* in their everyday errands and conversations, they were not only referring to the plots of these programs, but also to images, advertisements, magazines and diverse commodities that were interspersed with the plots of *telenovelas*. I could observe that not only did people talk about *telenovela* plots, their contents and characters, but they also talked extensively about *telenovela* actors, their diets, the spas they frequented, the food they ate, their gymnastic programs, their fashion and their plastic surgeries.

My ethnographic fieldwork foregrounded that informants experienced *telenovelas* not as a delimited and circumscribed narrative, but rather as a dialogic flow, with innumerable articulations and connections.[8]

My ethnographic material also foregrounded a discrepancy between how informants presented and reflected upon their watching practices in interviews and essays,[9] and how they spontaneously and more unreflectively appropriated, circulated and reiterated different elements from *telenovelas* in their everyday lives.

155

Telenovelas and social positioning: Possible and actual worlds
Selective viewers

> Wonderful bodies undress in front of the camera and invade our homes as if this was a very normal thing to do. [...] Children are reached by the sex wave propagated through *novelas* since these are one of their best amusements. (Lilian, 18, undergraduate student. Excerpt from a classroom essay.)

Most of my informants associated *telenovelas* with two particular definitions of popular culture: *Telenovelas* were either seen in contraposition to high culture (and thus understood as vulgar, shallow, low culture) or as being part of a commercial mass culture.

By affirming that watching *telenovelas* was not part of their own interests, informants positioned themselves as active and selective viewers. The practice of watching *telenovelas* was very often mentioned as being a marker of a non-prestigious age, gender or class. In fact, most of the people with whom I talked were eager to point out that they were not addicted to *telenovelas* – if they had anything else more interesting to do, they would not hesitate to stop watching. Therefore, in my informants' reflections on their watching practices, watching *telenovelas* was currently said to be part of someone else's interests: adults assumed that younger viewers were less critical and more easily persuaded to imitate the plots of *telenovelas*; women (rather than men) were often said to be the ones addicted to *telenovelas*, and less educated and poor people were targeted as being the ones most likely to be influenced by *telenovelas*, the explanation being that they were unable to distinguish between fiction and reality. For instance, Bruno, a 19-year-old, lower-middle-class student affirmed:

> *Novelas* encourage young children and adults to behave like fictive characters, to wear the same clothes, [...] to think in the same way.

By affirming their position as active and selective viewers, my informants were situating themselves on the right side of a widespread discussion about the negative effects of television on unprepared viewers.

Helping people

Still reflecting on *telenovelas'* impact upon (often unprepared and uneducated) viewers, several of my informants mentioned that *telenovelas* could be an instrument to "help people", thus giving their viewers access to certain kinds of information:

> *Novelas* show so many clothes, and then if people want to open a shop, then they look at the fashion in the *novela* and start to sell the same thing. So I think people

watch [*telenovelas*] to learn. There are lots of things to learn. And there are also lots of wrong things, too. (Meire, 18, live-in babysitter)

Here are some further examples of the ways in which my informants talked about how *telenovelas* gave viewers access to diverse and important information:

People with less education, for instance, can be introduced, when watching a *novela*, to different, unimaginable cultures. [...] They can obtain new and important information that can seem to be basic and obvious for us who are well educated. For instance, the importance of using condoms and the existence of other birth control methods. They can understand the gravity of an abortion – many people don't know that it is a crime – and they can get to know more about diseases, such as leukemia, which was dealt with by the *novela Laços de Família* (Family Links, Globo,[10] 2001). And, to the rich people [viewers] it might be astonishing to know and see how people live in shantytowns and how people suffer in order to survive. *Novelas* show the unknown... People belonging to different universes learn, get informed and entertained through [watching] *novelas*. (Júlia, 20, middle-class undergraduate student. Excerpt from a classroom essay.)

In *Porto dos Milagres* (Harbor of Miracles, Globo, 2001), they show people from Bahia, their love affairs and their problems, and they criticize in a subtle way the governor of that state. It is good that *novelas* deal with social problems. We like to see our faces reflected in the faces of the characters, because then we can share the same knowledge and try to solve our tensions. We can also think: "Thank God these things don't only happen to me!" (Bárbara, 18, undergraduate lower-middle-class student. Excerpt from a classroom essay.)

Novelas might teach something. Globo's *novelas* are a good example. Their plots contain information about cancer, AIDS, homosexuality, abortion and even traffic rules. (Marcelo, 19, undergraduate student. Excerpt from a classroom essay.)

I recall a scene from a *novela*. I felt imprisoned by it, by all the suffering [expressed] in that moment, and I could see myself in that actress, I could feel her problem as if it was mine, and I felt anguish about that situation. When the scene was over, I started to reflect on some social problems. This scene from *Laços de Família* (Family Links, Globo, 2001) enacted by Carolina Dieckman, who portrayed the tragedy of a person suffering from leukemia, worked as a way to educate the Brazilian people. We stopped and reflected on what can be done to help people who are suffering in a hospital or even at home. (Adriana, 25, lower-middle-class undergraduate student. Excerpt from a classroom essay.)

Examining the excerpts above, one can see what kinds of information were considered to "educate", "teach", or "help" (young, and/or uneducated, and/or rural, and/or female) viewers: information about sexuality and sexual practices (use of condoms, AIDS, abortion, homosexuality, pregnancy), about social issues (diseases, violence, social campaigns), about gender relations (parents who separate), and about class (unimaginable cultures, people who live in shantytowns).

Television works as a common reference among Brazilian viewers. It is a means to spread messages and information throughout a country that is fractured by enormous social inequalities. When Meire affirms that "people watch [*telenovelas*] to learn", she is representing a shared opinion among most of my informants: *telenovelas* work as a means to introduce new fashions (spas, clothes, looks), new technologies (computers, liposuctions, plastic surgeries) or simply "new stuff" (new unexplored landscapes, cars, household devices).

According to these informants, television programs (and *telenovelas* especially) help viewers gain access to information that is otherwise unequally distributed. Television and *telenovelas* translate unknown situations and milieus into recognizable events and places, offering viewers a cognizable basis for understanding and living within a complex and unequal Brazilian reality.

Viewers play an active role in the processes of repetition, appropriation and reiteration of elements from *telenovelas*. These processes of reception are generated, however, within particular social, economic and cultural contexts. In other words, viewers' backgrounds and experiences do play a role in the way they relate to the flow of *telenovelas*.

Consumption

Looming references to necklaces, earrings, shorts, bracelets, CDs, fashion, beautiful persons, beautiful goods, and beautiful stories from the *telenovela* flow kept reemerging from my informants' conversations and essays. These elements from *telenovelas* were connected to physical appearances and the body, and associated with transformations, productions and social mobility. Messages, products and texts coming from *telenovelas* worked as guidelines for people's perceptions of themselves and of Brazilian society.

Several informants pointed out some of the commodities and consumption habits introduced by the *telenovelas*:

> *Novelas* tell people what to wear, what to buy, how to cut or wear their hair, what to eat... (Marcelo, 19, undergraduate student. Excerpt from a classroom essay.)

> Fashion in Brazil is the fashion that appears in *novelas*. Music from *novelas* becomes national hits. (Luiza, 18, middle-class undergraduate student. Excerpt from a classroom essay.)

> *Explode Coração* (Bursting Heart, Globo, 1995-6) showed people the importance of personal computers. It taught people that computers are good for the future. (Eglei, 22, drugstore clerk. Excerpt from an interview.)

Telenovelas introduce a myriad of commodities to millions of viewers. As anthropologist Robert Foster[11] suggested, in some cases, "consumption choices appear to form the basis for nationality as a collective identity" (1999:265). *Telenovelas* offer an accessible relationship with "Brazil" as a nation. They invite people to access the commodities and consumption practices that typify Brazilian life. Drinking the same beer as the *telenovela* character, wearing the same shoes as a female lead, visiting the region where a *telenovela* plot takes place – the appropriation, circulation and reiteration of commodities related to *telenovelas* has become a way to access a collective Brazilian identity.

By the same turn, considering *telenovelas* as a Brazilian mass product, one can suggest that consumption of this product might produce a feeling of belonging, a feeling of collective participation in national rituals and national passions.

The appropriation, circulation and reiteration of slang, idiomatic expressions, and proper names coming from *telenovelas* – quite a common phenomenon among my informants – is yet another illustration of how participation in the flow of *telenovelas* produces a feeling of collective participation and belonging: Márcio and Gustavo, both undergraduate students, appropriated the slang "*corpos malhados*", "*corpos sarados*" that circulated throughout different *telenovelas* to describe well-trained bodies. By using these expressions, they marked their position as up-to-date, trendy and urbane young men. Andrea, a 30-year-old, middle-class housewife had a dog named "Lindainês", after a character from one *telenovela*. Sandra, a 19-year-old housewife was called "Regina Duarte" [the name of an actress] by her cousins. The fact that her appearance reminded people of the actress Regina Duarte was something that made Sandra very proud. Marina, an 18-year-old babysitter, told me that she was using the expression "*Pedro Afonso, meu filho*" ("Dear little Pedro Afonso") to playfully scold Ivan, the baby she took care of. "Dear Little Pedro Afonso" was a pejorative expression, used by a female character to scold and reprimand her oppressed husband. Marina's reiteration provoked laughter among the people who heard her.

Narrating gender

Several female informants became engaged in the fantasies of seduction, love and happiness from different *telenovelas* as a means to mold and retell their own experiences, thus giving them the shape of fictive, commonly and nationally shared stories, faces and problems. These young women might, for instance, describe their beloved as someone who looked "a little bit like", or "exactly like", the actor who played a certain character in a certain *telenovela*. Their engagement in *telenovela* narratives constituted a way for them to make their own story recognizable, interesting and thrilling, much like a *telenovela* plot. As mentioned earlier, my male informants were more reticent to acknowledge any kind of interest in *telenovelas*. They were "not interested", "didn't have time to watch them", or "didn't have an opinion about them", even though many of them seemed to be aware of the general intrigues of present and past *telenovela* plots. *Telenovelas* were assumed to be "women's business", and it was harder to obtain the same kind of information from men that I managed to obtain from my female informants. This difficulty in gaining access to the opinions of male informants per se can be seen as an illustration of social positioning: By disavowing interest in *telenovelas*, men were positioning themselves within a traditional heterosexual divide that separates men (and their supposed preferences for action and sports) from women (and their supposed preferences for romance and *telenovelas*).

Class matters

Having foregrounded some tendencies and repetitions in the way my informants related to and engaged themselves in the *telenovelas*, I wish to make it explicit that the ways in which this insertion is thought of and negotiated within society are associated with different nuances. For those informants who lived under harder material conditions and had to confront prejudices and oppression on a daily basis, *telenovelas* could be a way to bring pleasure, amusement and information. *Telenovelas* were, moreover, a way for them to find strategies (that sometimes succeeded, sometimes not) to make their voices heard, to make themselves visible and recognizable as complex subjects. The dialogue between Meire and Marina quoted at the very beginning of this article crystallizes this notion. From the way many of my informants told their own life-stories using elements appropriated from *telenovelas*, it can be understood that, through their reiteration of these elements, they wanted to see themselves as complex subjects: not only poor (and black and rural) servants, but also interesting, intelligent, and seductive persons.

Middle- and upper-middle class informants are also engaged in the *telenovela* flow as a source of pleasure, leisure and information, and as a means to try to reinforce or improve their positions. Unlike poorer informants, however, they did not need to untether themselves from certain stigmatized social positionings. Instead, they worked towards reinforcing their social status by trying to make their lives and their bodies – to quote an informant – as "beautiful as in the *novelas*". A dialogue between Cláudia (18-year-old, middle-class high school student) and her friend Fátima (19-year-old, middle-class, high school student) illustrates this:

> *Cláudia*: I remember a necklace that Adriana Esteves [an actress] wore in a *novela*. It had a little pearl in the middle… It was so trendy! But I didn't buy it.
>
> *Fátima*: There were also the earrings. Everybody was wearing them.
>
> *Cláudia*: Yes, everybody! And last summer it was a pair of shorts. The same ones that are shown in the vignette presenting *Malhação*[12] [a *telenovela*], you know? Everybody was wearing them. […]

Fátima: I saw a nice bracelet in a shop. But I didn't buy it. Then I went home and saw that same bracelet in a *novela*. The next day I went back [to the shop] and bought it. [...]

Cláudia: Do you remember, Fátima, when we went out to buy the CD with the songs played in *O Rei do Gado* [The King of Cattle, a *telenovela*]? We were so silly! Instead of buying two different CDs and recording from one another, we both bought the same CD.

Fátima: And the worst thing was that we only liked three songs on the whole CD. So after only a little while we got tired of listening to it!

Conclusion

The aim of this article was to present and discuss some of the ways in which young informants become engaged in *telenovelas*. What impact do these programs have on young viewers? Do they shape the way viewers think and act?

I argued that viewers actively interact with the flow of *telenovelas*, but the way they relate to this flow is colored by the particular socio-cultural contexts within which they are positioned. Informants respond to *telenovelas* as willful attempts to demand entrance into circuits of recognition. They engage themselves in *telenovelas* because for them, as an informant once put it, *telenovelas* reveal "something that every Brazilian would like to have come true". This "something" is the desire to be *someone*; the desire to be recognized as a subject within Brazilian society. The material presented here could be seen as an illustration of different attempts to gain access to circuits of recognition in Brazil. An excerpt from an informant's essay spells this out:

> Our lives are very different from those of the gallant lead or of the young beauty in the *novela*. All *novelas* have a happy ending, just like fairy tales. Poor people get richer, couples get together, marry, and have children… all problems are easily solved and the evil always repent. Brazilians see that world of fiction as their own world and they hope that their problems will also get solved easily, just like magic. (Patricia, 20, undergraduate student. Excerpt from a classroom essay.)

Notes

1. World Bank. 2001. World Development Indicators: Distribution of Income or Consumption. http://www.worldbank.org/data/wdi2001/pdfs/tab2_8.pdf
2. According to Reis, E.P. 2000. Modernization, Citizenship and Stratification: Historical Processes and Recent Changes in Brazil. In *Daedalus* 129 (2): 171-194; and Schneider, R. 1996. *Brazil: Culture and Politics in a New Powerhouse*. Boulder, Colo.: Westview Press.
3. According to http://www.worldscreen.com/latinamerica.phg and www.tv50anos.hgp.com.br

4. Haraway, D. 1991. *Simians, Cyborgs and Women – The Reinvention of Nature*. London: Free Association Books.

5. Stam, R. 1989. *Subversive Pleasures. Bakhtin, Cultural Criticism and Film*. Baltimore and London: John Hopkins University Press.
    Walkerdine, V. 1997. *Daddy's Girl: Young Girls and Popular Culture*. Cambridge and Massachusetts: Harvard University Press.

6. In 1997, during my most extensive period of fieldwork, eleven *telenovelas* were broadcast (10 of them in prime time, i.e., between 7 and 9 o'clock in the evening). Of these eleven *telenovelas*, two were imported from Mexico and the rest were produced in Brazil. The research presented here is based on viewers' reception of Brazilian *telenovelas*.

7. Beltrão, M.S. 1993. Interpreting Brazilian Telenovelas. In: *Serial Fiction in TV – The Latin-American Telenovelas*. Edited by A.M. Fadul. São Paulo: ECA-USP.
    Fachel, L.O. and Oliven, R.G. 1987. A Televisão e Outras Falas: Como se Reconta uma Novela. *Ciências Sociais Hoje* (1987): 80-93.
    Tufte, T. 1993. Everyday Life, Women and Telenovela in Brazil. In *Serial Fiction in TV – The Latin-American Telenovelas*. Edited by A.M. Fadul. São Paulo: ECA-USP.
    Vink, N. 1988. *The Telenovela and Emancipation – A Study on TV and Social Change in Brazil*. Amsterdam: Royal Tropical Institute.

8. See Machado-Borges, T. 2003. *Only for You! Brazilians and the Telenovela Flow*. Stockholm Studies in Social Anthropology. Stockholm: Almqvist & Wiksell International.

9. I noticed a relationship between age and the way people reported about their viewing practices. The younger the viewer, the easier it was for him/her to admit his/her likes and dislikes about *telenovelas*, their characters and plots. Adult informants articulated their relationship to these programs less overtly. The trend shifted again when it came to older people whose opinions about *telenovelas* were expressed more overtly.

10. Globo is the major television network in Brazil and the fourth largest in the world. According to Globo's own statistics (http://www.globo.com.br), it reached in 2001, 99.52 percent of the Brazilian territory, which corresponded to 37,743,062 households with television or 161,080,257 inhabitants.

11. Foster, R.J. 1999. The commercial construction of "New Nations". *Journal of Material Culture*. Vol. 4(3): 263-282.

12. *Malhação* (Pumping Up, broadcast by Globo since 1995) differs partly from other *telenovelas* in that it does not end. It is called a 'soap opera' even in Portuguese.

South Korean Television Drama in Asia

Doobo Shim

The *Korean wave* is a newly coined but widely circulated term in Asia in recent years. It refers to the popularity of South Korean[1] TV dramas, pop music, movies, fashion, food, and celebrities in Asia – especially in China, Hong Kong, Taiwan, Japan and Vietnam – and it is reported that such 'fever' is extending to Myanmar and other Southeast Asian countries (Kim, J., 2004). The Associated Press reported in March 2002: 'Call it "kim chic". All things Korean – from food and music to eyebrow-shaping and shoe styles – are the rage across Asia, where pop culture has long been dominated by Tokyo and Hollywood' (Visser, 2002). In this article, I will discuss the development of the Korean wave, in particular television dramas related to youth.

What is the Korean wave?

The Korean wave in Asia apparently started in 1997 when China's national China Central Television Station (CCTV) broadcast a Korean television drama serial called *What Is Love All About?* – a story about a family consisting of an extremely paternalistic father, a submissive mother, and their children with more modern values – which became a smash hit among television viewers in China. Audiences asked for its re-broadcasting during prime time, and the drama achieved the second-highest ratings in the Chinese television history (Heo, 2002).

After that, the demand for Korean television dramas exploded across Asian countries, especially those with large Chinese population. In the context of increasing television airtime because of broadcasting liberalization measures, which swept across Asia in the 1990s, Korean programs, which were relatively cheaper but having good entertainment quality, were popular imports for Asian broadcasters.

163

Television drama

In Korean, and also in other Asian, television environment, the word 'soap opera' is actually not used. Instead, 'television drama' is used referring to a wide spectrum of fictional dramatic programs including both what Americans call soap opera and prime time mini-series. While the word 'sitcom' is recently in circulation being considered as a new genre imported from America, as a hybrid between the drama genre and comedy genre, 'soap opera' is not expected to be in circulation because its function has always been there in the term 'television drama'. Korean television dramas have an average run of two to three months and come to a climactic close. While there are daily dramas, more popular ones air twice a week at night with each episode running about 50 minutes. Therefore, while retaining the melodramatic quality with continuing-story format, Korean television dramas are distinguished from soap operas in a strict American sense, many of which last for decades with an endless stream of conflicts, troubles, dilemmas, and crises, and are studio-based. In Korean television dramas, a love between the son of a rich family and the daughter of a poor family, or vice versa, and their respective family lives are the main motivator for plot development. Recently, social satire and more realistic difficulties faced by the youth are added in the plots. Because of their popularity, television dramas command the highest advertising rates of all television genres.

After Korea's and Japan's co-hosting of the (football) World Cup in 2002, the Korean wave reached the shores of Japan. It peaked with the television drama serial *Winter Sonata* – a touching love story about a woman and her boyfriend suffering from amnesia, also featuring beautiful winter scenery of Korea – which was broadcast twice in Japan on NHK (Japan Broadcasting Corporation) satellite in 2003. In response to the audience's demand, NHK aired it for the third time on its terrestrial network in summer 2004 on Saturdays at 11:10 p.m. Although it was a third run, the program, nicknamed *Fuyusona* in Japanese, enjoyed an average of 16-17 percent share in the Tokyo area. The Japanese public broadcaster is reported to have a plan to re-run the television drama for the fourth time in late 2004, this time with subtitles instead of dubbing meeting the local audience's wish to enjoy the 'genuine Korean feel' (Kim, H., 2004).

When the Korean actor Bae Yong Jun, who played the lead role in *Winter Sonata*, visited Japan on 3 April 2004, about 5,000 local female fans flocked to the Tokyo Haneda airport to welcome him. The crowd caused traffic jam and one woman fainted from over-stimulation and was evacuated to a hospital (*Korea Times*, 2004). During this visit, NHK president Katsuji Ebisawa presented Bae with an Award of Appreciation for his role in the popular program (Kim, K., 2004). Hopping on the bandwagon of Bae's popularity, Japanese Prime Minister Junichiro Koizumi is reported to have told supporters of his Liberal Democratic Party that he would try hard to enjoy a similar popularity as that of Bae (*Straits Times*, 2004).

Based on television dramas' popularity, Korean films have also attracted large numbers of cinemagoers in Asia, to the degree that the Korean film industry is being touted as the 'New Hong Kong' (Leong, 2003). Korean films are now regular fixtures in movie theatres across Asia. About the same time when Korean television dramas and films became popular among young people in East and Southeast Asia, both Chinese-language remakes of Korean pop music and their original songs became favored among youth in China, Hong Kong and Taiwan. It led to a huge Korean-pop fandom in these countries including Japan. Korean boy band H.O.T. topped the pop charts in Taiwan and China in the late 1990s; singer Ahn Jae-wook was voted the most popular star in China in 2001; and teenage girl singer BoA's album clinched the top spot in Japan's music charts in 2002. It is now common that Korean singers and bands give their concerts in these countries.

Against this backdrop, Korean pop stars have huge influence on Asian youth consumer culture, including food, fashion, make-up trends, and even plastic surgery. In Beijing and Taiwan, it is common that the local youth groups decorate their backpacks and notebooks with photographs of their Korean stars. In Vietnam, the 'Korea Tribe', or *Koreanophiles*, sprouted up among young people who walk the streets dressing like the stars in Korean television dramas. In particular, so popular are Korean actresses that their ardent fans in China and Taiwan are reported to visit cosmetic surgeons to change their facial features to resemble their stars (Joins.com, 2001; *Straits Times*, 2002a and 2002b). Korean television drama-themed travel packages have been created in these countries, leading to a huge increase of Asian tourists to Korea. According to the government-run Korean Overseas Info Service (2004), foreign tourists to Gangwon-Do province, where many scenes of the popular television drama *Winter Sonata* were shot, increased to 110,000 in 2003 – a figure that more than quadrupled from that of 2002.

Success factors of Korean popular culture overseas

Why are Korean television dramas so popular in Asia? Considering that 'popular culture is first and foremost a pleasure of recognition' (Ang, 1985), the cultural proximity factor (Straubhaar, 1991) plays an important role for Korean television dramas to attract Asian audiences. However, since Iwabuchi (2002) notes that the reason behind the Japanese audiences' consumption of Asian popular culture lies in their domestic agenda, there is more than the cultural proximity factor in the Korean wave phenomenon. In her fan letter to Bae Yong Jun, a 50-year-old Japanese woman wrote:

> Korean TV dramas remind me of the good times Japan had in the past. I think it's the nostalgia that draws people to Korean dramas (Korean Overseas Info Service, 2004).

According to Iwabuchi (2002), Japanese consumers of Asian popular culture attempt to recover something they believe their society has lost or is losing. On the other hand, Visser's (2002) observation of the Korean wave in Vietnam is also insightful:

> South Korean TV dramas provide the tightly controlled communist country with an enticing glimpse of the outside world.

In other words, unlike the Japanese, Vietnamese audiences project their national desire for more comfortable lives in their consumption of Korean television dramas.

Considering the fact that television dramas are above all leisure commodities, their entertainment values should not be neglected in this discussion. Thus, it is worthwhile to inquire into the matter how Korean television dramas have attained such high internal entertainment values. Before they are making inroads into foreign markets, Korean television dramas have to survive in their home market where three terrestrial networks air as many as more than 30 television dramas per week (Yi, 2004). While at the same time criticizing television dramas for having the 'same old' formula of storylines, Korean audiences avidly consume them to such a degree that television dramas often record remarkably high ratings of more than 30 percent share, with some even over 50 percent. Some persons attribute this phenomenon to Koreans having few options in leisure time (Shin, 2001). However, I would argue that despite the worn-out storylines these television dramas play their cultural roles well in the Korean society.

Television is the central storyteller of culture today, especially television dramas transmitting and sharing a culture's values and beliefs. In addition, in a pluralistic and democratized society, television also plays the role of a cultural forum. Television does not force a certain social value as propagandas do, but provides audiences with opportunities to think about, discuss and debate their culture and social agendas. In this process, television dramas provide a cue of cultural questions such as: 'Who are good guys and bad guys?', 'What is the meaning of success?', 'Which life road should I take?', or 'Is my life happy?', etc. In other words, Korean television dramas are good storytellers and cultural fora that have an ability to touch the right chord of both Korean and Asian sentiments with sufficient entertainment qualities.

In addition, the fact that Korea is one of the countries with the most developed new ICT (information and communication technology) infrastructures, with more than 75 percent of Korean homes having broadband Internet connections, has contributed to Korean television dramas' quality improvement. As such, many Koreans spend their time being connected to their computers, watching television dramas, playing games, chatting, and attending virtual schools online. A study shows that an average Korean netizen spends 1,340 minutes (more than 22 hours) a month online, in contrast to 641 minutes (less than 11 hours) for an average online user in the U.S.A. (Feldman, 2004). It is even said that the incumbent Korean president Roh Moo-hyun was elected President in 2002 thanks to the advanced penetration of information infrastructure in the country. When major newspapers were dismissing him as a dangerous leftie, Internet-based alternative news sites like www.OhmyNews.com, Internet weblogs and his online fan club www.nosamo.org played important roles mobilizing voters, especially among the young generation, to support him.

In the light of these facts of two-way communication, audiences have expanded their roles in television production processes in Korea. According to the traditional mass communication model devised by Wilbur Schramm (1954), what links the audience to the producer is 'feedback'. However, feedback in this model is indirect, delayed, and inferential. After airing a show, television executives have to wait a few days or weeks to learn the program's ratings figure – and ratings are composed of quantified numbers so that executives only infer from them what they have to do to improve the program. When a media critic wrote his or her critique about a television show, it would only appear in the newspaper the next morning, at the very minimum. For individual audiences to give feedback to producers, they had to resort to means such as letters ('delayed') or telephone (often 'indirect').

The Internet, however, has sped up the feedback process so that audiences leave their responses to a television program even at the same time they watch it on the television networks' message boards. For popular television dramas, more than 300 audience feedbacks are written up on their Internet message boards after each episode. Korean audiences even form cult-like Internet fan clubs of their favorite television dramas. They produce parody on the dramas in the form of magazines, newspapers and posters. When a synopsis of a drama serial is revealed, which the fan club members dislike, they pressure the producers to change it so that a heroine, who is supposed to die, 'revives' in the next episode. When young people, who usually form the core of popular culture consumption, tend to spend more time on the Internet and with mobile phones rather than watching television these days, it is television networks that have to show their appreciation for these fans' enthusiasm for television dramas. In addition, because these ardent fans are online opinion leaders about the programs, and form the guaranteed market for the dramas' sales of video-on-demand, DVD and other secondary products, networks cannot disregard their fandom. Networks and television drama productions often invite fan club members to locations, arrange meetings with their stars, and even allow them to play minor roles in television dramas (Gu, 2004).

Conclusion

In this article, I have described the popularity of Korean television dramas and other popular culture in Asia. There may be diverse analyses of the success factors for the Korean television dramas. While the cultural proximity factor has been offered as a reason for the rise of intra-regional cultural flows in this media globalization era, further research shows that different countries have different reasons for their consumption of popular culture imports from neighboring countries. As an alternative theory, I have noted the fact that Korea is the world leader in high-speed broadband access. In fact, the main age group (19-25 year olds) of television drama fan clubs overlaps with that of main online users. Based on such enthusiastic youth fandom of television dramas at home, Korean media have developed their popular culture into export capacity, engendering the Korean wave.

Note

1.   After this, Korea refers to South Korea, or the Republic of Korea.

References ˙

Ang, I. (1985) *Watching Dallas: Soap opera and the melodramatic imagination*. London: Methuen.
Feldman, M. (2004) 'Lessons from Korean digital democracy', *Korea Herald* 29 March. p. 20.
Gu, H. (2004). 'Drama bodyguards: Change the lead role's fate', *Joong-Ang Ilbo* 16 July. p. 22.
Heo, J. (2002) 'The "Hanryu" Phenomenon and the Acceptability of Korean TV Dramas in China', *Korean Journal of Broadcasting 16* (1): 496-529.
Iwabuchi, K. (2002) 'Nostalgia for a (Different) Asian modernity', *Positions 10* (3): 547-573.
Joins.com (2001) 'A Pop Culture Wave Rolls on', 10 September. [http://www.joins.com, accessed 22 January 2002].
Kim, H. (2004) 'The fever of Winter Sonata not cooling down', *Joong-Ang Ilbo*. 28 July. p. 24.
Kim, J. (2004) 'Korean drama and kimchi popular in Miyanmar', *Kookmin Ilbo*. 8 October [accessed from www.kinds.co.kr]
Kim, K. (2004) 'Korean heartthrob hits Japan's shores', *Korea Herald*. 10 April. [accessed from www.koreaherald.co.kr]
Korea Times (2002) 'Winter Sonata' actor gets warm welcome in Japan. April 5.
Korean Overseas Info Service (2004) 'Korea Wave crashes on Asian shores', August 26. [accessed from www.korea.net]
Leong, A. (2003) *Korean Cinema: The New Hong Kong*. Victoria, Canada: Trafford.
Schramm, W. (1954) *The process and effects of mass communication*. Urbana, USA: University of Illinois Press.

Chilean Tweens and Reality Shows

María Dolores Souza

There are many signs of the emergence of a new social group called Tweens, a segment of children ages 8 to 13, who display the attitudes and behavior one would expect of older children, but who are still quite young, "in between" childhood and adolescence.

These children are more autonomous than earlier generations, they are well informed, have opinions on many social and world matters, want to be heard, and know a great deal about technology, social trends and consumption.

The phenomenon has been studied in different countries in Europe, the U.S. and Australia, among others, mainly by market researchers. However, there is also a growing body of literature on this topic stemming from the social sciences. In the words of Martin Lindstrom:[1]

> This generation has been tagged the 'age of compression'. Almost every aspect of today's tween-ager is different from what we have seen among past generations...
> (p.1) Living in an interactive world involves so much more than having access to the internet. It means a whole new way of seeing... (p.3) They think in an interactive dimension. (p.3)

Though most of the research has been conducted in Western countries, other cultures and developing countries have also been taken into account in Lindstrom's book and elsewhere,[2] and there is sound evidence that in Chile this phenomenon has reached urban schoolchildren, that is, 86 percent of the school population.[3]

In the following, I will make some reflections on the way Tweens relate to television, and to reality shows in particular, based on research conducted in 2003 and 2004 by the National Television Council of Chile. One study is an evaluation of reality shows[4] through focus groups of children and adolescents 7 to 17 years old, conducted in Chile's capital city, Santiago.[5] Only the six focus groups of younger children up to 13 years old have been taken into account in this article (there was a total of ten groups covering the entire age range). Another study is a quantitative investigation of Chilean Tweens,[6] comprising 400 interviews with children and 150 with parents, also in the city of Santiago. A third study is qualitative[7] and involves 29 groups of children 8 to 13 years old from urban and rural areas all over the country.

It has been said that Tweens are well informed and have a say. On the one hand, they are at ease with technology – often teaching their parents how to use new equipment. They also handle money, and have an important influence on the purchase of family consumer goods and on leisure activities.

On the other hand, they not only know what is happening around them or "out there" in the world, but they also have a somewhat pessimistic view of the life of adults and their future. They view their parents as stressed and worried people, and they feel that neither the future of the world nor that of the country look very promising. They know about conflicts, wars and abuse and are worried about the environment.[8]

They value the family and want to have a good communication with their parents, but they often have the impression they are being "examined" when having a conversation. It is as if parents always initiate conversation, asking questions about school and leisure, so as to exchange information instead of having a "real talk".[9] In social interaction at school and otherwise, Tweens do not want to be patronized and expect to be treated by adults on an equal basis.

The role of reality shows

It is no wonder that Tweens want to see TV programs targeted at older people, including adults. They do not like "childish" programs and have a special interest in the lives and whereabouts of young people on the screen. They want to find out the ways the characters interact with each other, handle their love and sex lives, and solve their problems.

In this context, reality shows and certain other television genres for adolescents and adults, such as soap operas and Latin American *telenovelas*, are a fertile ground for Tween interests. This can be seen in Table 1 (valid for 2003, when most reality shows were broadcast on Chilean open TV – as opposed to pay TV).

It must be stressed that not only are several reality shows and *telenovelas* among the top rated programs, but also that the absolute ratings of both genres are even higher than shown in the Table, considering that the first four programs were broadcast simultaneously by the two leading television channels in the country.

Moreover, in the top ten ranking in the table, no children's programs are included, only a *telenovela* targeted at adolescents (the one called *16*).

Table 1. **Top ten programs on open TV among 10- to 14-year-olds, January – July 2003** (ratings)

Program	Genre (country of origin)	Rating (%)
Protagonistas de la Fama (Main Characters of Fame) The series is about youngsters living together in a house during the show season (three months). They take lessons in song, dance, acting and other types of performance. Each week they compete with each other and the losers have to leave the house.	reality show (Chile) non-fiction – entertainment	32.9
Puertas Adentro (Indoors – referring to maids working and living at their employers' family home) This is the story of a maid. Her boyfriend leads a group of homeless families and takes his girlfriend's employers' land illegally.	*telenovela* (Chile) fiction – entertainment	17.1
Machos (refers to male chauvinists) A male chauvinistic and authoritarian father has seven adult sons, one of whom is gay. The plot revolves around the father's life, including his sons and his mistress.	*telenovela* (Chile) fiction – entertainment	16.7
Protagonistas de la Música (Main Characters of Music) A group of youngsters is placed together to live in a house for three months. They take song lessons and compete every week with each other in a music contest. The losers leave the house.	reality show (Chile) non-fiction – entertainment	16.4
16 (years old) A series about a group of school students and their relationships and conflicts with each other and their parents.	*telenovela* (Chile) non-fiction – entertainment	16.0
Festival de Viña (Music International Contest) This festival has been held each summer in the touristy city of Viña del Mar by the sea since 1959. Broadcast of the program began in the 60s.	international music festival held in Chile (Chile) non-fiction – entertainment	15.6
Mujer Rompe el Silencio (Woman, Break the Silence!) Recreation of real human dramas told from the women's point of view.	docu-drama (Chile) fiction based on journalistic research	14.9
Gala Rojo (gala of a reality show called 'Red') The final of *Rojo*, a song and dance contest among youngsters.	song contest (Chile) non-fiction – entertainment	14.0
Mea Culpa (Latin: My fault) Real-life case stories of delinquency and murder, with some fictional recreations of events.	real-life documentary (Chile) non-fictional journalistic program	12.6
Protagonistas de Vuelta en Casa (Main Characters Go Back Home) Finale – youngsters who where living together for the show go home.	reality show ("finale") (Chile) non-fiction – entertainment	11.5

Source: Time Ibope 2003

Tweens' consumption of reality shows

When Tweens are asked to talk about their favorite TV programs, in the first place they spontaneously mention a number of reality shows.[10] They identify six main features of reality shows broadcast in Chile:

- youngsters who do not know each other
- youngsters who are living together
- youngsters who are isolated in a home
- their privacy is exposed using hidden TV cameras
- their behavior is spontaneous (not sketched)
- they compete with each other in an arts contest.

Children 8 to 13 years old identify the basics, or 'game rules', of reality shows and know that the key element is spontaneity – the most important difference in relation to other TV shows that are completely formatted in advance. Still, Tweens doubt the truth of this spontaneity. They think that many conflicts are induced, that some versions of reality shows resemble game shows, or music contests in search of new young talents, with little space for natural behavior.

Tweens are frequent consumers of reality shows even though the programs are "under suspicion". The children say that once reality shows made their appearance on the Chilean screen, their television consumption went up for two main reasons. First, they watched them every day or frequently so as to follow up in detail the development of the events. Second, Tweens found that reality shows resulted in a new TV-watching time table – at night, because of some late evening reality shows – something that used to be only occasional and not systematic.

Some features of Tweens' consumption of reality shows are:

- planning beforehand to watch the shows
- watching the whole show
- high concentration on the screen
- high socialization of what is seen.

Or, in their own words:[11]

> I didn't watch TV at night so often before, but now I kind of organize myself so I can see it [reality shows] in bed at 11 p.m. so I don't miss a thing.

> You have to really follow up the stories because otherwise you get a little bit lost.

There are differences among Tweens with respect to the frequency of reality show consumption. Some are *habitués* and watch the shows every day; others do it a few times a week. In both cases, Tweens tend to watch them in the company of siblings or even their parents, mostly the mother:

> My mother likes it [reality shows] and sometimes she watches with us; otherwise, she asks us to tell her [what happened].

Tweens say that parents try to prevent them from watching the late shows during school periods (a restriction they try to overturn), but generally they do not feel that their parents try to forbid consumption of reality shows due to their contents.[12] Tweens are aware of their parents' critical attitude toward some aspects of the programs, such as body exposure and bad language, but in that sense the children tend to repeat their parents' opinions, with which they agree in many cases, at least manifestly:

> My father says that the things they talk about [in the shows] are not fit for kids my age.

> They [the shows] are very vulgar, I remember Daniel handing a towel to the cheer-leader when she was taking a shower, the towel was too small, she could not possibly cover herself up with it...

> That [program] has a lot of swearwords, it is too much!

Younger Tweens (under the age of 10) feel a little ashamed when speaking about scenes containing overt 'making out' or sex. It also seems that there are gender differences in their conduct in front of the screen – as expressed by the children themselves – and when talking about the subject with others.[13] Boys tend to say they like erotic scenes, while girls say they do not feel comfortable watching them. This is how two 9-year-olds, a boy and a girl, refer to sex scenes on TV:[14]

> When they go to bed, it is nice, it is the best! (boy)

> It is embarrassing... sometimes, when I am watching a movie, and they start to have sex, I cover myself up with the sheets. (girl)

It has to be said that sex scenes were an important topic of debate in newspapers and among parents before and after reality shows came to Chile in 2002-2003. As in most countries, many features of the programs were criticized and reflected upon, but Chilean television – as opposed to Argentinean and Brazilian TV – showed self-regulated products not at odds with Chilean society, which is much more conservative than most other Latin American societies. There was no nudity[15] or explicit sex scenes to see.

What motivates Tweens to watch reality shows?

Why, then, do Tweens watch reality shows? First, these children want entertainment and excitement from television, and this is their main reason for watching reality shows:[16]

It is funny, I like competition.

It is exciting when they confront each other, even best friends can say 'I don't like you', so it is shocking.

The entertainment and excitement induced by reality shows are also associated with suspense and curiosity:

I like gossip so I love it when they [the program makers] interview their families and show their houses.

Second, what motivates this consumption is identification with young people on the screen. Younger Tweens look forward to adolescent experiences:

It is like a real *telenovela*, it is like making a report on a person just like us.

It is about the lives of older kids, most of them have boyfriends or girlfriends... we do not yet... Things that happen to us are boring.

Besides, there is a learning process. For some kids reality shows are a way to 'teach' parents and other adults about the life of young people.[17] At the same time, Tweens want to learn social behavior themselves:

They show the lives of young people like us... this is also a way of showing adults that we are not as bad as they think we are.

[The programs] teach you how to ease up conflicts so you can learn to live together and adapt a little.

Finally, reality shows are instrumental to socialization. The programs become a subject of conversation among most TV consumers, so they help Tweens to exchange opinions and compare attitudes:

Everybody is talking about it, you can't be left out.

In sum, reality shows are entertaining and educational in Tweens' views, and help them integrate themselves in the peer group.

A positive but somewhat critical view of reality shows

As seen above, Tweens like watching reality shows and try to do so even against parental rules. Yet, they are not uncritical and express some doubts about and objections to the programs. Tables 2 and 3 show the main positive and negative aspects of reality shows, according to Tweens.[18]

Table 2. Positive aspects of reality shows according to Tweens

Reality shows show the lives and world of young people.

They teach us how to live together in harmony.

They help young people to better themselves, overcome difficulties and value personal efforts.[19]

They show people from different social groups interacting together; they present different worldviews.

They show positive role models for how to deal with conflict and for how you would like to be treated.

They show you an ethical and ideal self (fidelity, trustworthiness, how to be a "nice person").

Table 3. Negative aspects of reality shows according to Tweens

Bad language

Too much interference of intimacy

Indecent body exposure

Idleness, the house is in a complete mess

Negative role models: intrigues and rivalry

Conflicts induced by program makers

The positive aspects tend to refer to ethical and ideal standards, such as moral values, hard work and somehow social equity, i.e., appreciating the visibility – through television as a medium – of different social groups, rich and poor,[20] especially the latter group, which normally does not have an entertainment value and in that sense is absent from (or stigmatized on) the screens.

With respect to negative aspects of reality shows, what makes Tweens sad or even mad is the perception that some programs induce conflicts among young participants so as to highlight drama, and show emotionality to its limit. On the one hand, Tweens feel sorry for participants in tears and distress, but on the other, they resent the television industry, which, in their view, uses emotion and drama as instruments for getting higher ratings:[21]

They [the program makers] would do anything to get good ratings.

They make each other fight on purpose.

As regards bad language, there is certain ambivalence among Tweens, as they admit this is the way most people speak and it is very common among youngsters. Nevertheless, they have the feeling that sometimes participants in reality shows tend to overdue it, on account of the special situation they are in, i.e., being in front of TV cameras.

The effects of reality shows on Tweens' conduct

The issue of the "effects" of television is always controversial. There are indeed a great number of books and articles referring to this subject, especially when TV violence is included.

In 2002-2003, there was a fierce debate in Chile[22] – in the press and in social interaction in general – about reality shows. People feared what was to be shown on the screen, and critics pointed to violence against human dignity and decency. The National Television Council had to release a public statement to reassure the audience that there would be serious supervision of program contents.[23]

After a while, reality shows appealed to the audience, especially the young, and some of the programs' dynamics – especially group and dyad dynamics – began to manifest themselves in people's social behavior. There is one particular case referring to "face-to-face" confrontations between two people – something frequently used on the shows – to discover the true motivations of the other party, as well as the truth in general.

There was a time when people in many places – at school, at work or in social daily interactions with family and friends – talked about and even started to use the dynamics of "face-to-face". Other TV programs and media, such as radio and newspapers, also started to cover debates or confrontations between public figures, like politicians, football players and others, referring to these events as "face-to-face" dynamics, aimed at getting people to say what they were concealing and to solve problems.

Of course, this phenomenon included Tweens and youngsters more than anyone else, due to their natural longing for truth and their distaste of hiding or twisting real facts and feelings. This characteristic of Tweens was made explicit in one of our studies in which Tweens depicted adults. One of the main characteristics of adults, according to the children, was that "they do not always tell the truth" (an opinion held by 73% of the Tweens interviewed).[24]

In this context, some dynamics seen on reality shows were, thus, adopted, seriously in some cases or as a matter of speaking in others. In the first-mentioned case, we can positively say that there was a conscious decision among viewers to resort to a dynamic that could be proved useful, i.e., 'speaking out' what you are concealing as a way of making relationships more honest and transparent. In the second case, there was the adoption of a label that could explain any discussion or debate, for example, if you were told "you are ground", you knew that you had made a mistake, according to the other party. Concepts of reality shows were used in social life exactly as they would be used in the shows.

Furthermore, other concepts and behaviors of reality shows were incorporated into daily life – seriously or as a game: words, nicknames, and sentences that had been heard and seen in the programs were imitated, such as, for example, the label "to be in suspense" when a participant in one reality show is sent away to a lonely place called "the chapel". Another example is the sentence "you have been threatened by coexistence",[25] which means that someone is behaving badly toward his or her partners in the house. This, and some other social dynamics within the programs, was imitated as a way of role-playing in meetings at school or other places:[26]

In the class we play that we are "threatened" because of cheating on exams...

Me, my cousins and my brothers always copy what they [the characters in reality shows] learn in acting classes...[27]

Besides imitation of some concepts or behaviors in real life, there was a redoubled interest among the young in popular dance, singing, theater and modeling lessons, because throughout watching reality shows the young viewers felt these aspects could become ways of making their living and pursuing their dreams:

I would like to be an actress, so I watch what acting classes are like [in reality shows].

After almost a year of reality shows, we see the decline of this genre on the Chilean screen, and the above-mentioned effects seem less obvious. What we noticed is similar to any trend in modern life, with its rapid change and new fashions.

What actually remains is the way of relating to social objects like reality shows as well as other television programs. We have seen that Tweens learned "the rules of the game" of reality shows and took these rules very seriously, but at the same time the programs were "under suspicion". Because Tweens know about television, they know that it is a commercial industry that "sells" programs, and they know, as well, that audiovisual language has its own special features, i.e., that you can use music, background sounds, lights and cameras in a specific way so as to have certain effects on the audience.

Television and reality

At this point, it is interesting to refer to the way reality shows fit or 'make a difference' within the general television grid. Because Tweens have a very good understanding of TV programming, they also have an opinion about how well television represents reality, social diversity and, especially, young people.

177

Tweens have two main critiques with regard to the way television tends to reflect people's lives. The first objection refers to a black and white, polar view of reality on the screen: the utterly negative view and the utterly positive one, which, according to these children, are too distant from daily life:[28]

> Life has to be shown as it really is, I do not want TV programs to show us that everything is nice and good and that we are going to live happily ever after.

> They show you the good-looking girls, but they will never show you poverty.

> On the news they show everything that is bad and negative about Chile; for instance, if there is an interview with students, they show you the ones who do not know what to answer, but they do not show the ones who do know.

> I do not watch newscasts, because they only show sad things.

Tweens expect to experience a sense of proximity, especially when watching non-fictional TV genres; they want programs to be credible, and therefore complex, with nuances, reflecting real social life, real people and a real country. They feel that television only tends to show two opposite sides of reality, the bright side of glitter – beautiful and popular people with shallow talk – and the dark side of marginality – poor people, crime and distress.

The second objection to television is the perceived general absence of youngsters on the screen and, specifically, the absence of average children and young people. Tweens have the perception that when children and youngsters appear on the screen, the portrayal is of victims of social, family, health and other problems:

> I would like to see more children because there are too many adults.

> What you see are extremely poor kids, they always show the same ones.

> You see handicapped kids.

Other studies[29] point out that children and young people think the most common portrayals of youngsters in the news are as delinquents or other criminal offenders. Moreover, Tweens feel that television does not reflect their interests and concerns:[30]

> And by the way, they [in TV] do not talk about any important subjects.

> I would like to see [journalistic programs] with young panelists who would have opinions like ours.

In light of these two critiques – and demands – reality shows represent an alternative of seeing average young people. Reality shows, even though they have an entertainment purpose, are complex programs. They contain a certain reflection of everyday life and show that the search for glitter and success does not hide social dynamics like efforts, hopes, conflicts and rejection. At the same time, participants have diverse social backgrounds.

Final remarks

We can say that reality shows came to fill a gap that Tweens had already identified in Chilean television programming.

- First, television is still the main medium of this age group, with the means to show them the world.

- Second, Tweens are eager to know what life really entails.

- Third, they are curious about society and the people around them, especially about the lives of young people whom they see as an ideal self.

- Finally, Tweens see themselves as fully thinking individuals and therefore they like products and television programs targeted at older people.

Thus, reality shows fulfill in many ways the expectations, claims and tastes of Tweens regarding television, especially because these programs are entertaining. Much of Tweens' interest in reality shows combines excitement with the cognitive challenge of complex content, the representation of social diversity and the possibility of instrumental learning. Therefore, the response of this new social segment of children to reality shows entails high viewing ratings and emotional involvement – including simultaneous acceptance and critique.

Notes

1. Martin Lindstrom: *Brand Child*. London and Sterling VA. 2003.
2. There is some research in Brazil, as well, done by the Mc Cann Erickson Co, see "Os poderosos pré adolescents". *Revista Veja* No. 8, 26 february 2003. Editora Abril (Veja Magazine, 'Abril' Editions, Brazil).
3. According to the Chilean Ministry of Education, see: http://www.mineduc.cl
4. Study No. 1: "Evaluación del Género Televisivo: Reality Shows". Consejo Nacional de Televisión. March 2003. (In Spanish) See: http://www.cntv.cl
5. Santiago belongs to the Metropolitan Region, which concentrates 40% of the Chilean population.
6. Study No. 2: "Informe 8/13: Los Tweens chilenos". Souza, María Dolores; Vidal, Maribel; and Cucurella Jorge. Consejo Nacional de Televisión & Mc Cann Erickson Co., Chile, 2003. (In Spanish). See: http://www.cntv.cl

7. Study No. 3: "Zoom Tweens: Tres estudios cualitativos". Consejo Nacional de Televisión. March 2003. (In Spanish) See: http://www.cntv.cl
8. Study No. 2 – see note 6.
9. Ibid.
10. In the second place, they mention youth programs. Study No. 2 – see note 6.
11. Study No. 1 – see note 4.
12. We must say that reality shows did give rise to a social debate in Chile because of the display of intimate scenes in other countries like Argentina and Uruguay.
13. In this case with the researchers of study No. 3 – see note 7.
14. Study No. 3 – see note 7.
15. People in *The House* took showers wearing their underwear.
16. Study No. 1 – see note 4.
17. This aspect has been further studied by the French scholar François Jost from the parents' point of view, i.e., parents are watching reality shows as a way of "seeing" what happens behind the closed doors of their adolescent's bedrooms. See books and articles at: http://www.ina.fr
18. Study No. 1 – see note 4.
19. Reality shows in Chile include song, dance and acting competitions.
20. The Chilean population is very divided into different social classes according to economic power and social influence.
21. Study No. 3 – see note 7.
22. This has been the case in most countries where reality shows have been broadcast.
23. Something the National Television Council institution normally does with all television programs.
24. Study No. 2 – see note 6.
25. In Spanish: "amenazado por convivencia".
26. Study No. 1 – see note 4.
27. Young characters in reality shows took acting, song and dance lessons while they were living together in a house.
28. Study No. 3 – see note 7.
29. "La voz de los adolescentes. Percepciónes sobre Seguridad y Violencia en Buenos Aires, Montevideo y Santiago de Chile". UNICEF 2001 (a study conducted in Argentina, Uruguay and Chile among adolescents).
30. Study No. 3 – see note 7.

The Idea of Learning
Young Viewers of Reality TV in the U.K.

Annette Hill

Can young adults learn from watching reality TV? In this article I consider the role of information within young viewers' experiences of popular factual television in the U.K. In its early incarnation, reality programming was often categorised as infotainment precisely because programmes such as *Police, Camera, Action!* or *999*, blurred boundaries between information and entertainment. Contemporary reality formats such as *Pop Idol* or *Big Brother* are closely associated with light entertainment genres such as talent shows or game shows, and therefore retain few links with traditional infotainment series. What follows in the rest of this article is an exploration of the way young viewers (aged 11-18) make sense of information in popular factual programmes.[1]

Information and entertainment

The suggestion that we can learn from watching reality TV is not common to discussion of the genre overall. The topics that dominate debate about reality TV in the media mainly refer to issues such as voyeurism, or quality standards. However, the first wave of reality programming in the late 1980s in America contained a range of programmes that were all, in one way or another, about information. *America's Most Wanted*, or *Crimewatch UK*, offer information to the public about law and order, and invite the public to offer information about criminal activities to relevant authorities. *Animal Hospital*, or *Children's Hospital*, offer information to the public about healthcare, and encourage viewers to care for their own children and companion animals in an informed manner. Although certain types of reality formats (i.e., reality game shows) have moved away from the origins of the genre, this does not mean to say all reality programming no longer informs viewers about a variety of issues.

A core feature of popular factual television is that it presents information in an entertaining manner. The origins of reality programming point towards a close association with tabloid news. Although the tabloid news connection is often used as evidence of the 'dumbing down' of factual television, the connection can also be used as evidence of the way reality TV attempts to present information to audiences who want to be entertained. The type of young viewer that chooses to regularly watch popular factual television is the type of viewer that tends to tune out of other traditional factual programming such as current affairs, or documentary. Therefore popular factual television serves an important function as a provider of "entertainment and diversion, with its knowledge-providing role as a secondary function" (Corner 1999: 117).

Watching reality TV

The way young viewers discuss reality TV highlights an uneasy relationship between information and entertainment in these formats. The majority of young viewers dismiss the idea of learning from popular factual television precisely because they perceive it as 'mindless entertainment'. The commercialisation of reality formats such as *Pop Idol* is a factor in understanding why young viewers categorise contemporary reality programming as 'mindless entertainment'. The popularity of reality talent shows, and accompanying merchandise to the series, increases the entertainment value of the programmes whilst at the same time decreasing the informative value of the programmes.

For example, the Beech family were fans of *Popstars*, and talked about the series on a regular basis. The Beech children, three girls all in primary school, learnt some of the songs and dance routines performed by the budding 'popstars' Hear'Say. In a discussion about *Popstars*, the mother and eldest daughter both made light of the potential learning elements of the series:

> *Interviewer*: Is there anything to be learnt from *Popstars*?
>
> *Rachael*: She's [her sister] got a Hear'Say top on.
>
> *Vivienne*: That's what she learnt... how to spend money on the merchandise! [laughs] She got Harry Potter and she wanted Hear'Say.
>
> *Interviewer*: Did you buy the album?
>
> *Sally*: Yes, we got the album and the single.
>
> *Vivienne*: Yes, joined everybody else.
>
> *Interviewer*: Did you learn anything?
>
> *Sally*: Well, about being famous... [laughs]
>
> *Vivienne*: Absolutely nothing!

Sally: What it's like to be famous, that's about the only thing I learnt from it... and the things they write about you in the paper! [laughs]

Vivienne: How easy it is to get there! Thousands of people can sing... I don't think they learnt that much. They did enjoy that one but, erm... there's nothing... well, perhaps there is something educational, I don't know, but if there is I can't see what it is [laughs].

The conversation is peppered with jokes about the merchandise and the marketing of celebrities in the series. When the daughter mentions *Popstars* in relation to learning about 'what it's like to be famous', her comment does not so much underscore potential learning elements in the series as negate there is anything really to learn in the first place. The final point made by the mother suggests that *Popstars* is so successful, and entertaining, that it is difficult to 'see' how it can be 'educational' at all.

Another reason why young viewers are so dismissive of the idea of learning from reality programming relates to the stigmatisation of 'learning' itself. In terms of what the sociologist Pierre Bourdieu (1986) refers to as cultural capital, reality TV has low cultural capital, as it is commonly referred to as mindless entertainment, and therefore has little value in the cultural marketplace. Of course, issues concerning 'quality' come into play here, as reality TV is often used as a barometer of low versus high quality factual television. But, there is another way of looking at the value of reality TV. For popular audiences, especially younger audiences, the value of reality TV is that it is entertaining. Davies, Buckingham and Kelley (2000) discuss the value children place on children's television. Citing Bourdieu's work on cultural capital, they argue that "children's assertions of their own tastes necessarily entail a form of 'identity work' – a positioning of the self in terms of publicly available discourses and categories" (2000: 21). For children, television is 'good' when it is engaging, action packed, funny, and, above all, entertaining.

The following extract from a discussion by a group of young female viewers (aged 12-14) illustrates the distinction between information and entertainment for young adults:

Rachael: No, but I think that's what I liked about *Big Brother*, 'cos you don't have to take anything in from it that much, just like watching it.

Kim: It was kind of interesting, though you don't have to learn about it. People our age aren't really interested in finding out information about how, like, stuff happens.

Clare: You learn that at school.

Kim: Like if they'd showed you, erm, like learning stuff, I don't think it would be half as interesting.

These viewers associated learning with work, and work with school. They made a distinction between *Big Brother* as engaging ('interesting') and as non-engaging ('learning stuff'). Most importantly, they did not wish to extract, or 'take', anything away from their viewing experience other than the pleasure of 'just' watching *Big Brother*. Another extract, this time from a group of young male viewers, serves to emphasise the stigmatisation of 'learning' for young adults:

> *Max*: When I watch TV, I don't watch it to like learn something, I watch it to enjoy myself, unless it was something like really, really interesting
>
> *Michael*: Normally I watch TV when I'm either bored or… well, then to entertain myself, but then I don't usually think about 'Oh, what have I learnt from this?' I just enjoy watching it.
>
> *Max*: I think it's good… I wouldn't watch a programme if it's called the Learning Programme but some programmes I think can be really good and at the same time you can like learn stuff but you don't actually realise it. But if the programme actually showed that it was a Learning Programme, I wouldn't watch it.

There is a distinction being made between informal and formal learning in television programmes. Formal learning ('the Learning Programme') is clearly associated with primary features of a programme, whereas informal learning is more associated with secondary features. What comes first is entertainment, and any secondary pleasures may include the possibility of learning, but are optional extras. Compare the above quote with the following from an adult viewer:

> I like learning programmes, I think I do now, more than anything. Sadly, but I do, yeah (43 year old self-employed builder).

For young viewers, formal learning is associated with school, and with being an adult, and if a television programme advertises itself as 'a learning programme' then it loses its attraction and becomes a teacher rather than an entertainer.

Informal learning about life

Despite having a natural aversion to 'learning programmes', some young viewers are open to the idea of learning about life as a by-product of watching an entertaining reality programme. Young male viewers are especially attracted to reality programmes such as *Police, Camera, Action!* or *Big Brother*. In discussion of these programmes, viewers talk about the idea of learning from social observation. Take this discussion about crime by a group of young male viewers (aged 12-14):

> *Interviewer*: Is there something about *Police, Camera, Action!* that you can learn from?

Mike: Don't steal a car.

Michael: There isn't really anything you can learn from it, it's just good to watch really.

Grant: Learn how to go at 130 miles an hour and not go into anything.

Richard: You learn that you can't, you can't really get away with it, the driver knew he was being followed 'cos as soon as he got out the car, he looked up.

Mark: It kind of, kind of gives the message that, erm, you shouldn't do stuff like that 'cos the police have all this new technology like in the helicopter, that they'll be able to track you down. And even though I wouldn't steal a car, after seeing that, people would probably be less likely to. And also, I think, they don't show some things on that programme 'cos the people who do get away, they probably wouldn't show on that programme.

Mike: Yeah, 'cos it shows up the police force as not being good.

First, there is a joke about learning from *Police, Camera, Action!*, a favourite reality format for this group of viewers, and the usual dismissal of learning 'anything' from a programme that is 'good to watch'. But, what follows on from this discussion is an exploration of how the programme can teach people 'that you shouldn't do stuff like that'. What is more, these young viewers have also learnt that the programme only selects successful stories of law and order in order to teach viewers not to engage in criminal activities. Here, the 'message' of the programme gets through to these viewers, and at the same time they critically reflect on how these crime stories are selected for viewers.

In another example, a group of young female viewers (aged 15-18) talk about social learning in relation to *Big Brother*, the favourite type of reality format for this group of viewers:

Interviewer: Is there anything that is informative about *Big Brother*?

Angela: Well you learn about people.

Hilary: No, it's only like you always get caught lying.

Laura: No, it is informative when they go in that room and they start giving their opinions on people...

Angela: I think you can learn a lot about people from that.

Laura: Yes.

Angela: You can see the way people behave, the way they behave around TVs, on their own, the way they deal with things 'cos they're locked up... I mean... When people think of it they think first of all 'Oh, no, you can't learn' but you can. Do you know what I mean? It's really interesting to watch people, you know, in an environment where everyone is seen all the time...

Sally: I think *Big Brother* was a lot more interesting and more informative than *Animal Hospital*.

Emma: Yeah, it's like people skills, you learn to see how people react to certain situations and it's like they're shut in a house all the time, with each other, they can't get away from each other and it's like how they either put their difference aside and try and get on or they have stand-up rows, or... it's just how they get on and the way you relate to it really.

Nicola: Well, erm, what I got from people at school was that it wasn't for the informative part or anything it was just basically bitching about other people, they were just like 'I don't like him, I don't like her, I think he should win...' that was all basically it was, it was just entertainment.

Sarah: Definitely. It was a lot more light-hearted.

Angela: Yeah, it's like entertainment but you still can... you know what I mean, you can still like see things, you can learn things. No, you don't necessarily learn things from it but it shows you things like, you know, people's attitudes or whatever.

Again, there is the familiar dismissal of the idea of learning from watching *Big Brother*, this time framed in relation to gossip and entertainment. But, there is also debate about how viewers can 'learn about people' by watching the activities of the contestants in the *Big Brother* house. Thus, the discussion moves backwards and forwards, assessing various responses to the series as 'light-hearted' or more serious, depending on the way viewers perceive the activity of 'people watching'. There is hesitation about what to call this type of learning ('you don't necessarily learn things from it but it shows you things'). But there is also an open debate about the idea of learning from watching a reality format such as *Big Brother*. For these young viewers at this stage in their lives, watching the way people behave in social situations is potentially informative because they are still forming their own understanding of socially acceptable and unacceptable behaviour. Younger adults have a vested interest in gathering as much knowledge as they can about 'the way people behave' because they are still learning how to conduct themselves in various social situations, in particular situations involving peers. Reality game shows such as *Big Brother* provide a useful opportunity for young adults to learn about something that matters to them. As one viewer suggests, watching a contemporary reality format such as *Big Brother* can be more informative than a traditional reality format such as *Animal Hospital* because young adults can relate to the content of one more than the other.

Conclusion

The way that viewers dismiss or qualify the idea of learning from reality programming highlights a shift in understanding the role of information in reality programming. Reality game shows such as *Big Brother* combine a number of different elements, psychological facts, social observation, personal experiences, games, to create an innovative popular factual programme that offers informal learning opportunities for young audiences about being a young person in the twenty-first century. Such examples indicate the potential for contemporary reality formats to provide 'modes of casual, inferred knowledge' (Corner 1999: 117) for popular young audiences.

Debate amongst young viewers about learning in reality programmes suggests such viewers are engaged in critical viewing practices. The fact that some viewers are critical of the idea of learning would suggest there is something they have learned from watching reality TV. For example, when the young girl who watched *Popstars* said all she learnt from it was how to be famous, she intended her comment to suggest she didn't watch the programme to learn about life as a popstar. However, her comment is evidence of learning, as she has learned that *Popstars* is not the kind of format that foregrounds information about the entertainment industry; at the same time she has learnt about the media by watching how the programme has turned its contestants into celebrities. The idea of learning therefore relates not only to how viewers might learn from popular factual television, but also how viewers might learn not to value learning from particular reality programmes. When young viewers critically reflect on the idea of learning in reality TV they are reflecting on the development of the genre itself.

Note

1. This article is an extract from Annette Hill: *Reality TV: Audiences and Popular Factual Television* (Routledge 2004). The research presented in this article is drawn from a multi-method research project conducted during 2000-2001. The research aim was to provide information and analysis regarding viewing preferences and strategies across all age ranges for a variety of reality programming, available on terrestrial, satellite, cable and digital television in the U.K. Funding for the audience research project discussed in this article came from the Economic and Social Research Council, the Independent Television Commission (ITC) and Channel 4. Quantitative and qualitative audience research methods were used, in conjunction with analysis of the scheduling, content and form of reality programmes. The data from the quantitative survey was conducted using the national representative sample (over 9,000 respondents aged 4-65+) of the Broadcaster's Audience Research Board (BARB). Qualitative focus groups were also used, consisting of 12 groups of male/female viewers, aged 11-44, in the social category C1C2DE (skilled and working class, and lowest level of subsistence), living in the South East of England. Family in-depth interviews were also conducted over a six-month period.

References

Bourdieu, Pierre (1986) *Distinction: A Social Critique of the Judgement of Taste*, London: Routledge.

Corner, John (1999) *Critical Ideas in Television Studies*, Oxford: Oxford University Press.

Davies, Hannah, Buckingham, David & Kelley, Peter (2000) 'In the Worst Possible Taste: Children, Television and Cultural Value', *European Journal of Cultural Studies* 3, 1: 5-25.

Reality TV – The Mechanisms of a Success

François Jost

With the broadcasting of *Loft Story*,[1] the French version of *Big Brother*, in April 2001, a wave of so-called *télé-réalité* (reality TV) began to sweep over France. Since then, the programmes ranked under this label multiplied, adopting the international formats: *Koh-Lanta* (Survivor*)*, *Star Academy* (Star Maker)*, The Bachelor*, *La Ferme des célébrités* (The Simple Life), etc. If this phenomenon is not amazing in itself, insofar as it gradually reaches a large number of countries, its name, on the other hand, merits examination.

If, almost all around the world, the programmes mentioned above were designated by the word "reality show", a word that had been used in France to qualify some programmes such as *Perdu de vue* (Chi l'Ha Visto [in Italy], Who Saw Her?), *La Nuit des héros* (1991, The Night of the Heroes), or *Témoin No.1* (Crimewatch), M6 – the channel that broadcast *Loft Story* – invented a new expression, *télé-réalité*, for launching the programme. As a result, it emphasized two ideas, which were, moreover, at the centre of the debates that accompanied the appearance of the programme. The first idea was that these programmes touched reality better than any other previous programme, and at least much more than the "reality shows", whose name in France has an inevitable connotation of spectacle due to the French meaning of "show". The second idea was that, with this new generation of programmes, television experienced a real revolution, a break, the beginning of a new era.

I would like to demonstrate in this text that these arguments, on the contrary, are those of any consumer marketing, based at the same time on the promise of novelty and the logic of supplement (television promises more reality as some washing powders promise whiter laundry), and that the force of these programmes lies exactly in the success of a marketing approach that knew how to deal with some already tested televisual recipes, with the ideologies of the present and the expectations of the targeted public. Unlike *Big Brother*, which is on for its fourth season in numerous countries, *Loft Story* stopped in its second season in France because of its weak audience, and its imitation *Nice People* had only one season. On the other hand, *Star Academy*, the French adaptation of *Star Maker*, is on for its fourth season and has an audience that, although it is not as large as that of *Operación triunfo* (Pop Idol) in Spain, remains important. I shall thus choose the example of *Star Academy* for dissecting the mechanisms of the success of *télé-réalité*.

Star Academy, the reconciled school

When, at the end of 2001, TF1 launched *Star Academy*, M6 accused the rival channel of plagiarism: how TF1, which some months before had decried *Loft Story* and "garbage television", did dare to use a device so original as to lock young people into a castle and film them! Although, finally, TF1 was not condemned, this denunciation of a channel by another one proves, to the good listener, that any new programme is rather the transformation of a previous format than a radical break (in the same vein as the "style sheets" on the computer program Word are always based on previous formats). This continual *deformation* of television programmes makes the point of departure of the analysis relatively arbitrary, because, in truth, we can never isolate the format that would be an indubitable origin. This phenomenon, which was noticed in relation to literature,[2] is even truer of television.

Thus, let us start with this observation: *Star Academy* is a second generation product, a product of the after-*Big Brother* or the after-*Loft Story* period, which reflects the success of the programme of M6 and optimizes it, as the marketing consultants say. This optimization is made according to the principle of Russian dolls, which is at the heart of the serialization of the television apparatus: From a formula which works, a device or theme or the most efficient sequence is taken in order to reconstruct a new formula. In this particular case, the mechanism is based on two features of *Loft Story*:

- *The reuse of the apparatus of the web cam.* When everybody has the possibility of making a spectacle of him-/herself only by using a small movie camera connected to his/her computer, television had to invent a formula that blends this desire for exhibitionism/voyeurism with the penetration of a lived intimacy. Such a blend is promised when the set of the programme is designed in the image of an apartment loft.

- *The capacity of "sampling" TV programmes*, to use the vocabulary of the DJ (disc jockey), who makes new pieces by mixing samples of pre-existing musical numbers. In addition to the gestures of everyday life reserved for live broadcasting, *lofteurs* (the persons on the loft in *Loft Story/Big Brother*) must ceaselessly play roles in games whose rules are dictated by the "owner", i.e., the producer. These tests vary considerably from one country to another, but all have in common that they play with the television culture. The candidates have to imitate or to make a pastiche of their favourite sequences (karaoke, awards ceremony, demonstration of samba or hip-hop, etc.). For the candidates, these activities offer a test-bed where anyone can give evidence of his qualities: one of her sense of rhythm, another of his humour or eloquence, still another of her skill, and these qualities will be decisive for their hopes of winning.

Star Academy is based on one of the main *criticisms* formulated against *Big Brother*, namely that the last-mentioned programme shows idle young people, who become famous without doing anything. How can one show the intimacy, about which TV viewers are apparently crazy, without giving the feeling that it is the main part of the programme? In order to resolve this question, the new format inverts the hierarchy of both features, which I have just isolated above in relation to *Loft Story*. Instead of everyday life being in the foreground and the games taking second place, being on television to demonstrate what one knows and can do is the first purpose of the programme, and the invasion into private life is simply the fallout of life in a boarding school.

As regards avoiding the artificial aspect of the loft and its too openly IKEA-character,[3] it is situated in a castle, yet decorated in the minimum luxury. Certainly, the daily programmes report scenes of life within this group of young people – conversations, dressing and, especially, time-limited phone relationships with the family or close partners – but they emphasize especially the work of these pseudo noblemen: singing lessons, dancing lessons, morning jogging, and so on, so that the daily summaries shown in access-prime-time announce the weekly prime time on stage. More than a life of luxury, in which the only concern would be – as in the loft – to put on make up, to sunbathe or to chat, *Star Academy* shows on film the learning process to which the inhabitants are subjected. They believed that show business was made by luxury and a carefree attitude, and they discovered that it was a profession requiring a great deal of work. Such is, at least, the morale that Pascal Nègre, Chairman and Managing Director of Universal France, expresses in concluding the final of the programme.

What do the programmes show us except the daily back stage of the weekly shows? They show some young people locked in a boarding school, maybe luxurious, but run according to severe rules. Those who did not finish their breakfast before jogging time are forced to do without it; those who make noise during the lessons are asked to leave. (To Jean-Pascal, who does his gymnastics exercises while grumbling, the professor shouts: "If you bawl, you go out!") Supreme guard of this small world, producer Alexia Laroche-Joubert (also producer of *Loft Story*) periodically receives the apprentice singers in her office to teach them some lessons of life, scolding them occasionally if they do not sit straight in their chair. In a vast room lined with glass-doored bookcases containing rows of bound books, she addresses her pupils, at a good distance, behind her perfectly tidied-up desk, hardly soiled by one or two files:

You were on borrowed time during this week. You are now in another configuration. It is you who is going to be judged. And it is Jennifer who is on borrowed time. I am going to ask you to draw from your energies because, during prime time, it is you that one is going to judge. (5 January, 2002)

In other words, the apprentice singers have to integrate the mission of any singer who performs on a TV channel in prime time – making audience rating. Sometimes, the lesson is simpler:

You must work because it may happen to you regularly – on December 25th, on January 1st, on December 31st, you may be the lead to be on stage and thus to work. (end of December, 2001)

Every week, candidates are subjected to an evaluation in each of the practised activities (dance, self-expression through movement, singing, etc.) and the audience follows the jury's deliberations about their performances. *Star Academy* is, thus, the positive opposite of the image of the school conveyed by the media. In this utopian place, young people learn only what they like and any "incivility" is repressed: No question of being late or being lazy! No question either of questioning the authority of a professor or of the director! The last day, the pupils and teachers fall into one another's arms with many embraces and shared tears!

If the first quality of a programme is not to arouse objections from the heart of the family, thus to be *less objectionable*, the success of *Star Academy* is comprehensible. To relatives who regret the acquiescence of the teaching profession and to the children who blame the school system for the boredom of taught subjects, *Star Academy* offers the image of a reconciled school, where adults and teenagers work together towards the successful fulfilment of a common aim. *Star Academy's* success owes a great deal to this nostalgic model of the School, which gathers children and adults, as has since been proved by other successful ventures. For instance, we see this model in Christophe Barratier's film, *Les Choristes* (The Choristers), where a supervisor transforms the life of the pupils of a very repressive boarding school by organizing a choir, as well as in the programme *The Boarding School of Chavagnes* (M6, 2004), which stages teenagers living in a boarding school of the 50s under the quasi-military authority of a supervisor. In this program, laughter, lax dressing, gossip, etc., are severely chastised. The very large audience ratings among French 11- to 14-year-olds (70.3%) and 15- to 24-year-olds (61.5%)[4] suggest that current pupils find symbolic pleasure in the spectacle of this continual repression, sufficiently far from the contemporary universe. If the nostalgia is easily understandable for the oldest TV viewers, who see there images that remind them of memories, true or not, it is certainly not the key to the success among younger people. I prefer to see there a new confirmation of a feeling that lives in every TV viewer and that, naturally, is far from being to his honour: sadism. The teenagers take all the more pleasure in seeing this discipline from another age applied to others! As for the television channel, it gives itself an attractive role: Whereas its news shows daily the spectacle of school dysfunction, in particular of the violence that reigns there, it shows that another discipline is possible, one that reigns over the pupils for whom it is responsible.

The sadism of the TV viewer

Why do we look every day at the television spectacles that would be a source of horror for us if we lived them? Because the position of the TV viewer is sadistic, by definition, if we admit with Freud that sadism "consists of an activity of violence, a demonstration of power against another person taken as object".[5] Let us remember the spectacle – the word is shocking – of this small Colombian, Omeira, swallowed inexorably by a stream of mud without any help and, notwithstanding, shot by cameras for television viewers all over the world… What can explain why the whole world was able to and urged to look at her image on the screens, if not the transformation of the suffering subject into a pure visual object?

If the TV viewer can watch such images with greediness, it is because he enjoys not being where others suffer (some have a feeling of pity and turn the television set off). The reception of information from the world always supposes an implicit comparison of the other's situation with the viewer's own situation. Television channels know that very well, and they ask: "Would the same thing be possible in our country?", as soon as a disaster occurs abroad. The TV viewer is, thus, by definition a self-centred being who takes a certain pleasure in contrasting the comfort of his/her own situation with the misfortune of the other. And if, by chance, the spectacle seems unbearable to him/her, the ultimate demonstration of power against the other is to channel-flick or "zap him", i.e., to remove the other from the viewer's horizon.

All this returns us very naturally to *Loft Story* or *Star Academy*. To the feeling of being everywhere, seeing everything, these programmes add that of having an effect on reality by giving the viewer a vote. Any gossip may become a judgement immediately transformed into action… What magician would be capable of managing such a metamorphosis, if not television? One element still strengthens the hypothesis of sadism: the fact that TV viewers always voted against the explicit happiness of the candidates, preferring to separate those who seemed to have feelings for one another (the first season of *Loft Story*), and to cause a man and a woman to win who, counter to the purpose of the game, did not form a couple. It amazed all those who imagined the TV viewer as having the features of a Harlequin romance reader to note that the spectator was seemingly formed at the school of Aristotle's *Poetics*! Or, to cast this differently, that he/she made choices corresponding to what he/she expected from the television narrative in general.

As Aristotle says, if there is "mutual hostility, what one does or wants to do to the other one arouses no pity"; tragedy springs up in the heart of the alliances (among the family), when violence becomes part of it.[6] From this point of view, by separating the couples, the audience reveals its narrative competence! It knew how to manage situations in a way that would boost its own interest in the continuation of the events. Moreover, in order to recreate this generative "alliance" of tragedy, many programmes of *télé-réalité* impose a double constraint on the candidates – that of forming a team in everyday life, in the organization of the household, in the games, and of finally beating all the others to win the game (this is particularly true of *Survivor*).

Human beings who look like us

This relation of domination of the person on the screen by the TV viewer is essential and can also be explained on the narrative side. For understanding this, it may be helpful to take in account Aristotle's criterion of the elevation of the character. I shall consider, from this point of view, that the narrative, fictitious or not, causes the viewer to face two types of characters whom he always judges with regard to himself.

On the one hand, there are the heroes who seem superior to other human beings because of their superior qualities or behaviours (*high mimetic mode*): policemen with great powers of deduction (*Columbo*), an incorruptible teacher (*l'Instit'*, The Teacher) or an individual endowed with exceptional courage (*La Nuit des héros*).

In that case, identification with the characters is made through respect and admiration. The TV viewer undergoes in a sense what Bergson calls "the appeal of the hero", which "pulls the other one by the force of the emotion and to the judgment of whom we subject then in imagination our behaviour".[7] Even if the mechanism is the same, be it a narrative of reality or a narrative of fiction, the effects are different. Everyone can willingly agree to be surpassed by heroes of pure invention, but it is never very pleasant to see oneself put in one's place by heroes of everyday life. By dint of presenting supermen, *La Nuit des héros* eventually reduced the common TV viewer to very little indeed.

Regarding the second category of narrative, that which tells the story of characters equal to the social environment and to other human beings (*low mimetic mode*) – policemen confronted by doubt and personal difficulties (*NYPD Blue*) or the young lawyer haunted by the problems of being single (*Ally McBeal*) – we identify with the heroes thanks to their humanity and we maintain complicity with them.

Obviously, there are still other ways to situate fiction (with characters from the superhero to the smallest one) with regard to its spectator, but these two modes are illuminating for understanding the relation of the lovers of *Loft Story* or *Star Academy*. This opposition between a series with high mimetic mode – which revolves around an exceptional individual, fictitious or not – and a series with low mimetic mode – which favours groups of and the relations between "ordinary" individuals (*Hélène et les garçons*, *PJ* [8]) – is just like the disaffection to the experts and the progressive valuation of the anonymous of which we are victims. Any politician knows that a good local testimonial is better than ten statistics, at least for the voters. The television news obeys the same principle. Journalists prefer the portrait of an unemployed person to curves depicting the evolution of unemployment.

Everything takes place as if the discourses on proximity had a profound effect on television. Whodunits as talk shows or reality shows are increasingly interested in persons who look like us, with their failings and their anguishes. *Loft Story* glorifies what is the most everyday and at the same time the most commonplace: to get up, dress, eat, to seduce… the most heroic act of all. Watching these *lofteurs* who have difficulty getting out of bed and who bicker about how to make orange juice, results in our becoming the heroes of everyday life.

Seeing them celebrated, then, by all, while they did nothing exceptional, elevates anyone who thinks that media fame is a toss of the dice and that luck is enough to be promoted to the foreground. In proof, moreover, consider that, during *Star Academy's* first season, one of the least vocally bright, Jean-Pascal, nevertheless received votes from a large majority of the audience, who liked above all his behaviour in life. While the song "idols" of the 60s were at first untouchable stars, whose private lives we entered bit by bit, the young singers of *Star Academy* are at first friends and then singers, so that the teenager sometimes has the impression of seeing one of his/her close relations succeed.

Between transgression and regression

Where does this feeling of familiarity and pleasure in contemplating the commonplace come from? Doubtless it comes partially from the type of reality created by a programme such as *Loft Story* or *Star Academy*. Seemingly, the specific device of these two programmes is to abolish the separation between the "front stage", where social representation takes place with its actors and its public, and the "back stage", where the actors escape the glances of the public: "a back region or backstage may be defined as place relative to a given performance, where the impression fostered by the performance is knowingly contradicted as a matter of discourse".[9] If cameras are everywhere, any place becomes, it seems, a front stage (hence the first media discussion about *Loft Story*: Is there a movie camera in the toilet?). Why does this gliding towards the front stage delight a part of the public? On the stage of the social life, the actor must be responsible for everything that occurs in the representation, Goffman says in substance. To the extent that the public is used "to interpreting the signs", he continues, the actor has to avoid any gesture or any behaviour that would damage the meaning of his whole role, as well as a dissonance that provokes a sometimes fatal break of tone in the execution of a piece.

These particular types of clumsiness are to be avoided:

First, a performer may accidentally convey incapacity, impropriety, or disrespect by momentarily losing muscular control of himself. He may trip, stumble, fall; he may belch, yawn, make a slip of the tongue, scratch himself, or be flatulent; he may accidentally impinge upon the body of another participant. Secondly, the performer may act in such a way as to give the impression that he is too much or too little concerned with the interaction. He may splutter, forget his lines, appear nervous, or guilty, or self-conscious; he may give way to inappropriate outbursts of laughter, anger, or other kinds of affect which momentarily incapacitate him as an interactant....[10]

Confront this text with the actions gathered in the summaries of *Loft Story* or *Star Academy*, and you will not spend much time before finding it illustrated in picture or sound. Jean-Pascal's success during *Star Academy's* first season, which I evoked above, is completely due to his "clumsinesses" of the first category, which aroused the anger of some journalists and the affection of a part of the audience for whom he was long one of the most popular, in spite of his weak qualities as a singer. As for the clumsiness of the second type (spluttering, uncontrolled laughter, and so on), the success of collections of out-takes proves to what extent they also have the favours of TV viewers.

By proposing tests intended for the back stage (during the prime time show), the producers favour all the behaviours that should stay in the back stage and, obviously, the editors pay particular attention to the choice of extracts to be broadcast. If not, how can we explain that the "worst moment" lived in *Star Academy* by Jennifer, the first winner, was, according to her statements, when one of its inhabitants forgot to close the door of the toilet he was using?

If *Loft Story* represents the reign of the slip – in the very wide meaning that Goffman gives this term – *Star Academy* is completely based on the idea that it is necessary to show what is usually hidden. Contrary to the social norm requiring that we hide "the nasty job" from the public, *Star Academy* decides to dedicate the programme to the back stage of the singer's profession. Instead of making apparent only the ease of the song interpreted in playback (as in the 60s), the difficulty is shown.

In short, it is less a question of making visible all the spaces in the front stage than of making visible the learning, with its failures and sweat, to give a triple symbolic profit to the TV viewer. This is a reinsurance of authenticity: By privileging the clumsiness, the editing suggests that *lofteurs* are below social norms, that they play no roles, contrary to the TV viewer in his/her everyday life. So, the world of the loft, without "facade", with its imposed set, would be truer than ours. This privilege granted to acts that break with the correctness of the front stage makes the public participate in a sort of carnival in which everything is reversed. What is to be avoided in society becomes here the standard, and the "passage" (performance?) on television – front stage above all – does not adhere to the usual conventions.

Goffman notices that "backstage behaviour has what psychologists might call a regressive character".[11] By putting the back stage in the foreground, by making it reach the television space, *Loft Story* and *Star Academy* legitimize this regression, which explains partially the pleasure the young public experience in following these programmes. While children are sometimes excluded from the social scene by parents because of the possible impropriety of their behaviour (for example, during a dinner with important guests), these broadcast role-playing games propose a world just like the one they live in the back stage, a world where human beings would drop masks and be such as they are, without facade. The media popularity of *lofteurs* or apprentice singers comes less from their professional qualities or from their gifts than from their capacity to gain fame thanks to behaviour normally reserved for the back stage.

To the pleasures of regression is added that of infringing, which represents the trespassing of the border separating the back stage from the front stage. Obviously, television did not invent this pleasure. Contemplation of the images stolen by *paparazzi* from movie stars or from political personalities is subsumed under the same mechanism. Britney Spears' acne, the silhouette of a princess making love at the edge of a swimming pool, or the nudity of a president of the Republic attract the public because they humanize the stars, these human beings who surpass us.

Nevertheless, seized by telephoto lenses, the images maintain these heroes at a distance: Their behaviour looks like ours, but not their world. For this reason, in spite of all the invasions into their private lives, the stars are no more and no less human than the Gods of Olympus, so close to us in their passions and so distant in their powers.

The *Loft Story* and *Star Academy* actors are nothing but heroes, in the sense of the Greek mythology, i.e., people who dream about immortality. In the image of the TV viewer – like all the characters of the low mimetic mode – they seduce all the more in that they show their defects and their clumsiness. The mediocrity of the intimate behaviours, showing the proximity of the filmed daily world to the TV viewer's universe, reassures him of his own capacity to become a celebrity, if an opportunity occurs. Hence there is sympathy both for those who stay "natural" (Jean-Pascal in *Star Academy*) and for those who rise (Loanna in *Loft Story*). This identification with the behaviour rather than admiration for talents almost thwarted the projects of Universal, partner of TF1 in *Star Academy*: The public did indeed become infatuated with the most unrefined of the pupils, as it was generally recognized that he did not know how to sing. And the channel had to intervene by diverse means to ensure his elimination (notably by blocking the switchboard allowing people to vote for him).

Gathering the family

One may still find some other reasons for the success of programmes such as *Loft Story* and *Star Academy*. The reasons I have developed explain nevertheless at the same moment why the entire family may meet around the programme and why each member finds an interest there. By offering an image of an unreal, reconciled school, *Star Academy* gathers children who find a continuation of their dream of a school where they would do only as they like. By giving an image of rigor, the programme answers to the criticisms that parents often formulate concerning the laxness of current schools.

The choice of the songs worked on by the young people is federative: Contrary to the traditional entertainment programmes, which were based on the last successes of the song and which pushed aside the generations, *Star Academy* makes work the successes of yesterday, which satisfies the oldest spectators; by choosing participants who look like the current high school students, the youngest viewers are satisfied. But television does not do this to stretch out a mirror: It gives to these young viewers the opportunity of enjoying their observer's position, and of finding in others' lives the narrative schemes that usually move them in the fiction. The relation of domination by the spectator over familiar human beings, almost friends, who are loved especially because they break everyday bans on the social stage, a relation in which the spectator is free to create idols or to exclude his fellow human beings, always maintains mastery over them.

Notes

1. The principle of this programme, broadcast in April-July 2001 and April-July 2002 on M6, is the following: Eleven candidates are locked in a loft for seventy days. The public eliminates the candidates by voting until there is finally one couple. There is a daily summary and a weekly prime time programme that mixes sequences in studio, reports and sequences from life in the loft. A psychiatrist and a psychologist are also present in the studio. Programming is 2 hours and 45 minutes delayed with regard to real time. The final on July 5, 2001, was watched by 49.6% of the audience.
2. Cf. Gérard Genette, who asserts that any text is derived from a previous one, *Palimpsestes*, Paris: Seuil, 1982.
3. IKEA is a chain of inexpensive furniture shops.
4. According to the research firm Médiametrie.
5. Sigmund Freud, *Métapsychologie,* coll. Folio Essai, p. 26.
6. Aristotle, *Poetics*, French translation, coll. *Poétique*, 53 b 14, Paris: Seuil [ca. 300 B.C.], p. 81.
7. Henri Bergson, *Les Deux Sources de la morale et de la religion* [1932] 1958, PUF, p. 30.
8. *PJ*, abbreviation of Police Judiciaire, is the title of a French series with a format very similar to the American series *NYPD Blue*.
9. Erving Goffman, *The presentation of self in everyday life*, New York: Doubleday Anchor Books, 1959, p. 112.
10. Ibid., p. 52.
11. Ibid., p. 128.

Reality Shows in Cyprus
New Media "Fallout"?

Nayia Roussou & Michaella Buck

Reality shows are a product of the 90s, with *Survivor* and *Big Brother* being considered the forerunners of the genre. Charlie Parsons, who originated *Survivor*, described his work in the following terms:

> The inventor of reality TV? No, but I consider myself to be the pioneering producer who took documentary into a controlled environment and created a new kind of television. (quoted in Brenton & Cohen, 2003: 44)

The same originator describes reality TV as "a hybrid of four forms: the docu-soap, game show, drama and talk show". (quoted in ibid: 57)

The reality show contains different features, such as the relationship of the actor to reality (docu-drama), reality time concepts, e.g., events spread over a long time and over many episodes (soap operas), competitiveness (game shows), fluctuations of emotion (drama) and efforts towards the justification of self (talk shows). Above all, the reality show is a constructed world where the pecking order, once believed to be the sociological wrapping paper of Darwinian theory, is quite all right, under the rigorous surveillance of an authority figure that tries to transform yesterday's *inconnus* into tomorrow's celebrities. This recent programme genre may not require actors or scripts. It may be a particular space-based production (with all events in a house, on an island, or the like), but the artificiality of the situations in which the contestants are placed, the restrictions they have to face while on camera and the efforts towards survival (of the fittest one might add), have been the object of discussion and criticism on the part of different writers. One of the most important questions concerns the "reality" in reality shows. It seems that viewers have a deep suspicion about the "real" nature of the behaviour of the contestants, believing that they overact for the camera with the mask they put on, slipping away "in moments of stress and conflict, revealing the concealed 'true self' or 'real face' of a contestant" (Brenton & Cohen, 2003: 51).

Let us look at the famous reality show *Survivor*. The basic scenario of *Survivor* is simple. Sixteen contestants (called "castaways") are dropped off in an isolated environment (in Borneo, Australia, Africa, etc.) and are divided into two tribes. The tribes have to provide themselves with shelter and food and, besides these activities, compete in various physical and mental challenges. The losing tribe has to vote to remove one of its members. The tribes eventually merge, whereby former enemies become team-mates, and the individuals start to compete against one another until the final, when the two remaining contestants get votes from the jury (the out-voted contestants) and one of them wins a million dollars. In our opinion, the appeal of the show lies less in its "reality" than in the underlying fantasies and conflicts the show enacts and that viewers can experience vicariously.

In many reality shows, psychologists enter the process to measure how well participants would hold up under the trying circumstances of life on the physical edge, without proper shelter, food and sleep (*Survivor*), how they will interact with each other or deal with intrigues and conflicts with different types of personalities locked in the same house (*Big Brother, The Bar*). For instance, how will a highly energetic extrovert get along with a severe introvert who dwells on details? Or how will a worrying individual cope with the difficult circumstances? The purpose of psychologists is to help people make the best of who they are, rather than – as is more usual – look at their worst traits.

According to Levak (2001), who was the psychologist to screen the *Survivor* contestants, psychologists are looking for character types, people who stand out because they are obnoxious, passionate, or unique types of personalities. At the same time, even the most unique person will not win with a complete breakdown on TV, and therefore psychologists also look for self-destructive tendencies in participants. They want to avoid fragile people who cannot deal with trauma and deprivation. Being cold, wet, hungry, thirsty and alone influences thinking, coping ability and requires considerable denial. Based on his personal experience, Levak characterizes contestants as supernormal people in terms of resilience and self-confidence (ibid).

On the other hand, Brenton and Cohen (2003: 92-93), analyzing the role of the psychologists and psychiatrists who participate in these reality shows in support of the contestants – both prior to their selection for participation when they have to go through interviews, screening processes and personality tests, and during the show when the out-voting processes begin and people have to leave the show, or again after the end of the show when they have to provide "after-care" – come to the conclusion that these experts are "primarily, production-side consultants, mind crew". In other words, their prime professional goal is to help the programme carry on, by supporting the contestants to reach this end.

Kellner (2003: 109) believes that the way we perceive people is mediated by media images, stating that:

> looks, image and style become more and more fundamental constituents of social identities, shaping how people are publicly viewed and defined.

How, then, are the looks, image and style of the younger generation – both participants and viewers – affected by reality shows in which the contestants are moving in a semblance of freedom, but with the oppressive presence of cameras and microphones all around and the threat of expulsion from the arena of competition? In other words, how is the social identity of these contestants affected in a forum where competition is raised to the level of adversity and the ethos of fair play, which is legitimate in a world of mercantile utilitarianism, is turned into a Darwinian struggle for the survival of the fittest in the specific game – be it a farm, an island, a house with a big brother watching, or a singers' contest, where the winner will harvest the loot of glamour, fame and money? Perhaps this kind of adverse ethos should not surprise us, as identity politics in the past few decades, according to Kellner again (ibid: 116) "have become in general heavily media oriented, with contending groups articulating and circulating their views through the media". This media strategy or perspective is now being literally applied, not to groups but to individuals, by placing them in enclosed encounters to test their viability and survivability in conditions of stress and competition, a transfer process that should not perhaps surprise us, as social identities and their relationships to reality are inextricably interwoven with social, professional or economic competition.

However, where does the responsibility of the media lie in relation to the moral and psychological dimensions implied in the process of this entertainment genre, which establishes and promotes looks, images and styles of real people who, at least, have made it to the production studio and whose sleeping and waking hours, and discussions, arguments and activities throughout the day, are of interest to a nation of viewers daily, for weeks or, sometimes, months? Brenton and Cohen (2003: 104) remind us that:

> Entertainment is frequently the foremost purpose of broadcast mental health presentations but the mental health professional must never allow entertainment considerations to outweigh or dilute the principles of ethical mental health practice.

Because reality shows are comparative newcomers on the television scene, data about their influence on viewers and contestants are not forthcoming. That is why we believe this article, organized in two parts – about viewership as well as three cases of reality show contestants in Cyprus – makes a contribution to the area.

Viewing of reality shows in Cyprus

With the end of the public television station monopoly (Cyprus Broadcasting Corporation) in Cyprus in 1990 and the arrival of other TV channels, the commercialization of television placed a new set of values before Cypriot viewers, young and old. Many of the programmes broadcast by private stations (of which

Antenna 1 and Mega are extensions of channels in Greece) are produced in Greece and sometimes shown either as repeats in Cyprus, or in the case of very popular programmes as live broadcasts.

There are today (2004) five private TV channels broadcasting on a national level: Mega, Antenna, Sigma, Alpha and Lumiere, a subscription channel. There are also several private local channels broadcasting in the island, in Limassol, Paphos and Larnaca.

Reality shows first reaching the island were those produced in Greece and, as early as 1998-99, the Greek-produced reality show *Epitelous Mazi* (Together at Last) was very popular among Cypriot audiences; however it was essentially a talk show attracting mainly adult audiences.

Reality shows popular among young people on the island began being aired in 2001, with *Big Brother*, produced by Antenna 1, Greece, and transmitted live in Cyprus. The high ratings obtained by the show led to other channels broadcasting similar reality shows and in the next three years, the reality shows presented in Table 1 – all originating in Greece and imported from there – were shown in Cyprus with the ratings given in the table, according to the age-group indexes used by AGB. The percentages indicate "the AMR (Automated Meter Reading) of the programme, in relation to all viewers of the specific target" (http://www.agb.com.cy).

It is obvious from the table that, on average, the two age groups most highly attracted to these shows are teenagers and adolescents, i.e., the age groups 13-17 and 18-24. These results are not surprising. During adolescence, insecurities concerning social acceptance and a need to belong, accompanied by a fear of banishment, are very strong (Erikson, 1980). The shows remind us of cliques in school and high school in relation to which inclusion or exclusion can be felt very dramatically. These characteristics during adolescence are probably one reason why so many teenage viewers watch the shows.

The most popular reality shows among the two younger age groups are summarized in Table 2.

Even though *Big Brother 2 Final* earned the highest ratings among the older age groups, too, the percentages in Table 2 are exceptional.

It is also understandable that the younger generation is most attracted to the reality shows transmitted in Cyprus since 2001 if we bear in mind that in the first reality show that became popular on the island, *Together at Last* mentioned earlier, Cypriots never seemed to participate. Cyprus is a small, closed society and airing personal or family problems on television would leave an individual highly exposed to the public. However, after that young Greek-Cypriots began participating in the Greek-produced reality shows, beginning with *Big Brother*. Presenters always made special mention of the participating Cypriots and this was, probably, a further motivation for participants from Cyprus, as well as a further attraction for wider Cypriot audiences. Young Cypriots also participated in *The Bar*, co-habiting in a house and in the evenings working in the bar on the ground

Table 1. **Audience ratings of reality shows in Cyprus 2001-2004 by age groups** (per cent)

Year	Channel	Title*	13-17	18-24	25-44	35-54	18-54
2001	ANT1	Big Brother	33.6	37.0	26.4	23.7	26.3
2001	ANT1	Big Brother Final	55.8	54.7	50.5	48.5	50.8
2002	MEGA	The Bar	34.5	30.3	28.2	25.6	27.2
2002	MEGA	The Bar Final	79.6	71.0	63.2	53.1	59.7
2002	ANT1	Big Brother 2	24.5	24.9	19.9	20.5	20.9
2002	ANT1	Big Brother 2 Final	98.9	99.7	74.4	84.5	81.4
2002	ANT1	Fame Story	28.7	31.2	17.5	13.8	18.4
2002	ANT1	Fame Story in Concert	48.7	44.5	39.9	36.1	42.8
2002	MEGA	The Farm	20.4	26.3	24.7	21.4	24.5
2002	MEGA	The Farm Final	13.9	27.5	33.1	27.4	31.8
2003	ANT1	Fame Story in Concert	34.2	36.5	16.2	10.9	17.1
2003	MEGA	The Farm	13.9	12.4	13.2	13.4	13.1
2003	MEGA	The Farm Final	11.5	41.4	14.7	15.8	18.9
2003	ANT1	Mission	11.9	12.6	10.4	11.7	11.5
2003	ANT1	Mission Final	5.9	7.8	6.1	4.9	6.5
2003	MEGA	Popstars	35.2	24.0	21.0	16.5	20.8
2003	MEGA	Popstars	30.3	29.3	8.2	11.6	13.6
2003	MEGA	Survivor	34.6	29.7	25.6	25.4	26.5
2003	MEGA	Survivor Final	53.5	52.9	42.8	43.9	47.1
2003	ANT1	The Wall	17.9	29.9	13.7	11.8	15.0
2003	ANT1	The Wall	39.1	43.7	32.5	26.9	31.2
2004	ANT1	Fame Story 2	26.4	37.6	21.5	19.2	22.6
2004	ANT1	Fame Story 2 Live	100.0	53.3	18.7	28.2	25.2
2004	ANT1	Mission Final R/R	18.1	19.2	9.5	15.5	15.1
2004	MEGA	Super Idol	36.4	44.4	28.7	24.6	29.4
2004	MEGA	Super Idol Final	56.7	47.2	50.7	45.6	47.6

* *The Farm* features people of different age groups living together in a farm doing different chores. In *Mission* a group of participants camps in a military setting and undertake different action projects related to "military" expeditions. *The Wall* is a reality show in which two groups of participants live under extremely contrasting conditions – rich or very poor and primitive. The groups exchange visits in the different settings. The contents of the other series are briefly mentioned in the text of the article.

Table 2. **The two highest audience ratings of reality shows in Cyprus 2001-2004 among 13- to 17- and 18- to 24-year-olds, respectively** (from Table 1) (per cent)

Year	Channel	Title	13-17	18-24
2002	ANT1	Big Brother 2 Final	98.9	99.7
2004	ANT1	Fame Story 2 Live	100.0	
2002	MEGA	The Bar Final		71.0

floor, serving "clients" who essentially were audience members, and discussing the aired programmes with them.

Other programmes in which Cypriots participated were the singing reality competitions *Popstars* and *Super Idol* and more recently *Fame Story* – something natural as quite a few Greek Cypriot singers are making a successful career in Greece. Besides, the concept of a reality singing competition has proved to be very attractive for young people who feel they can, or would like to, make a career in singing. A start in a singing competition, set in the framework of a reality show with expert training and guidance for young aspirants in song and dance, is glamorous. However, all three shows had numerous young participations from Greece, with just few participants from Cyprus.

When *Big Brother 1* was being aired in 2001, the more conservative circles in Cyprus criticized the violation of young participants' personalities, as well as the creation of new lifestyle standards, which prioritized publicity and glamour, media coverage and a heightened sense of competition that cultivated more self-centredness among young people – both among participants and viewers – as the sole goal was to outstay all others in the house of *Big Brother*, thus winning fame, money and recognition. When *Big Brother 2* and *The Bar* were introduced in Cyprus in 2002, the Federation of Parents' Associations on the island lobbied against the shows in the House of Representatives, as they believed that these shows were demoralizing their children. The TV channels did not stop the shows from being aired, of course, but moved the series to later hours of transmission, from 9.00 to 10.00 p.m.

In these programmes, the cameras were constantly tracking all the movements and behaviours of the young participants, and it was therefore difficult to know which behaviours were natural and spontaneous and which were affected and assumed because of camera recording and live transmission. We will now deal more with the climate and culture of these shows by presenting three partici-pants in reality programmes.

A winner, a loser and a quitter

The three reality show participants can be called a "winner", a "loser" and a "quitter". The "quitter", Marios Kleanthous, 20 years old, participated in *The Bar*. He quit in the middle of the show and wrote a book about his experiences that was published in Greece and titled *BARethika ke fevgo* (I got fed up, I am quit-ting).[1] The "loser" is a young woman, Lina Kawar, 26 years old, who participated in *Popstars*, but was voted out of the show, mainly because she could not sing in Greek (a fact the producers were aware of from the start). The third contestant, Stavros Kyprianou, 19 years of age, was a "winner" in *Super Idol* and has now got an agent and is embarking on a career in Greece.

The first two contestants, the "quitter" and the "loser", gave us personal interviews in August-September 2004. The third participant, the "winner", said he was "too busy" to give an interview, so we use here another interview he gave to the pop magazine *Selidhes* (Vol. 657, 1 August 2004, pp. 31-32).

Considering the very exploratory nature of this study, we used personal in-depth interviews with open-ended questions (which was also the method used in the printed magazine). The three types of contestants would provide, we believed, varied reactions to reality shows. Using a list of questions, we focused on the contestants' personal experiences and feelings regarding the shows and their own performance. Ample time and space were given in our own two interviews for the participants to explore their remembered experiences of the show in as much detail as possible. Tapes were transcribed and analysed to identify key themes and categories. The translated interview of the winner from the pop magazine contained questions that to a certain extent facilitated our approach to the other two interviews, as the magazine questions to the "winner" tried to delve into his feelings about and attitudes towards the show as well as his predicament in the show.

The interviews

The interviews generated a great deal of material about the contestants' experiences of the respective shows and the impact of the shows on their personal and professional lives. In this article, we offer a descriptive account of only some of the most salient themes. A more fine-grained analysis will be provided in the future.

Initially, our informants found it exciting to participate in the reality show and to strive for victory. There was, however, a striking difference between the expectations of the committee in the cases of *Popstars* and *Super Idol*, as described by the contestants. Lina Kawar ("loser" in *Popstars*) said they expected the girls to have a good singing voice, but also to be able to dance and perform. The girls' band they would form from the winners of the contest – called Hi-5 – would, Lina said, be modelled after Spice Girls. That is why, she said, one of the coloured girls seemed to be good, because

> she had beads in her hair... when they wanted to make the dance, they gave her an Afro look, like the coloured girl in the Spice Girls, so they were trying to give that image of the young hippie to the girl, like in Spice Girls.

In the reality show *Fame Story*, Lina said, the organizers tried to make a Britney Spears out of the winner Kalomira. For Lina herself, however, "she was always going to sing, and the competition was just an experience" on her journey, nothing more.

In contrast, the "winner" in *Super Idol*, Stavros Kyprianou, was not very good at dancing or performing, but had a good singing voice. He was continuously proclaimed the winner by the votes of both the invited audience and the television audience. Throughout the different elimination stages of the contest, however, the committee constantly pointed out to Stavros that he should sing a song by Parios, or in the future do a duet with Parios, a well-known Greek pop singer from the island of Paros. Parios depends for his fame almost exclusively on his voice, not on his star power or performing abilities. He is also an aging singer, which is why a young Cypriot – from another island – appeared to be a good successor to the Greek idol. Characteristically, magazine commentator Christina Skordi, who interviewed Stavros in the magazine *Selidhes*, describes his success as follows:

> Counter to existing trends, without stylish techniques and without the appearance of a "super idol", with authentic simplicity, Stavros managed to find himself among the top ten contestants and to eventually win, with his voice as his only advantage.

Stavros himself stated in the same interview:

> Fame has no influence on me whatsoever. I belong to the type of people who are not easily influenced and I'm not gonna change. For the time being my feet are well on the ground and that's how I plan to stay.

In *The Bar* there were no singing demands, so to be a winner one had to be diplomatic and careful in her/his verbal and non-verbal expressions. The "quitter" Marios Kleanthous, who quit *The Bar* halfway through the programme, revealed uncertainty in response to the question regarding the impact of the fame and popularity participants gained during the show:

> Fame has no influence, only I started to be more careful with my manners because more people know and recognize me now.

Talking about the short-term influence of popularity, the interviewees' answers are more "the socially accepted responses" than accurate or objective evaluations of their talents. The reality is that huge popularity and love of the public helped them to publish and sell the book (the "quitter"), or led them to contracts on the pop music scene (the "winner"). The long-term influence is almost unpredictable, depending a great deal on their personality qualities, such as discipline, hard work and ability to glean something from fame, the interviewees said.

Reality show finalists usually enjoy enormous status and popularity, glamour, and attention of the media and cameras, which cause them to have great illusions about themselves. However, publicity does not last and it can, if allowed, upset one's life and future, as happened to a young farmer who won Greek *Big Brother I*. Having quit his farming job during the show, he found himself looking for a new job after the show, forgotten by those who just recently had worshipped him.

Common to all three informants were the negative feelings accompanying the voting system. Having to vote out their fellow players of the game without any real reason or explanation and seeing how those who lost went through difficult emotional situations, were in conflict with the three contestants' personal values. None of our informants experienced any satisfaction of the type "Fine, they are out and my chance to win is higher". They experienced the opposite: sympathy. The role of "togetherness" plays a big part in the lives of young people and was also reflected in the responses of our interviewees. They experienced the voting out of fellow-participants as very disturbing and a blow to the morale of the whole group to such an extent that the psychologist had to be called in to talk to them, relieve their depression and brighten up the climate. Marios Kleanthous (the "quitter") offered a variety of explanations for the contestants' bitterness and pointed at several frustrating elements:

> The most traumatizing experience was watching how people around me are being kicked off the show and how difficult it was for them to cope with this defeat. It was one of the reasons I quit.

Another reason was, of course, that, whereas for him it was all a game, he soon realized he was surrounded by "conflict and intrigue", with insults and four-letter words populating the contestants' vocabularies.

Lina Kawar ("loser" in *Popstars*) also expressed her disappointment with the judges' panel:

> Judges knew exactly what they wanted from the first time they saw a girl, but because it was a reality show they had to drag it out and sometimes they would insult us like: "You look like a lady of the night with your make up on."

However, she is ready to offer perhaps an "accommodating" explanation, as well:

> Judges were cruel because they wanted to get a reaction out of us because that's the whole reason we are there – viewers want to see us laugh and cry.

She further felt that this oppressive approach was characteristically illustrated on the eve of the day she was going to leave the game: Even though they told her she would have to leave the next day, she still had to learn two verses of a new Greek song, as well as some new dance steps. That, she said, "was the stressful, the most stressful time".

If the role of fame in their lives was a hidden topic that was not easy to talk about, the traumatic experiences regarding the voting procedure let loose many emotions and unresolved conflicts.

207

Discussion

When we watched different programmes in repeat broadcasts after the interviews, quite a few of the points made by the Cypriot contestants were verified on different occasions in the programmes. For example, in one episode of *The Bar* on August 18, 2004, the entire programme was full of beeps, obviously in order to mute four-letter words used by the participants, a fact reminding us of the "quitter" Kleanthous' remarks about the atmosphere of intrigue and bad language used in the show. Quite a few of the participants, if not all, looked unhappy and behaved nervously, jumping on each other about different things, whereas some of them seemed to feel rather lost. Characteristically, responding to a question from a fellow contestant about whether she was really "herself", one of the girls retorted with: "Which one is yourself? Can you really be yourself, at the end of the day? In some phases, yes, I am myself."

In another repeat broadcast on August 15 on the same channel, one of the ten last contestants in a reality song contest, Maria, upon being voted out, complained publicly to the panel of judges that "her mobile messages had not reached their destination and she hadn't been receiving any mobile messages herself, either", insinuating there had been interventions in her communication with people outside the building of the contest. In the same programme, another remaining contestant was modelling his overall appearance, style and singing after a popular Greek-Cypriot singer, already famous in Greece.

In a repeat broadcast of *Fame Story*, also a reality song contest, on October 3, one of the contestants, who was quite overweight, was protesting at the top of her voice against the panel of judges who, even though she had lost about 100 kilos in order to participate in this contest, were out-voting her from the very first day, not even giving her a chance to learn anything new at all in singing or dancing.

Our observations must, naturally, be interpreted with great caution, as the three interviewed contestants comprised only a very small "sample" from Cyprus, whereas most of the contestants in the reality shows in question came from Greece. However, despite this basic limitation, our exploratory study generated a number of themes that may have heuristic value in guiding future investigations. The main findings that emerged were:

- the contestants' belief that the winner does not need to be the best, but needs to be attractive to the viewers

- the contestants' uncertainty about acknowledging the impact of fame on their lives

- the contestants' traumatic experience of the voting system.

In one sense, reality shows map the world we live in, not only because of contestants who decided not to live with the feeling "I could participate but I didn't do it", but mainly because participants must endure an enigmatic situation, where cheating is not possible. This enigma somehow mirrors the real world's law of the jungle in which the winner is the strongest.

In contrast to society, which may appreciate the player who is playing fairly but in the end still celebrates the winner, the informants appear to give humble, not self-revealing responses regarding the role of popularity on their lives. Probably, they assume that this type of response will be accepted by the readers and will not harm their image.

However, lack of certainty in relation to the voting procedure was expressed. In our opinion, even if it is painful for the contestants, the enormous appeal of reality shows is found exactly in the voting process – the worse for the contestants, the better for the audience. In spite of being fabricated, the shows create a reality of physical and social stress and then allow the audience to witness the exposure of human character through the contestants' interpersonal responses and interactions. Contestants have to struggle to balance the competing sides of their nature. To varying degrees, we all are involved in a similar balancing of actions in our lives. Reality shows probably play on a deep-seated fear of rejection and humiliation (Shapiro, 2002). Contestants may be kicked off the island (*Survivor*), out of the bar (*The Bar*) and the song contest (*Popstars*, *Super Idol*), and audiences internalize their fear. All people need love and acceptance (Maslow, 1970), and all of us to some extent worry about losing them. Watching how others have to confront this fear, how they scramble to fit into a group and find their role and acceptance, makes us cringe, but on the other side brings us some pleasure. And it seems that, today, looks, image and style are taking a meaningful place in the consciousness and social ideology of both contestants' and young viewers' concepts and value systems.

Further research

It is clear that further research into personal feelings and experiences of the contestants in reality shows is necessary. Even if our pilot study has identified important issues, they require more extensive exploration in the context of a larger sample of informants. It is hoped that the findings of a next phase of the investigation, involving more contestants, will provide a framework that can contribute to greater clarity about the validity of the impact of reality shows on contestants and, perhaps, audiences.

The conclusions of this preliminary study constitute, we believe, a type of theoretical "fallout" that is different from audience reactions, or TV audience relationships that we are familiar with in numerous empirical academic research studies about media functions. This is media fallout that seems to be delineating new parameters of the TV audience's (young in this case) relationships, which may begin through programme participation, but continue into other strata of the lives of both participants and non-participants. Some specific reminders of the general points drawn from the study could be the following:

- Reality shows, especially those involving art contests, seem to aim at pro-liferating acknowledged stars, such as the Hi-5 girls' group in *Popstars* modelled after Spice Girls, or Stavros Constantinos from the island of Cy-prus in *Super Idol*, modelled after the well-known singer Parios from the Greek island Paros. A good reminder to the point is Brenton's and Cohen's (2003: 91) remark that "conceptual artists create templates for installation in the world"; the conceptual artists here are obviously the panel judges, who are trying to model new singers after existing stars in national or inter-national forums.

- Reality shows seek to impose the organizers' decisions on the participants and to train them to comply with discipline and authority. Brenton and Cohen do remind us, after all, that "reality TV is a game of power" (ibid: 1).

- Reality shows seek to immunize young people to their loss of privacy and their adaptation to competition, the cynical acceptance of difference or of trauma and indulgence in self-interest which accompany the process of turning "scars into stars" (ibid: 101).

This is a new type of fallout being created by a new type of programme that is currently gaining ground – all over the world – and that deserves more attention and further analysis.

Acknowledgement

The authors thank M.A. Psychology student Marianna Charilaou for transcribing the interviews.

Note

1. "Barethika" is a pun on "bar", which in Greek is also the first syllable of the word "barethika" (I'm fed up).

References

Brenton, S. & Cohen, R. (2003): *Shooting People*. USA, Library of Congress.
Erikson, E.H. (1980): *Identity and the Life Cycle*. New York, Norton.
http://www.agb.com.cy
Kellner, D. (2003): *Media Spectacle*. London, Routledge.
Kleanthous, M. (2002): *BARethika ke fevgo*. Athens, Livanis Press. (in Greek)
Levak, R. (2001): Survivor, *Psychology Today*, Vol. 34, No. 5, p. 51.
Maslow, A. (1970): *Motivation and Personality* (2nd ed.). New York, Harper and Row.
Selidhes, Vol. 657, August 1st, 2004, pp. 31-32.
Shapiro, B. (2000): Who's afraid of being kicked off the island? The psychological appeal of Survi-vor. *Journal for the Psychoanalysis of Culture and Society*, Vol. 7, No. 2, pp. 274-280.

"But It's Not Real"

South African Youth's Perceptions of Reality TV

Nathalie Hyde-Clarke

Reality shows have dominated South African television over the past five years. The various channels (SABC1, SABC2, SABC3 and M-Net) have all broadcast some form of reality show in the past. Initially these shows were the British and American versions: *Survivor, The Amazing Race, The Apprentice, The Block, Popstars*, and *Idols*. Audiences have since been privy to South African versions of a variety of these shows, including *Big Brother* and *Project Fame*.

Big Brother was probably the first South African reality show to create a storm of controversy. This series centres around twelve contestants who are confined to a house for one hundred and six days. Each week the audience watching the show votes one 'housemate' out. There are cameras throughout the house, taping all activities of the housemates 24 hours a day. In the debate, there were questions around the content, which often featured nudity, sex, the use of risqué language, as well as racist comments. Although the *Big Brother* series was broadcast on a paid channel (M-Net) and subject to an age restriction (16+), highlights were edited and accessible to the general public during its daily two-hour 'open time' from 17:00 to 19:00. The airing of the questionable material (even though most of the controversial behaviour occurred outside open time) was hotly contested in the media throughout the duration of the three series *Big Brother 1* (2001), *Big Brother 2* (2002), and *Big Brother Africa* (2003).

In spite of the age restriction, many young people admitted to watching *Big Brother*. Even if the age restriction was adhered to among some families, due to the public nature of the debate in the major newspapers most were aware of the events that had occurred and the topics under discussion

This article will explore the responses of 60 teenagers (16-19 years with a concentration on 18-year-olds) to some questions about reality TV in South Africa, and about their perceptions of the *Big Brother* phenomenon. The responses were taken from a survey conducted in September 2004 and three group discussions.

The study was carried out among the top third students of the first year of Media Studies at the University of the Witwatersrand, Johannesburg, South Africa. This sampling strategy was preferred as it enabled the researcher to target students with a more nuanced understanding and comprehension of South African popular media. The unique aspect of Media Studies at the University of the Witwatersrand is the broad representation of all races in South Africa.[1] Thus, the study was assured of receiving data from a range of races, cultures and social backgrounds, although it should be noted that at the same time the sample is both small and consists of top students, which is why it is not representative of any larger groups of the South African population.

There were two parts to the study. The first was the distribution of a questionnaire that comprised five open-ended questions, designed to gauge how respondents understood the genre of reality TV, and their perceptions of the three *Big Brother* series. The second part included three small group discussions (with 20 students in each) discussing the findings of the questionnaire in more detail, and expanding the discussion to greater social issues.

Youth's thoughts on reality TV

'But it's not real' was the first response about reality TV in one discussion group. The participants were bemused that this genre would indicate a certain 'truthfulness' about the way 'real' people act in 'real' situations – only to watch scenarios that they felt were staged, thus manipulating the behaviour and responses of the programme participants involved. They also found that participants chosen for the series often were not representative of South African society. In fact, a few agreed that the players were more representative of a South Africa gone by (white, middle-upper class)[2] than of the new contemporary South Africa – in spite of the fact that South African reality shows had only begun to emerge in 2000/2001, six years after the first democratic elections. It is arguable that the audiences would have changed during that time.

The position that there is little real about reality TV persisted in the survey, where more than half of the respondents identified the constructed nature of the genre. Although most respondents appreciated the shows for their entertainment value, the reasons for a more critical stance included: the commercial nature of television programming; the need for players to 'show off' for the cameras and the audience at home, coupled with the incentive to win a large prize; the strategizing and alliance building with people with whom one would not normally associate; the false or extreme setting of the show; the intervention of the host or outsider; and the form of challenges or mini-competitions. One respondent maintained that reality TV was actually a combination of a game show and a situation comedy. Another felt, based on personal experience, that it was completely staged:

I've been on a 'real live' show, a youth talk programme. They called us in and told us what to ask. What's real about that?

In contrast, supporters of the genre accepted that whereas there may be an element of the surreal (being stuck in a house with the same people for many weeks), once the initial period of discomfort had passed, players' responses were 'real enough'.

These frameworks would prove quite useful when analysing the reactions of the youth to the specific series *Big Brother*.

Big Brother in South Africa

Big Brother 1 was a big success from the outset. Measurements showed that it had captured a 24 per cent share of the South African audience in its first five weeks – an increase from 15 per cent on M-Net in the weeks prior to the launch (Moodie, 2001, p. 1). More than 5,000 new subscribers to the channel registered in the first ten days, and there was an increase in advertising revenue (Koenderman, 2001, p. 99). Yet, in 2002, the television audience measurements indicated that *Big Brother 2* drew fewer viewers than other South African shows featuring on the public service broadcaster, SABC (South African Broadcasting Corporation) and the free-to-air commercial station etv. The most popular series for the debut week of *Big Brother 2* were actually soap operas, one American, *The Bold and the Beautiful*, and one South African, *Generations* (Seery, 2002a, p. 7). According to these statistics, *Big Brother 2* only accounted for 21 per cent of the available viewers during open time (17:00-19:00). The series' live eviction shows on Sundays proved to be the most popular, watched by as many as one million viewers (of the total available South African audience, estimated at 17.6 million). Although this figure seems comparatively small, it should be noted that, due to the cost of subscribing to M-Net, the viewers represent a higher income bracket – an important attractor for advertising revenue (Seery, 2002b, p. 10.). According to Seery (2002b), the viewing audience of M-Net in that year totalled 1,559,000, of which *Big Brother 2* was capturing 47 per cent.

From a commercial perspective, more people subscribed to M-Net during both seasons of the show. This could be linked to an increase in the general level of interest in reality shows among South African audiences. According to various views aired in 'Letters to the Editor' columns in major South African newspapers and the survey conducted at the University of the Witwatersrand in 2004, the decline in *Big Brother 2* viewership amongst M-Net subscribers was attributed to the lack of novelty in the second show: Not much had changed, the venue was the same, and the audience knew what to expect.

Big Brother Africa managed to entice a larger audience than both the previous shows. This was mostly due to the larger area in which the show was broadcast – continental as opposed to national – and the fact that the contestants were very different from those who came before. In the first two programmes, the majority of contestants were white and all were from South Africa. In the third series, there was only one white male, and contestants represented twelve different African countries.

The show was broadcast by M-Net to more than 40 countries. In 2003, the number of M-Net subscribers had grown to 1.3 million, 80 per cent of whom lived in South Africa (Robinson, 2003, p. 39). Carl Fischer, Director of local production at M-Net, said: 'It makes business sense: African content attracts subscribers' (cited in Robinson, 2003, p. 39). This sentiment was reflected in the study with 16- to 19-year-olds where many cited the differences in culture as a determining factor that caught their attention, in spite of concerns that the contestants did not represent the majority of people living in Africa, instead reflecting the higher strata of African society. Although the 12 contestants were from twelve different African countries, they all spoke English, indicated an interest in hip hop and designer clothing (Hollands, 2003, p. 3), and appeared to be from middle class families – not at all representative of the continent's population, which falls largely into the lower income category.

The public debate

Although a commercial success, the large and diverse audience created complications for the producers due to audience members' interpretations of decency and language. There were a number of complaints about the airing of pictures of nudity (bare bums), and one of the more 'conservative' countries, Malawi, cancelled the show due to its 'immorality' (Sapa, 2003, p. 3). This was partly due to the different means of broadcasting elements of the show. In South Africa, only M-Net subscribers could access the show 24 hours a day. However, in countries such as Malawi and Namibia, the show was aired on free-to-air channels, making it available to all television-owning audiences for up to one hour daily (catering to approximately 30 million people on the continent without a M-Net decoder or DSTV, digital satellite television).

Interestingly, even though subscription numbers were up for *Big Brother Africa*, advertising sales had decreased by as much as 25 per cent compared to the first two shows in the first few weeks. This was altered slightly after a sex scene involving South African and Ugandan housemates, proving the adage that 'sex sells' (Maggs, 2003, p. 60). Many, both in the public debate at the time and in the study in 2004, felt that this scene was intentionally broadcast with a view to increasing interest in the third series. A similar scene had been edited out of *Big Brother 2* due to 'broadcasting guidelines' (Kast, 2002, p. 12). Clearly, the broadcasting of the sex scene, a controversial 'shower hour' (when the audience watches the contestants taking a shower, either in the nude or a swimsuit or underwear) and the apprehension about the casual displays of intimacy – that some felt condoned the notion of casual sex in an age when HIV/AIDS is a large concern (Wax, 2003, p. 1) – meant that *Big Brother Africa* was hotly debated in public forums, such as newspapers and magazines.

As mentioned, this was not a new debate. Arguments surrounding the type of content aired and the behaviour encouraged had also been put forward during *Big Brother 2* in 2002, when 'Letters to the Editor' questioned whether the media were encouraging promiscuity (McIntyre, 2002, p. 12).

The issues of race and racial relations were also raised during all the *Big Brother* shows. In the first two shows, where black contestants were in the minority, white men won both versions. Organizers stated that one of the reasons for the lack of black contestants on those shows was the low number of entries from that group. However, applications for the second show reflected more entries from men than women (at a ratio of 3:2), and more from black than white persons (Mufweba, 2002a, p. 3). The race debate reached new heights in *Big Brother 2* when only non-whites were nominated for the first eviction – causing one contestant to state: 'White people have taken our land' (Mufweba, 2002b, p. 7). In 'Letters to the Editor' in *The Star*, viewers discussed whether *Big Brother* was a 'racist game for racists' – questioning whether the rules were designed for white players, and saying that in the spirit of nation-building, black participation needed to be enhanced (Mduba, 2002, p. 9). Although sentiments such as these created quite a stir, the producers were not too concerned as they maintained that the housemates were discussing real South African issues. Mr Fischer (Director of local production at M-Net) was quoted as saying:

> I don't believe that these kinds of conversations don't happen around the dinner tables all around South Africa (Mufweba, 2002b, p. 7).

Yfm[3] presenter Thomas Masengana reaffirmed this view:

> This is society. Blacks and whites don't know one another. We are seeing a South Africa that is changing, and if anything else, this is exactly what the show is proving (Mufweba, 2002c, p. 1).

In contrast, *Big Brother Africa* was predominantly black, with only one white male from Namibia (a contentious decision in itself). Although this alleviated much of the racial tension in the house, it still had an impact on the audience, as the number of white South African viewers appeared to dwindle (Sowaga, 2003, p. 5).

As mentioned before, there were also concerns raised about the language used, specifically by viewers SMS-ing. SMSs from viewers' mobile phones were first introduced in *Big Brother 2*. The messages were scrolled across the bottom of the television screen. Initially, Afrikaans and English swearwords appeared regularly, as well as slang phrases for genitals and sex. While there were warnings reading 'no under-16s', this did not seem to stop children from tuning in and sending SMSs themselves (Smit, 2002, p. 1). When confronted by viewers angry about the language, producers claimed that all the SMSs were being filtered through a blocking system, but that the system did not recognize some slang phrases and was being updated regularly (Smit, 2002, p. 1).

Youth's perceptions of Big Brother's controversial content

How did the youth in the study perceive the *Big Brother* phenomenon? Given that the majority of those surveyed were between 14 and 16 years old at the time *Big Brother 1* was launched, were they aware of the media debate about controversial material?

The great majority of the respondents in the survey and group discussions were aware of the debate on *Big Brother* in the media. However, many felt that the debate itself was staged so as to attract more viewers to the show – to watch for the scandalous behaviour of the housemates. One participant in a group discussion said:

> The debate was popular, but it didn't solve anything. There's this tension in South Africa between people being very sensitive to issues that seem indecent, and people wanting to be seen as liberal.

A respondent to the questionnaire even mentioned that it had become a standing joke in the family that they only watched the 'shower hour for the naughty bits' after reading about it in the newspapers. Still another's parents had banned them from watching *Big Brother* altogether, even during open time, due to the nudity and language.

This raised an interesting question: Should the networks be allowed to air nudity, sex, obscene languages and racist comments under the guise of reality TV? The resulting comments proved interesting. A few of these are listed below:

> If you want to watch something real, then expect to see the less flattering side of human nature.

> It's a part of life, it's around us everyday, it's hypocritical for parents to judge and say we can't watch.

> People wouldn't watch otherwise, no one wants to watch people talking about nothing all day.

> My parents won't talk about sex, so I need to get information from somewhere. What better way than through TV?

It should not be watched by children, there should be an age restriction. (This respondent was not aware that there had been an age restriction for *Big Brother*.)

All TV has obscene language. If you don't like it, don't watch it.

It's immoral to show such things, particularly in our culture (the black culture). It should be stopped, the younger people will want to act like that, experience things.

These comments provide insight into how young people may see reality TV as a reflection of the attitudes and behaviour exhibited in society. They may see the comments made by contestants as an accurate expression of how they are viewed by society, and adjust their perception of themselves accordingly. This is probably truer of younger viewers. Does this mean that participants in the programmes may become role models or protagonists? If so, the unscripted nature of reality shows may be potentially dangerous for social improvement in societies in transition – particularly if voiced bias is acted out.

The survey also pointed to a generally cynical perception the young people in the study have of South African society, that is, belief in a society that may be represented in shows like *Big Brother* as being racist, uncouth and overtly sexual. The respondents were definitely displaying a 'take it or leave it' attitude to this material being aired on television, which may be interpreted as a form of acceptance of such media content or a degree of resignation that such material is unavoidable in the world today.

Concluding remarks

South African media managers may face a conundrum between producing material that will facilitate the media's role as an agent of social change, and producing popular material that attracts audiences due to its controversial nature. As with a large number of developing countries there is a genuine need for television content to transmit meaningful messages to youth. Given the possibility that teenagers may identify with and emulate television characters, it is important to monitor the type of personalities displayed on television – even in reality shows. This is particularly pertinent in an environment where young people may genuinely believe that they receive more 'educational' information from television than from their immediate family.

Reality TV based on local content offers an alternative to the largely stereotypical world of entertainment media imported mainly from the U.S. That in itself makes local reality TV attractive to South African audiences. The type of content produced may be contentious, but it adds to the appeal of the programme. It also means that younger viewers will be interested in finding out what the fuss is all about. Even though reality shows with elements of nudity and strong language may have an age restriction, this will not deter issues from being discussed by major news providers. As such, the barrier between what is real and what is manipulated should be clearly defined for the youth in South Africa.

Notes

1. In 2003, there were 24,381 students registered at the University, of whom 15,820 are black. In Media Studies' first year, 80% of the class is black, Asian or coloured. The majority of first years are 18 years old.
2. It was decided that this is especially true of shows such as *Big Brother* and *The Block*.
3. Yfm's (Youth Radio) main target audience is black youth.

References

Hollands, B (2003) Unique African Big Brother starts. *Daily Dispatch*. 26 May. p.3

Kast, G (2002) What BB wouldn't let you see. *The Star*. 5 September. p.12

Koenderman, T (2001) *Big Brother* is really big. *Financial Mail*. 28 September. p.99

Maggs, J (2003) Subscribers go Bonkers. *Financial Mail*. 4 July. p.60

McIntyre, M (2002) Is media encouraging promiscuity? *Saturday Star*. 10 August. p.12

Mduba, S (2002) BB a racist game for racists. *The Star*. 22 October. p.9

Moodie, G (2001) *Big Brother* proves that its bite is as big as its bark. *Sunday Times*. 28 October. p.1

Mufweba, Y. (2002a) New BB faces race dilemmas. *Saturday Star*. 18 May. p.3

Mufweba, Y (2002b) *Big Brother* confronts race issue. *Saturday Weekend Argus*. 10 August. p.7

Mufweba, Y (2002c) Race spat is no blow to BB2's popularity. *Saturday Star*. 10 August. p.1

Robinson, S (2003) Reality TV, African Style. *Time*. 23 June. p.39

Sapa (2003) Conservative Malawi pulls plug on Big Brother. *The Star*. 7 August. p.3

Seery, B (2002a) *Big Brother* may be watching the house but not many viewers are watching *Big Brother*. *Saturday Weekend Argus*. 17 August. p.7

Seery, B (2002b) Tills ringing for BB2. *Saturday Star*. 7 September. p.10

Smit, A (2002) *Big Brother's* dirty SMS row. *Citizen*. 31 July. p.1

Sowaga, D (2003) Sponsors are not queuing up at BB Africa's door. *City Press*. 29 June. p.5

Wax, E (2003) Africa is watching *Big Brother*. *Cape Argus*. 16 July. p.10

Reactions of Nigerian Youths to the Reality Television Show Gulder Ultimate Search

Eno Akpabio

Nigeria's usual television menu changed somewhat in June 2004, when what was hyped as the country's first reality television show was aired on several stations. These stations included the Nigerian Television Authority (NTA) – the Federal Government owned station, which covers the length and breadth of the country – and a number of privately owned stations located in Lagos, the commercial capital (Silverbird Television, Murhi International Television, African Independent Television, Minaj Broadcast International, state-owned stations, as well as the South African Cable Satellite Network DSTV). The *Gulder Ultimate Search* took to the airwaves for one hour from 10.00 to 11.00 p.m. during a period of 21 days.

The Nigerian-produced programme featured ten Nigerian youths marooned on Snake Island in Lagos. The programme organizers tried to portray humankind at the primal level, so the islanders had the barest of comforts. They lived in a hut, cooked on firewood, drank from calabashes… Throughout the duration of the contest, they lived close to Mother Nature in the quest for a treasure chest that would make the finder about US$ 20,000 richer, while the rest of the islanders would go away with an equivalent of about US$ 2,000.

To be selected to feature in the *Gulder Ultimate Search*, the contestants had to pass a rigorous physical and intellectually demanding exercise at Sea School in Apapa, Lagos. Many of those who had registered at the web site set up for the purpose fell by the wayside, being unable to cope with the regiment of obstacles they had to overcome. At the end of the exercise, only ten made it – Emmanuel, Ezugo, Joy, Julian, Latanya, Sandra, Seun, Stanley, Uche and Yewande.

The selected islanders were given a map of the island to serve as a guide to the treasure. They engaged in a series of tasks, such as running many kilometres, swimming, climbing, and playing games. The first ten days were meant to encourage bonding among the participants, and they faced various challenges in pairs. The organizers also deliberately underfed them and this led to frequent squabbles, which added to audience attention and delight.

On the eleventh day on the island, the participants were treated to a feast featuring various delicacies and, understandably, they gorged themselves. They were not reminded that evictions would start on that day. After the meal, they were given the task of running from the venue of the feast (Ghost Castle) to Mamba Camp. Joy (a woman) came last and was evicted. Gloom descended on the camp, and the sound of shouting and singing, a usual fare during the first ten days, died down. The contestants were now down to business. From then on to the eighteenth day, for one failing or the other, six other islanders followed suit (in this order: Latanya, Emmanuel, Stanley, Yewande, Seun, Sandra).

With all these evictions, only three persons were left – Ezugo, Julian and Uche – to find the treasure. Julian, formerly of the U.S. Marines, was at first the toast of viewers because of his leadership skill and charisma. (Provision was made for viewers to send text messages.) As the days went by, his desperation to win got the better of him to the extent that he manifested selfish and unbecoming character traits. He usually took offence and resorted to swearing and four-letter words at the slightest provocation. He also began to drop in viewers' estimation.

Even though he was the strongest of the ten islanders, he did not have the patience and intelligence to pull of a win. In the last stages of the contest, he was first to get to the point were the treasure was buried, but could not bring himself to discover it. It was Ezugo, who arrived last, who actually found the treasure. The calmness and intellect he had displayed throughout the contest finally paid off. When Julian discovered he had lost out, he expressed his frustration in full, issuing forth vigorous expletives.

The treasure chest contained a repackaged bottle of Gulder beer. The whole contest was to be used to reposition and relaunch one of Nigeria's oldest lager beers. The brand, which hit the market thirty-five years ago, had started to lose its market share – hence the show was intended to reverse the decline and breathe new life into the brand. Yinka Daramola (Group Account Director) and Akin Adesola (Creative Director) at Insight Grey – the marketing communication agency that handled the brand – gave further insight into the contest in a press interview.[1] They suggested that:

> The concept of the ultimate search was to present at the primal level man overcoming obstacles... such that when people observe the lives of these ten young men and women... and see the way they overcame these obstacles, you see the 21-day activity reflecting the longer term aspect of one's life. And as we surmount the obstacles, the brand celebrates our success; it now becomes the icon, the model of your struggles and eventual success.

These words go to show that Nigerian Breweries Plc, in bankrolling the contest, was very clear-eyed about what it intended to achieve – the contest was to refocus attention on the brand. And the way to achieve this objective was to present audience members with a show that had ingredients – conflicts, tension, suspense, challenges, etc. – guaranteed to keep them glued to the programme.

This leads us to some aspects of theories of reality-deviation of media contents.

Theories of reality-deviation

McQuail (1987: 196-199) discusses different theories of why media contents deviate from (social) reality. Some of the theories he puts forward are functional theory, conspiracy or hegemony theory, organizational theory, and the audience as determinant. Relevant here are, not least, the first and last variants – functional theory and audience as determinant.

It is generally agreed that the mass media have various functions, such as to inform, educate and entertain us. In doing this, the media are usually supportive of the values of society and try not to offend their potential audience (McQuail 2000: 80). Among other things, the media may try to "meet certain needs for models, objects of identification, value reinforcement", as well as engage in deviation from reality which ensures that the burdens of our existence are more bearable (McQuail 1987: 197).

The theory of the audience as determinant sees the deviations of media contents from reality as audience-driven. Among other things, the media are said to respond to the audience's demand for comforting myths, nostalgia and social amnesia (ibid: 198).

The organizers of the *Gulder Ultimate Search* appear to have been acting out the script of these theories. Wanting audience members to identify with the contestants in their struggles against the elements and the vagaries of nature is a throwback to the nostalgic African past, free of the complications of modern living. Audience members are thus enveloped in the myth that they can make it if they are determined and hardworking like the contestants. So they see in the contestants their models for overcoming various challenges.

The *Gulder Ultimate Search* show "transported" viewers to the world of the islanders – a temporary escape from the harsh realities of the Nigerian environment, with programme makers knowing well that audience members predominantly use the media for relaxation and escape (ibid: 198).

An exploratory research study

Marketing people's ingenuity when it comes to selling their product knows no bounds. They utilize the mass media to advertise the brand; they engage in sales promotion, point of purchase advertising and even pay to ensure their brands are portrayed positively in films, etc.

Nigerian Breweries Plc has taken marketing to another level in Nigeria by embarking on Nigeria's first reality TV show *Gulder Ultimate Search*. Going by reports,[2] ten cameras were placed at strategic points on Snake Island to capture every move of the contestants; there were sixty crew members of which five were from South Africa utilizing equipment worth US$ 400,000. By the time the cost of buying airtime in the various TV stations is thrown in, coupled with the money paid the contestants and other sundry expenses, the realization would dawn that this was indeed a capital-intensive endeavour.

The natural questions that would immediately trouble one's mind are: Was it worth it all? Do audience members now see Gulder beer as "the icon, the model of [their] struggles and eventual success"? Has there been a change in attitude or consumer behaviour as regards the brand? Did the concept of recreating the past positively connect with audience members?

An exploratory study was conducted with the intent to elucidate audience members' reactions to the *Gulder Ultimate Search* and what significance or meaning the programme had for them.

Focus group discussion was adopted as a research strategy for seeking to understand audience members' attitudes and behaviour (Wimmer and Dominick 2000: 119). Two focus groups of undergraduate students at University of Lagos and Ambrose Alli University, respectively, made up the respondents. The former university is a Federal Government owned institution located in Lagos, while the latter is a State owned university located in the Niger Delta region.

There were nineteen undergraduate students in all, twelve of the University of Lagos in the first focus group and seven of Ambrose Alli University in the second. More females (13) than males (6) took part. The majority (14) of respondents were between 21 and 30 years of age, whereas three were under 20 and three above 30. All the respondents were single.

Because respondents constitute a small group of university students, their answers are, naturally, not representative of any larger population strata.

A number of guiding written and oral questions allowing open-ended answers were posed to the respondents. These questions touched upon the recreation of primal existence in the show, association of the brand with struggles to overcome life's challenges, strength versus intellect during the treasure hunt, male and female contestants competing on an equal footing, comparison of values portrayed in the programme with African values, and relationships between the contestants.

Findings

Primal existence

There were sharp disagreements as regards the portrayal of primal level humankind struggling against the elements. Some respondents were of the view that the modern clothes and shoes worn by the contestants did not correctly reflect this – going bare-footed and wearing traditional African attire would have been more like it. Some other respondents were of the view that the island environment in addition to traditional drinking mugs, drums and preparation of meals using firewood were sufficiently representative of the African past. They felt that expecting participants to go bare-footed and scantily dressed would have exposed them to injuries from thorns, snake bites, etc., although these respondents conceded that participants, being urbanites, brought their upbringing to bear on their new environment and activities on the island.

Gulder beer as the embodiment of struggle and eventual triumph

The respondents identified the various challenges facing the participants as reflecting life's ups and downs. This sentiment was reflected both in their written and spoken answers and so could not be attributed to a bandwagon effect. Perhaps the participants see in the obstacle course of the programme the dire economic situation in Nigeria. There was also a consensus that with determination and will power one can overcome obstacles in the path to achieving one's goals and ambitions. Some of the female respondents identified with Sandra, the last female to be evicted, who had "survived" when some of the male contestants had fallen by the wayside.

However, the respondents did not see the brand as having any role or being an embodiment of life challenges and expected victory. In fact, their conscious attitude to the brand remained unchanged (at least in the short term). Some of the respondents do not consume alcohol and so their response was expected. Those who so consume alcohol indicated preference for brands other than Gulder. Some of the respondents even said uncomplimentary things about Gulder beer, such as causing headache, hangover, excessive urination, etc.

Physical activity vs. intellect

It was agreed that the tasks given the contestants were physically challenging with intelligence forming some percentage of abilities required. To corroborate this, a respondent pointed at Joy who appeared to be the strongest among the female contestants, yet she was the first to be evicted. Also, respondents pointed to Julian (formerly of the U.S. Marines) who was the strongest of the pack, yet he was not the one who eventually discovered the treasure.

Non-discrimination as regards tasks given male and female contestants

The male respondents were neutral on possible gender discrimination as regards tasks given. The female respondents had sharply differing viewpoints. Some felt that it was a *fait accompli* that a male contestant would eventually find the treasure, as men are naturally stronger than women. Another point in the favour of those canvassing this viewpoint is that the last three contestants were males. However, some other female respondents pointed to the fact that Yewande and

Sandra stayed longer than some of the male contestants. They also pointed to the fact that Sandra was the best swimmer among the whole lot on the island.

Comparison of values portrayed in the show and African values

As for values in the show vis-à-vis African values, two areas were hotly debated by the respondents: intimacy between contestants and the show's sleeping arrangement. Some respondents felt that physical embrace between males and females as well as acts such as a female contestant plaiting one of the male contestant's hair were un-African. Some others felt that there was nothing wrong or un-African about these behaviours. As regards the sleeping arrangement, some felt that there ought to have been separate abodes for the male and female contestants. Some other respondents were of the opinion that the sleeping arrangement was fine.

There was, however, agreement that lack of sexual relationship between the contestants corresponds to our values, which frown at such displays. One of the contestants[3] had told me that the organizers would not have discouraged sex during the programme. But the respondents felt that even though some of the contestants were quite close, the restraint they exhibited was a function of the values of society. Having sex on television would have been the height of irresponsible behaviour and would have been repulsive to viewers.

Respondents took exception to Julian's ill treatment of Yewande and felt that he was a bad influence on other contestants. His use of four-letter and swear words, obviously a carry over from his American sojourn, encouraged others to do likewise.

Conclusion

Gulder Ultimate Search elicited intense emotions from the focus group respondents, which meant that it was able to "transport" these and, probably, other viewers to the world of the ten contestants, that is, identification occurred with them as they ran many kilometres, swam many metres, climbed trees and other ingenious obstacles placed on their path in search of glory. In a way, the respondents saw in the struggles of the participants their own life story and felt that as the participants overcame challenges, the sky also is no longer their limit to achieving their goals in life.

Interestingly, no respondent reacted negatively to the evictions, nor did any of the respondents see this as a blow to their goals and ambitions. They all uniformly focused on the motivation to succeed. Minor meanings derived from the treasure hunt include humility and avoiding focusing too much on one's skills or abilities as "the race is not to the swift" (the Holy Bible, Ecclesiasts 9: 11).

The organizers of the programme wanted to use the show to breathe new life into their brand but – at least based on the findings of this exploratory study – ended up motivating these young Nigerian respondents to believe in themselves, to exhibit humility and ultimately more than before to achieve their goals and aspirations in life. However, a more positive attitude towards Gulder beer was not among the benefits derived from the programme.

Nigerian Breweries Plc and their marketing communication consultants – Insight Grey – must be commended for exhibiting proper understanding of Nigerian youths according to the theory of audience as determinant of media contents and packaging a show whose functionality was clearly apparent – motivating our youth to achieve what they want to achieve. The fact that the marketing objective apparently was not achieved is as it is sometimes: you win some, you lose some.

In any case, when the modern mass media are utilized in advertising products and services, the advertisers' expectation is creation of awareness and not measurable attitude change. Expecting the achievement of the latter would amount to asking for too much. Similarly, there is inconclusive evidence as regards the media's ability to change behaviour even though there is a natural concern about sex, violence and other appeals to the lowest common denominator.

However, the findings of this study as regards the *Gulder Ultimate Search* open up a world of purposes to which reality TV shows can be put from the purview of cultural norms. Instead of showing the whole activity of contestants on a daily basis, the show organizers edited the recordings into a one-hour presentation and effectively too, therefore bringing it in line with the cultural norms theory, which posits that through selective presentation and tendentious emphasis on certain themes, the mass media are able to get impressionable members of society to pattern their lives after such presentation (Folarin 1998: 69). The functionality of reality TV shows in tackling social ills and motivating young people needs further exploration in light of the effectiveness of the *Gulder Ultimate Search* in achieving audience identification with the contestants and their challenges.

Notes

1. *This Day*, the Saturday newspaper July 10, 2004, p. 10
2. *This Day*, the Saturday newspaper July 31, 2004, p. 36
3. Interview with Seun Bakare in this researcher's office in the Department of Mass Communication, University of Lagos, on Thursday September 9, 2004.

References

Folarin, Babatunde (1998). *Theories of Mass Communication: An Introduction*. Ibadan: Stirling-Horden Publishers.
The Holy Bible.

McQuail, Denis (1997). *Mass Communication Theory: An Introduction* (2nd edition). London: Sage Publications.

McQuail, Denis (2000). *McQuail's Mass Communication Theory* (4th edition). London: Sage Publications.

Wimmer, Roger D. and Dominick, Joseph R. (2000). *Mass Media Research: An Introduction* (6th edition). Belmont, California: Wadsworth Inc.

"This is it" – South African Youth's Reading of YizoYizo 2

John Gultig[1]

YizoYizo 2 is a thirteen-part television series commissioned by the South African Broadcasting Corporation's (SABC) Education Television in support of the national Department of Education's *Tirisano* (Let's Work Together) campaign. The series, flighted in the first half of 2001, was immensely popular, breaking the South African television viewership record that had been set by *YizoYizo 1* in 1999. *YizoYizo 3* was aired on South African television in 2004.

YizoYizo 2's aim was to *inform* viewers of some of the critical problems facing youth and schooling in South Africa, *raise debate* about possible solutions, and then evoke some form of *social action* to change these conditions. But, unlike many other educational dramas, *YizoYizo* producers decided that the veil had to be ripped off rather rudely: The drama, they believed, had be 'in-your-face' and controversial if it was to raise debate in the constituencies in which it wanted to raise debate.

Many of the issues that *YizoYizo* set out to tackle were issues that communities were loath to talk about: rape, sex between teachers and learners, rampant drug use, the glamour of gangs and crime. *YizoYizo's* challenge was to find a way in which these things could be revealed as they were, in all their ugliness, while still sending out a message of hope and of change. In other words, the drama had to communicate the idea that the ghetto could be fabulous.

Thus the title: *YizoYizo* is *s'camto*[2] for 'this is it', or 'this is how things are'.

YizoYizo 1 and *2* certainly did raise debate, in school, among youth and in the media. *YizoYizo 2* generated more than 20 broadsheet pages of newspaper copy during its 13-week run! It has become, at least in one large sector of South African society, a well-recognised, if controversial, television 'brand': It has generated tons of publicity, been accused of being too sexually explicit, of being culturally-insensitive, and of glorifying gangsterism and violence and encouraging copycat behaviour.

But the findings of our evaluation suggest a different and far more interesting picture of *YizoYizo's* impact on young viewers and, by implication, on the way in which youth read (interpret) media messages. Our study suggests that young people aged 13 to 20 read the series in a far more nuanced way and are more discerning than their parents or the media think they are. They are also *better* readers of television than their parents.

Far from being impressionable and easily influenced, South African youth demonstrate a high level of engagement with *YizoYizo* characters and a sophisticated understanding of the plot and the messages it carries. They are able to interpret the content of the series in an allegorical sense. Ultimately, the overriding message they took from *YizoYizo 2* was that of redemption and inspiration. Young viewers, it seemed, read *YizoYizo 2* as a story about ghetto fabulism.

Research method

In order to assess the impact of *YizoYizo 2*, we conducted a study in and around 22 schools in six provinces in South Africa. The sites were all characterized by a high poverty index and relatively little previous intervention by the national Department of Education, which manages schools in South Africa. The sample of 1,200 Grade 7 to 12 students was chosen to reflect *Yizo Yizo 2's* target audience. As a consequence most respondents were young African people in township schools.

The study had two phases, midway through the series and again once the series had ended. In each phase we conducted:

- surveys of about 1,000 learners (an additional 200 learners were added to the second phase survey in order to check for specific demographic differences)

- in-depth interviews with 200 teachers, principals, and parents

- about 50 focus groups with teachers, learners, and parents.

In addition

- a survey of 750 parents was conducted after the series was completed.

- diaries were written by about 20 teachers and learners throughout the series.

- school observations occurred for about a week during the series.

- discourse analyses of the series was conducted by three expert media analysts.

- a content analysis of press coverage of *YizoYizo 2* was conducted.

YizoYizo's approach

YizoYizo 2 is a consciously youth-orientated educational drama. This is evident in many of its rather unconventional – for educational drama – cinematic choices. It is shot in a style reminiscent of an MTV music video, with seamless and rapid cuts between scenes. It uses saturated colours and frequent use of wide-angle lenses to construct township and prison scenes that are at once real and fantastic. All of this is accompanied by a *kwaito*[3] soundtrack, punctuated by snatches of gospel and even opera. In some cases traditional prison songs are remixed as a gospel/kwaito hybrid.

While many of the cinematic choices might create a feeling of the hyper-real, *YizoYizo 2* also chose to have a dialogue track comprised almost entirely of a deep street *s'camto* – and in prison an even deeper and more inaccessible version of this township dialect. The prison scenes were shot in Diepkloof[4] and starred a recently released in-mate. The school and township scenes were meticulously researched. All of this gave *YizoYizo 2* a gritty realism that appealed to young viewers at an intense emotional level, our research showed.

It is this intensity of youth identification with *YizoYizo 2* that is interesting. Young people surveyed were generally positive about programmes like *Soul City*,[5] but what *YizoYizo* seemed to have been able to do was create a loyalty, a sense of ownership, by young viewers.

YizoYizo 2 has, contentiously among some, consciously drawn on existing youth culture to build its profile and thus viewership. A number of its actors are established *kwaito* stars. But it has also contributed to *building* this culture. One of the interesting aspects of *YizoYizo 2* is how it has become a popular culture phenomenon. Its CD has gone platinum, and some of the singers have gone on to become stars. Moreover, the press now uses it as a reference point to identify singers or actors.

The very tight 'niching' of the drama has led to significant generational differences in both the extent and quality of viewing. Our research shows that while some 70 per cent of both learners and parents interviewed in our survey watched an educational drama like *Soul City*, *YizoYizo 2* drew significantly more young viewers (around 85%) than older viewers (around 60%).

Different perceptions of YizoYizo 2

It seems that *YizoYizo 2's* formatting choices has led to a trade-off in breadth of viewership for an intensity of viewership among a particular segment. But it was not the controversial prison sex scene[6] that made the difference. While it did generate a lot of heat – far more in the press than in the minds of, particularly, younger viewers – it seems that while some, mainly older, viewers were shocked enough by this to turn off, many more turned on. And a significant number polled said they returned to watching *YizoYizo* a little later.

Older viewers, it seems, were anxious about *YizoYizo* 2 for two reasons:

- First, they found its determinedly youth style 'foreign' and alienating. They said the language – both verbal and body language – used in the series was offensive.

- Second, parents were uncomfortable about what they regarded as explicit renditions of sex.

Very few parents objected to the violence of *YizoYizo 2*, a common complaint of *YizoYizo 1*.

In many cases the parents and adults who objected most strongly were those who watched very few episodes of *YizoYizo 2*. Their discourse was characterised by an inability to remember character names (people were often referred to in terms of other roles they played), confused explanations of plot lines, and an inability to make the links between an undesirable act and its consequences. An inability to make the link between act and unpleasant consequence by adults was often translated into a belief by parents that their children would involve themselves in copycat behaviour.

In contrast, our research showed that young people were media-savvy; they understood when an act was depicted in order to discourage young people from taking part in this kind of act. They have grown up with television as part of the furniture in their homes. They understand story structures and make quick and good sense of often quite complicated visual cues. And they have all grown up in a democracy: They believe (in an often quite apolitical and possibly naïve way) that they, as individuals, have choices, that they can make choices that will change their lives, and that education is vitally important to all of this.

YizoYizo 2's impact

This media-savvy, allied with the extraordinarily strong identification young people showed with *YizoYizo 2* and its characters, lead us to suggest that youth certainly have been empowered by *YizoYizo 2* to make changes in their lives. This sense of empowerment is most visible around social issues like drug abuse, crime, or *communication* with teachers and parents – rather than direct classroom matters. It is also most often expressed in terms of individual actions rather than systemic actions.

The last point is, for us, interesting. A number of *YizoYizo 2* messages stressed systemic actions, like working with police through a community policing forum, or getting parents more involved in schooling through parent teacher meetings. While youth heard these messages, they were received in a lukewarm way. The images and story arcs from *YizoYizo 2* that resonated were those in which friends, parents or teachers put themselves out to help someone in trouble. So, for instance, learners were moved by Sticks' support for his friend Bobo[7] as he went through the agonies of drug withdrawal. And they remembered teacher Zoe's support for Mantwa[8] as she struggled to read.

This individualist take on key messages tells us quite a lot about the power and limits of educational drama:

- First, sophisticated television watchers – and South African youth are this – relate to what drama does best, namely, tell human stories about individuals (strongly developed characters) who overcome hardship (classic story lines). They are able to and do read these allegorically. This is so precisely because *YizoYizo 2* evokes their world and their dilemmas so powerfully. Television drama is not good at telling stories about inanimate systems, and youth read this as an attempt to preach. So while they hear the message, they remain unconvinced.

- Second, the lack of resonance of story lines related to systemic change may also have to do with the total lack of credible systems in which youth (and adults) read these messages. Any educational drama is but one of many stories circulating (and often competing) at anyone time. The strong attachment to individual stories of redemption, and the invisibility of systemic messages, may be a consequence of viewers knowing that the only possible form of action is individual action. The lack of systems is, in the thinking of people like Singhal and Rogers,[9] an impediment to social action. The lack of systems in our contexts might well mean that the emotional and messaging power of the drama may dissipate over time.

Message 1: Don't do crime

As we have suggested, *YizoYizo 2's* social messages – around crime and drugs particularly – were particularly strongly heard by younger viewers. The most common unprompted message that both learners and adults associated with the series is that crime does not pay:

> In the case of Papa Action and Chester,[10] they are showing that you can be the wise guy, but you will end up in jail. It doesn't pay to be a wise guy. (Gauteng, focus group, male learner)

The power of this message in *YizoYizo 2* was important as it effectively addressed the criticisms aimed at the first series. As regards *YizoYizo 1*, concerns were raised about the 'glamorous' portrayal of gangsters and criminal behaviour. One of the key aims of *YizoYizo 2* was to de-glamourise criminal behaviour and illustrate the consequences of this behaviour.

Probably the most powerful carrier of this 'de-glamourisation' message was the brutal depiction of prison life in *YizoYizo 2*. This message was carried in a number of story lines, most notably in the incarceration of the two *YizoYizo 1* gangsters Chester and Papa Action. All viewers commented often and unprompted, that the depiction of life in prison had convinced them that whatever short-term lure crime might have, it was not worth it.

Much of the controversy around *YizoYizo 2* has centred around a sixteen second prison sex scene in which a common prison practice of one (subservient) man – the formerly glamorous gangster providing a more powerful man with sexual favours – is depicted. The encounter occurs under a blanket and uses sound – mainly – to depict the progress and climax of the sexual act.

It is also contrasted with two other arguably more explicit scenes, one in which a prisoner is cut open and another in which Thiza[11] has casual sex with a schoolgirl.

While youth did comment on the prison scene, and did find the scene shocking, they did so for very different reasons to those expressed by parents and in the public debate, and they noticed other story lines, which parents simply did not.

While the public outcry – led by an ANC (African National Congress) Member of Parliament and fuelled by journalists – was characterised by moral and cultural condemnation, and called for the programme to be banned, youth read it as a cautionary tale. They read it in relation to the many other humiliations they saw prison heaping on Chester and Papa Action. They saw it as an act of power and abuse, they saw it as depiction of reality, and they opposed calls for *YizoYizo 2* to be banned:

> After seeing what happened to criminals in prison I am afraid to commit crime because I don't want to go to jail. In jail life is very difficult. Chester was forced to sleep with a man and I don't want to fall into the same trap. (Northern Province, focus group, male learners)

> I can say through the imprisonment of Papa Action they were trying to show us life in prison, most people think that in prison things are difficult, you eat terrible food, you find people with hot heads, all that sort of stuff. You end up being scared of jail and you avoid things which might take you there. (Gauteng, focus group, male learner)

Equally importantly, youth did not lose sight of other story lines. While the moral horror of the prison sex scene led to focus group discussions among parents that were dominated by this scene (particularly suggestions that male-on-male sex was culturally alien), youth spoke about the Hazel's[12] rape trauma, about whether Thiza was right to sleep with someone else because Hazel was 'pushing him away', and, significantly, they noticed that Thiza took a condom from his bag when he did indulge in casual sex.[13]

Message 2: Don't do drugs

Throughout the series *YizoYizo 2* shows the physical, mental and social consequences of drug use, in particular through tracking the story of Bobo, an addict, who with the help of the school and his friends manages to break his addiction.

Partly in response to criticisms that *YizoYizo 1* glamourised drug use, and encouraged young people to experiment with drugs, *YizoYizo 2* spells out the consequences of both its use and dealing in it. Youth read *YizoYizo 2* as saying:

- Drug dealers will be arrested and imprisoned, and this will occur mainly when the community comes together and works with the police.

- Drug withdrawal is a painful, difficult and terrifying process.

- Drug addiction leads to a loss of self-control and 'loss of dignity'.

- Ultimately, drug addiction leads to crime and the murder of innocent people (which, in turn, causes extreme pain to others).

The vast majority of learners (93%) understood *YizoYizo 2's* message about drugs and 16 per cent of learners said that the most important lesson *they* had learnt from *YizoYizo 2* was 'Don't do drugs':

If you use drugs you became totally destroyed. (2nd learner survey)

I learned that drugs shatter many dreams. (2nd learner survey)

Peoples taking drugs don't have a future. (2nd learner survey)

This was echoed in focus groups where learners spoke movingly of how disturbing they found the scenes in *YizoYizo 2* where Bobo battles to kick his habit, and of Sticks' (Bobo's best friend) trauma in supporting his friend through these times. The friendship was read as a powerful message of hope and of the importance of being a friend at all times, not just in good times.

An interesting finding was that while young viewers identified strongly with the realistic depiction of drug dangers, and with the strong characterisation of this story arc's main protagonists, Bobo and Sticks, they were a little cynical at the 'too-easy' resolution of the problem.

YizoYizo 2 had, in fact, attempted to address the criticism that *YizoYizo 1* offered very few solutions and resolutions that were too protracted, by programming 50-minute rather than 30-minute episodes, and as far as possible resolving story lines within episodes. In this instance, it seemed to undermine the story's credibility, probably because young South Africans are acutely aware of drugs and drug addiction.

Consequentialism

Yizo Yizo 2 deliberately used a 'consequentialist' approach to its teaching; in other words, think about your action because it has *consequences* and these are often personally unpleasant.

One criticism of this approach is that it leads young people to speak about not doing crime or drugs because of the consequences this would have for them as individuals, not because of any moral conviction or acknowledgement of the painful consequences for other people. While this is a vital first step in changing behaviour and developing deeper value systems among youth, it does emphasise external rather than internal agency. It tends to overshadow an assessment of the moral consequences of criminal or violent behaviour and depends heavily on perceptions of efficacy in the police and justice systems.

While the series did show the victims dealing with the consequences of criminal behaviour (the Shai family coping with Mrs Shai's murder, and Hazel and Dudu dealing with being raped), viewers tended to concentrate on the consequences for the perpetrator.

Message 3: Let's talk sex... but...

Yizo Yizo 2 wanted to get people talking about important social issues that were often not spoken about, for a host of reasons. Many of these related to issues of sexuality and, in particular, dealing with the trauma of rape.

The desire to talk

Most of the young people interviewed express a deep desire to talk to their parents about the critical issues they face, and which are raised by *Yizo Yizo*. They want to be heard and want to be taken seriously. Although talk about intimate issues like sex remains a difficulty, all groups recognised and accepted *Yizo Yizo 2's* message that this should happen. In this sense *Yizo Yizo 2* has put this issue firmly on the agenda, and created the space for talk to begin even though, in many instances, this still has not begun.

Again, where parents have begun raising issues it seems to be for reasons related to the unpleasant *consequences* of not talking. A number of parents said that although they found it difficult, and 'not within their culture', they realised that the 'dangers of this world' – HIV/AIDS, in particular – made it vital that they talk to their children.

Predictably perhaps, children and parents had very different ideas of what constituted talk and of what *Yizo Yizo* was saying to them about dialogue. Parents, mostly, used *Yizo Yizo* story lines as a deterrent: They told their children that if they didn't behave properly they, too, would land up in prison! Children regarded this as monologue rather than dialogue, which is what they want; they often said their parents didn't *listen* to them.

An interesting (and pleasing) finding was the fact that children read the *YizoYizo 2* message as one, which encouraged *them* to initiate talk. In many instances they dismissed the culture arguments and pro-actively raised these issues with parents. The fact that some 80 per cent of young people watched *YizoYizo 2* in family groups of some kind, suggests that intimate talk is still difficult; the conditions for it to increase are increasingly present.

The fear of copycat behaviour

Adults seemed to read *YizoYizo 2* as far more sexually explicit than either youth or our content analyses suggest it was. They often missed messages about condom use, or about intimacy without sex (told through the story of Nomsa's and Javas' relationship[14]). Instead, they noticed the prison sex scene, or Thiza's casual fling with a girl, or the fact that Nomsa and Javas were found in bed together by Nomsa's mother, or the relationship between Elliot (a teacher) and KK (a learner). While they seldom suggested that *YizoYizo* would encourage violent or criminal copycat behaviour, they suggested that they knew of 'many' instances where sexual activity had been encouraged. When prompted, most copycat reports seemed to be of a symbolic kind: stories of learners mimicking verbal and body language used in *YizoYizo*, or using the term *yizo* as a pseudonym for having sex.

Youth and adults read *YizoYizo 2's* sexual messages very differently. Thiza, one of the main characters, has casual sex with a girl from his school after being 'pushed away' by his girlfriend, Hazel. Many parents were appalled at this scene, were unhappy about the depiction of teenagers having sex, and were uncomfortable with having to watch scenes such as this with their children. They were concerned about the possibility that their children would imitate Thiza's actions, and start having sex. They often spoke of the girl as a 'prostitute' (although she is constructed in the series as a girl who has always 'fancied' Thiza), and accused her of 'tripping' (seducing) the hapless and forlorn Thiza into sex. Finally, many objected to the fact that she was 'on top' during sex. Almost no parent spoke about the important messages or questions, like:

- the fact that before having sex Thiza very obviously takes a condom out of his bag.

- whether Thiza was justified in resolving his grief and confusion through sex.

Young viewers, however, were not shocked or appalled by this scene, probably because for teenagers having sex is part of their reality, and part of the 'truth' that they believe their parents are trying to avoid. What is more interesting, is that when referring to this scene, it was almost always in the context of:

- commenting on Thiza's use of a condom. (Many compared this scene to the fact that in the series *The Bold and the Beautiful,* where 'people have sex all the time', one never sees anyone using a condom.)

- a discussion about how Hazel and Thiza are dealing with Hazel's rape trauma, one of *YizoYizo 2's* central story lines.

Dealing with rape

Dealing with the trauma of rape is a key *YizoYizo 2* message and is carried through two concurrent story lines and characters. One story is about Hazel, one of the lead characters and Thiza's partner. She was raped by her former boyfriend, Sonnyboy, a taxi-driver. The other story links Papa Action and Dudu, another schoolgirl. Dudu was gang-raped by Chester and Papa Action.

Dudu is represented as someone able to deal with her rape. She befriends and supports Hazel. Later, they form (with assistance from teacher Zoe) a rape support group. But Dudu's story arc is about the difficulty of testifying. She has to decide whether she will testify against Chester and Papa Action. Her father tries to discourage her from doing so because of the shame discussing the rape will bring on the family. Dudu eventually finds the courage to testify and, while Chester denies everything, Papa Action comes clean.

Hazel, on the other hand, is not able to talk about her rape, has recurring nightmares about it, pushes Thiza away, and, penultimately, attempts suicide. Later, through teacher Zoe's assistance, she is able to resolve her trauma by becoming part of a support group. The episode where Dudu finds the courage to testify was regarded by young viewers as the second most 'popular' episode. The reasons given by learners for liking this episode are moving and profound. Learners, especially girls, seemed to feel a great deal of affinity and sympathy towards Dudu, and expressed their admiration for her. Almost half of the learners who chose this episode mentioned Dudu's bravery and courage, and 40 per cent of the learners who chose this episode said they believed it would encourage people to speak out if they found themselves in a similar position. The way they talked about her indicates the extent to which they have formed a 'relationship' with her:

> It was so painful hearing someone explaining how she was raped. (2nd learner survey)

> Dudu showed us that we must not be ashamed about what has happened in our lives. (2nd learner survey)

Hazel's story also evoked intense sympathy from girls (but this often did not translate into 'wanting to be her friend') but a high degree of irritation from boys. Many boys saw her as 'selfish' and criticised her inability to talk about rape, something they never said about Dudu.

We can speculate as to why Dudu's and Hazel's rapes are responded to so differently by boys and girls:

- The *YizoYizo* story is read in a context where rape is horrifyingly common. This may explain why boys said they would have understood Dudu had *she* been traumatised (because she was gang-raped) but Hazel had very little excuse for her trauma (because she was raped by her former boyfriend).

- Hazel's internalised trauma also conflicts with a kind of overriding sentiment among young viewers, namely that they liked people who 'faced' their fears, and were brave enough to act to overcome these. Hazel's inner turmoil was not recognized as this.

- Finally, viewers did not recognise any girls as powerful characters (even though two women teachers were clearly central characters). In effect, it could be argued that despite attempts to do so, *YizoYizo 2* ultimately constructed too many of its 'strong' women as too one-dimensional and as victims. Hazel, for instance, is a rape survivor and, essentially, is the message carrier for this only. Zoe, the most popular teacher, is to be retrenched, and largely carries the story only of a caring teaching vocation. In contrast, male characters, like Thiza and Javas, have far more dimensions, and flaws, and are, ultimately, read as far more active and able.

The difficulty of telling a story about rape that leads to desirable social action remains a difficulty, it seems. (The *YizoYizo 1* evaluation also talks about the need to re-assess its communication strategy in this regard.) While a massive majority of learners identify it as wrong, they have more difficulty about understanding why, or what needs to be done to rid South Africa of this scourge.

In conclusion: YizoYizo as a redemptive story

If one were to judge *YizoYizo 2* from media coverage it would seem to be a bleak, sensationalist story about crime and violence.

Our research suggests that the target group read a very different story. *YizoYizo 2 did* choose a controversial strategy of reflecting South African youth and school realities as gritty, tough, and nasty; as the series' title suggests, 'This is it!', this is a reality dominated by crime, violence, drug abuse, and resource deprivation.

But virtually all the individual story lines were read by viewers as redemptive and inspirational. Ultimately they understood the programmers' desired message, that the 'ghetto can be fabulous'. They did this by showing how bad people can become better people, that people with initiative can overcome the constraints of ghetto life, and that all of this is made possible through perseverance and support from peers, families and teachers.

Had our research concluded after the first phase, conducted shortly after the prison sex scene episode, we might have concluded that viewers had read *YizoYizo*

2 as primarily sensationalist entertainment. Parents in particular, but youth also, dwelt quite a bit on issues of crime, sex and violence.

But even at this stage many young viewers (but not adults) had noticed and been moved by Thiza's journey. Thiza dabbled in crime and was present at the murder of KK's father. This proved a powerful lesson to him. He subsequently gives evidence against Chester's gang, despite being advised by his brother Jakes that this would be dangerous, and despite the possibility that he was laying himself open to criminal charges by testifying. Thiza also, voluntarily, offers to assist KK's mom run her shop as a means of redemption.

Research conducted after the series had ended was filled with respondent recollections of redemptive and inspirational moments and messages in *YizoYizo 2*. Many related to overcoming hardship, but others were more joyful, like stories of Supatsela School's (the fictitious township school in the series) technology competition triumph (see below), or the 'light' signified by the matric farewell after the 'dark tragedies' of *YizoYizo*, or the journey of one teacher from simply being a good teacher to being a good *and caring* teacher.

These messages about hard work and self-belief were identified by 20 per cent of learners as the most important lesson they had learnt from *YizoYizo 2*. In addition, 30 per cent of learners identified better behaviour, hard work and the encouragement of their fellow students as the positive improvements they could make at their school.

Supatsela's technology triumph

A thread running through the entire series was that of Supatsela learners involved in a technology project. First, they built a set of speakers that they used at their Valentine's Day bash. Then they made a go-cart that they ultimately entered into a schools' technology competition. The intended message was that technology could be fun.

Learners read the technology message as an inspirational message – it suggested that with hard work they could achieve a great deal. It was also read as a message that high levels of school resourcing does not matter as much as having learners and teachers who are resourceful:

> The Model C school[15] had technology [computers] but what they didn't realise is that the technology is in the mind. (Western Cape, focus group, mixed learners)

But learners also learnt that technology was fascinating. In some instances this is expressed in almost dreamlike wonder:

> I liked the part where Javas was looking at the gate opening up and in that he was watching it and wondering how it works. It opens our minds and makes us want to experiment. (Western Cape, focus group, mixed learners)

The 'technology is fun' message was received, powerfully. It seems that the combination of a charismatic protagonist (Javas), a story line that ran for almost the entire series, and a classic narrative structure (challenge, achievement, setback and ultimately victory) helped capture viewers' attention.

Papa Action's redemption

One of the 'dark' stories, about the redemption of Papa Action, *YizoYizo's* archetypal villain, also ran as a thread through the entire series. At the end of *YizoYizo 1*, Papa Action is arrested for rape and other criminal activities. He enters prison full of bravado but as the story progresses his partnership with Chester crumbles, he faces his drug addiction and, ultimately, publicly apologises for and confesses to his rape of Dudu.

Young viewers have always related to Papa Action, even while *they* said they hated what he did. This ambiguity was one of the reasons why *YizoYizo 1* was accused of glamourising gangsterism.

But with *YizoYizo 2* this fascination pays off, we believe. Young viewers (70%) understand the message that Papa Action confesses because he was truly sorry for what he had done rather than for some more self-serving reason. But because *they*, in some ways, identify with this charismatic character, *they* are thrilled that he is eventually able to turn his life around. Learners, it seems, are interested in his story because it could be a story about themselves, and so *they* invest something of themselves in the fate of this character. Thus, when he tries to change, he has the absolute support of their audience. It is also more likely that, because learners identify with this character and his struggles, *they* will hear the messages about the dangers of drugs and the possibility of turning one's life around:

> The suffering that Papa Action was in when he didn't take drugs showed I could change in life by stopping taking drugs. (2nd learner survey)

But, at the same time, they recognise very clearly that Papa Action has committed a crime, that the rape of Dudu was horrific, and that Papa Action deserved to be punished. They understood that his 'redemption' – his 'brave' action and his attempt to change his life – was a consequence of his punishment and rested on his willingness to sacrifice his future to 'make things right'.

YizoYizo 1 and *2* is firmly rooted in youth culture, and, ultimately, provides youth with a strongly inspirational and redemptive message. It tackles many of the critical issues facing young people in a provocative and undidactic manner. It uses production techniques that may in some eyes serve to create messages that are obscure or ambiguous. Yet our evaluation shows that, despite their parents' fears, young people interpreted *YizoYizo's* messages mostly as they were designed to be read.

The respect *YizoYizo* producers had in young viewers has been repaid.

239

Notes

1. An early version of this article was presented to the South African Association of Child and Adolescent Psychiatrists in September 2001. The article reports on an extensive research project undertaken by the South African Institute for Distance Education (SAIDE) and the Community Agency for Social Enquiry (CASE) between March and August 2001, involving over 100 researchers and fieldworkers. Sue Marshall (CASE), Siven Maslamoney (South African Broadcasting Corporation, SABC) and Helene Perold contributed to the initial version of this article.

2. *S'camto* is a township-based patois that uses Zulu, Xhosa, English and Afrikaans. It is commonly used by township youth.

3. *Kwaito* is a South African township version of hip-hop; it draws on American hip-hop and rap, gospel, and traditional South African rhythms like 'mbaqanqa'.

4. Diepkloof is a real South African prison situated on the outskirts of Soweto.

5. *Soul City* is South Africa's longest running educational soap opera. It uses radio, television and print and follows a far more conventional edutainment style. It is also screened by SABC Television.

6. The single most controversial scene – at least in terms of media coverage – was a prison scene in which a gangster 'hero' from *YizoYizo 1* is forced to have sex with a more 'senior' prisoner.

7. Sticks and Bobo are two parentless teenagers who live in a township shack and fare for themselves. In *YizoYizo 1* Bobo is revealed having a serious drug problem.

8. Zoe is the 'ideal' caring English teacher, contrasted in this series with either authoritarian old-style teachers or teachers who simply don't care. Mantwa is a flighty girl who tends to get through school with smiles and flirtatious moves rather than learning.

9. See Singhal, A. & Rogers, E. (1999) *Entertainment-Education: A communication strategy for social change*. London: LEA publishers.

10. Chester and Papa Action were the gangster 'heroes' from *YizoYizo 1*. They were young, rich, violent, and wreaked havoc in the community surrounding Supatsela School, the school in which the story takes place. They were arrested and imprisoned towards the end of *YizoYizo 1*.

11. Thiza is one of the two male heroes in *YizoYizo*. He is a senior student at Supatsela but is drawn into crime in *YizoYizo 1*, momentarily, but with devastating consequences. In *YizoYizo 2* he struggles to redeem himself.

12. Hazel is Thiza's long-term girlfriend. She was raped in *YizoYizo 1* by a taxi driver (and former boyfriend) and much of *YizoYizo 2* is about her trying to deal with the consequent psychological trauma, and about Thiza's inability to understand her reactions towards him in sexual situations.

13. This is significant because of the HIV/AIDS pandemic in South Africa. Some people criticized *YizoYizo 2* for not addressing this strongly enough.

14. Javas and Nomsa, senior school students, are the other two key 'role model' characters in *YizoYizo* (other than Hazel and Thiza). They have a long and loving but complicated relationship, which includes sex but is portrayed as being far more about love and respect.

15. 'Model C schools' *was* terminology used in the apartheid era to refer to a particular category of privileged white schools; the term is now used to refer generically to suburban schools that are open to all races. *YizoYizo* deliberately set out to suggest that 'township schools' – the old blacks-only schools that are still used only by black children because they are in poor, black, townships – could compete with privileged schools if they put their minds to it.

YizoYizo: This Is It?

A Critical Analysis of a Reality-based Drama Series

René Smith[1]

YizoYizo ('This is it'/'The way it is') is a drama series based on reality, aired on South Africa's national public service broadcaster, South African Broadcasting Corporation (SABC). The series was created by SABC Education as an 'edutainment' drama, designed to augment the national Department of Education's (DoE) educational strategies. Laduma Film Factory won the tender to produce the first series, *Yizo Yizo*, with Bombshelter/Bomb Productions also responsible for *YizoYizo 2 & 3*.

The series was 'groundbreaking' in presenting the experiences of black youths on television, in achieving consistently high audience ratings and in exploring the potential of the medium in bringing about social change (Smith, 2002). It has won numerous local and international awards including Avanti Awards as well as the Cinema Tout Ecrand Award for Best International TV Series at the 2001 Swiss Cinema and TV festival (Manyaka, 2002).

The half-hour first series of thirteen episodes was commissioned with the express aim of exposing what stakeholders describe as the 'crisis in education' and the general collapse of the culture of learning and teaching. The hour-long second series offers closure to and demonstrates consequences of issues uncovered in *YizoYizo* (e.g. rape, corporal punishment, criminal activity). The final series, *YizoYizo 3*, aims to explore some of the challenges facing young adults as they negotiate their way through higher education, unemployment, sexuality and HIV/AIDS.

According to stakeholders, *YizoYizo* aims to confront denial about the culture of learning, reflect the crisis in education, and create a platform for debate. In reflecting real-life impediments to learning, the creators of the series aimed to challenge existing models of educational broadcasting, which are seen as essentially 'message-driven' and which resemble a 'banking' approach to education (Maslamoney, 2000).

The series was informed by research to the extent that specific issues, themes and subsequent social messages are incorporated in an audio-visual text, which both entertains and educates. SABC Education contends:

11

Messages were designed to address core problems in schools. Carried by the characters and demonstrated through various stories in *YizoYizo 2*, the messages were based on research into real-life school situations (SABC Education, 2002: 9).

On-going attempts to evaluate the series' potential to bring about social change are reflected in macro research (SABC Education, 1999; SABC Education, 2002). Following the above, the series can be defined as 'entertainment-education' in that the series is constituted of messages, purposively designed to

entertain and educate, in order to increase audience member's knowledge about an educational issue, create favourable attitudes, and change overt behaviour (Singhal & Rogers, 1999).

Significantly, participants of focus group research consistently describe the first two series as educational or edutainment (Smith 2002).[2] This is confirmed in macro research where 26 per cent of learners 'spontaneously described *YizoYizo 2* as being educational' (SABC Research, 2002: 16).

This article begins with a contextual analysis of the series, followed by discussions on the meanings and messages implicit in a text, which purport to present authentic representations of township high school experiences. It highlights the contradictions of representing the *real* by questioning the imperative of including graphic images in representing real life experiences. The article employs a discursive approach in assessing the way in which the series engages violence and gender relations in particular (Hall, 1997). It adopts a cultural studies approach in assessing the relationship between the text, audiences and context and is informed by writings on black popular culture as well as a previous reception analysis on *YizoYizo 1 & 2* (Smith, 2000 & 2002; Dent, 1992).

Contextualising the series

About 75 percent of South African households have access to a television set and a recent national survey of South African youth confirms that television is the most popular form of entertainment among teenagers, with more than two-thirds of respondents saying they watch television more than five times per week (Kaiser Family Foundation, 2001).

The production of *YizoYizo* began as an initiative of SABC Education, in partnership with the DoE and its 'Culture of Learning, Teaching and Service' campaign (COLTS). The partnership was guided by a common vision 'to exploit the possibility, or the potential of television for education in this country [...]' (Maslamoney, 2000).

The primary goal of the first series was to 'confront denial' about the culture of learning and teaching in some township schools. Factors impeding this *status quo* include inadequate leadership, and lack of resources, parental involvement and learner organisation. Fundamentally, the series had to engage the challenge facing the DoE in getting people to, at the very least, acknowledge the 'crisis' in schooling. While the series was originally aimed at high school learners, educators and parents, its reach extended to the general public over eight years of age (Gibson, 2000).

YizoYizo 1 includes events occurring within a time frame of one academic year and exposes the harsh conditions of some township high schools. Learners are forced to negotiate their way through 'a general culture of violence': from the presence of gun-wielding youth, to corporal punishment, continuous and sustained harassment, bullying, drugs, and a general unsafe school environment. Simultaneously, *YizoYizo* audiences are bombarded by images of the general demise of a culture of learning and teaching, and the ever-present threats of violence within and outside school premises (rape, hostage drama, murder, attempted murder, harassment, bullying, corporal punishment, hijacking, 'community justice', etc.). Although the last few episodes of *YizoYizo 1* attempt to resolve some of these issues, a key concern remains the lack of closure for many of these issues and, more significantly in terms of entertainment-education, the lack of clarity around social messages.

The hour-long second series (aired almost two years later) allowed for the development of character and attempted to bring closure to some of the key issues raised in the first series (rape, drug abuse, crime). Significantly, perpetrators of violence are taken to task and survivors of rape begin a journey of healing. A culture of learning and teaching commensurate with the national Outcomes-Based Education is identified.

YizoYizo 3, the hour-long final series aired in 2004, continues to reflect a culture of violence, with the ever-present threat of 'San Jose's' thugs.[3] The series explores drug abuse and the tragic effects of addiction, eating disorders, xenophobia against fellow Africans, and sexuality. In addition, it reflects the ever-present threat of sexual harassment and HIV/AIDS. While the imperative to acknowledge the presence of violence and HIV/AIDS in the daily lives of all South Africans is commendable, the series' ability to deal with violence against women and HIV/AIDS in a sustained manner is questionable.

'This is it' – messages and meanings

YizoYizo is located within a context of socio-political injustices sustained by historically specific inequity and inequality. South Africans live amidst the very real threat of crime, hijacking, rape, harassment, etc. It is, therefore, important to question representations of violence in a dramatic form to audiences living the reality. For example, while the series aims to create dialogue about these very real challenges, it also uses violence for dramatic intent. As argued elsewhere, violence is used as

243

a cliffhanger in a few episodes of the first series (Smith, 2000). The anxiety, tension and suspense created around violent acts – through the use of music, camera shots and techniques – contribute to the drama of, and that is, *Yizo Yizo*.

The ability to authenticate real life experiences was of prime importance to creators. To this extent particular attention was placed on the use of 'street language' and the local music genre *kwaito*.[4] Authenticity is a significant research area in macro evaluations of the series. According to *Yizo Yizo 2's* evaluation, '[a]uthenticity is key to achieving a depth of identification between audiences and characters and facilitating genuine reflection' (SABC Education, 2002). Similarly, according to the creators of the series, this 'street language' is significant in authenticating the experiences of township youth and 'telling it like it is' (Gibson, 2000). However, it is interesting to note the evaluation of the first series found that although 'learners spoke about the series being "real" ', '[m]any felt that *Yizo Yizo* exaggerated the problems' (Research Partnership, 1999: 72).

While the first series alerted the South African viewing public to the conditions of schooling in some township schools, the second series focused more on 'dealing with' and finding solutions to problems and experiences exposed in the first series. As mentioned, the second series aimed to offer closure to some of the unresolved issues exposed in the first series. For example, a notable development is the incarceration of Chester and Papa Action, who terrorised some of the learners at 'Supatsela High' (a fictitious township high-school) and the community in general. Thiza's decision to turn state witness and testify against the thugs, demonstrates the importance of 'facing up to wrongs', or making 'the right' choices.

Yizo Yizo 2 aims to demystify gangster lifestyles as glamorous. The series explores the experiences of Papa Action and Chester in prison as they negotiate their way through prison 'rights of passage', which include sexual relations with other gang members to secure their safety. The scene involving Chester in sexual relations with a male inmate in exchange for protection in prison elicited the fiercest criticism, with calls for the series to be banned. Consequently, *Yizo Yizo* was debated in the media and even parliament (Home Affairs Portfolio Committee, 2001).

In supporting the DoE's 'Tirisano Campaign',[5] *Yizo Yizo 2* highlights the issue of literacy through Mantwa's inability to read at a level equivalent to her peers. In keeping with the broader education framework, Mantwa's English teacher, Miss Cele, adopts a 'learner-centred' approach and encourages 'critical consciousness' (Freire, 1970).

While *Yizo Yizo 1 & 2* has specific references to education and story lines revolve around 'Supatsela High', *Yizo Yizo 3* presents a different approach to engaging challenges facing young people. Activities take place within the inner city, at 'San Jose', Technikon, University, strip clubs or on the streets. Here the focus is on the experiences of youths, post-school. Audiences witness challenges facing central characters as they embark on higher education and, more significantly, personal development, sexuality, body consciousness, unemployment, and HIV/AIDS.

The final series is currently (2004) being evaluated to determine the reach and impact of the series. A noticeable feature of the final series is the emphasis on the drama of life, of challenges facing young people not directly connected to education and educational bodies. Significantly, certain stereotypes persist including that of Mantwa as temptress. The connection between her teasing behaviour and her being harassed and used by men is created. While this is juxtaposed with Snowey's self-affirmation, it is supported by images of scantily clad women as objects of the male gaze, of phallic associations, including women rubbing car bonnets and dancing against poles – all of which reaffirm gendered stereotypes perpetuated by the dominant patriarchal culture. The significance of these depictions is questionable, as they do not contribute constructively to the development of the story.

Mantwa's decision to leave her 'sugar daddy' and all the luxuries she dreams of because of her steadfast commitment to safe sex is commendable. So, too, is the choice to have one of the key characters, Gunman, discover and reveal his HIV positive status. However, the series does not truly interrogate and expand upon the very real experience and effects of HIV/AIDS and thus fails to engage the 'urgency of the HIV/AIDS emergency', a key priority of the DoE's 'Tirisano Campaign'.

In view of the extensive reach of the programme and of its overall aim to promote dialogue, I contend the series falls short of presenting a sustained approach to dealing with and offering solutions to the very real challenges of living with HIV/AIDS and the threat of harassment as a form of violence against women – a theme that is present throughout the series. It would indeed be interesting to assess the findings of the final series' evaluation, particularly in relation to the first series where

sexual harassment and rape features [were] one of the lowest scoring messages with only 1% of participants having learned 'must not harass or rape girls' (SABC Education, 1999: 44).

Macro research

The evaluation of the first series was conducted by a consortium including the Centre for the Study of Violence and Reconciliation (CSVR), Coordinated, Management Consulting, Helen Perold & Associates, and the South African Institute for Distance Education (SAIDE). Similarly, *YizoYizo 2: The evaluation of its impact on viewers* was conducted by The Community Agency for Social Enquiry (CASE) and SAIDE.

Aired on the most watched television channel (SABC1), *YizoYizo 1 & 2* were watched by over two million viewers and over 3.5 million viewers, respectively (SABC Research, 1999 & 2001). The most watched episode of the second series, episode eight (aired on 10 April 2001), had audience ratings indicating a reach of over four million viewers (SABC Research, 2001). While some parents claimed the series impacted negatively on the behaviour of learners, research highlighted the overwhelming positive response by learners to the second series.

In relation to the graphic approach taken in *YizoYizo 1*, '32% of parents, 27% of principals and 24% of teachers stopped watching the series at some point, mainly because they were embarrassed and shocked by the rape scenes and the abusive language'. While some learners stopped watching (11%), this was mainly due to their parents but also because they themselves felt 'embarrassed and shocked'. In terms of negative impact, '24% of learners and 33% of parents felt *YizoYizo* encouraged the use of bad language'.

According to *YizoYizo 2: The evaluation* (SABC Education, 2002), the following were some of the key findings:

- Among learners who said the series had a positive impact, more than 90 per cent felt that *YizoYizo 2* encouraged them to become more active in school life.

- At the end of the series, 75 per cent of learners who watched *YizoYizo 2* said criminals should be handed over to police, compared with 55 per cent who said this half way through the series (after episode six).

- 90 per cent of learners surveyed said they discussed issues arising from *YizoYizo 2* with their friends.

- About 71 per cent of learners who watched *YizoYizo 2* agreed that criminals could repent and become better people.

- The highest recorded scores in terms of messages were 29 per cent for 'do not take drugs', and 19 per cent for 'crime does not pay'.

In addition to these lessons, the series was complemented by on-going dialogue about issues raised in the series. The multimedia approach included supplementary material, which not only supported issues raised in the series, but also advanced the aims of *YizoYizo*. This approach included the distribution of print material as well as on-going radio and television initiatives in the form of talk shows primarily. Stakeholders refer to this approach, supported by the distribution of music in the form of the *YizoYizo* soundtrack and outreach initiatives, as a 'social action' approach (Maslamoney, 2004).

Setting the scene:
'In your face' approach to getting the message across

As mentioned, the aims of the series include creating dialogue and debate about township high schools and confronting denial about the present state of schooling (Gibson, 2000; Mahlatsi, 2000; Maslamoney, 2000). The following analysis questions whether or not these aims and objectives are compromised by the style of the programme. Key questions in this regard are: Is the inclusion of representations of violence necessary to the story? Are representations of violence and gender relations in *YizoYizo* necessary to articulating the ultimate aim of the narrative? What is the significance of having the series informed by real-life experiences?

The importance of meaning is embedded in interpretations by the creators, audiences and characters of the series. In other words, each stakeholder approaches the series with individual interpretations of the definition or definitions of violence. Addressing the issue of violence within a context of increasing social and personal violence is particularly difficult as one risks under-representing or exaggerating violent acts. That is, someone used to violent language and experiences involving car jacking, or robbery at gunpoint, may or may not interpret the language and images used in *YizoYizo* as violent or aggressive. While it is true that conceptions of violence are relative to one's living reality and experience, there are definitions of violence which include a basic functionalist approach (all that is physically and emotionally harmful), as well as an approach situated within the discourse of violence in television programming. With regard to the latter, violence is defined as

> the overt expression of physical force (with or without a weapon) against self or other, compelling action against one's will or pain of being hurt or killed, or actually hurting or killing (Gunter & McAlleer, 1990: 80).

Specific forms of violence, such as sexual harassment, can be defined as 'unwanted sexual conduct', including suggestive language (sexual innuendo). Gender-based violence includes

> physical, sexual, or psychological harm or suffering of women – including threats of such acts, coercion or arbitrary deprivation of liberty, whether in public or private life (Soul City, 1999: 5).

Based on the above definitions, there are indeed various acts that can be construed as violent within the series *YizoYizo*. These include criminal violence, such as car jacking (also referred to as hi-jacking) perpetrated by Chester on two separate occasions, the attempted murder of Mr. Edwin Thapelo and Zakes and the rape of Hazel and Dudu. These forms of violence are otherwise referred to as 'social violence' (as distinguished from political violence) inclusive of arson, assault, and the various forms of abuse (Thipanyane, 1992). Some other examples of violence (depicted or inferred) in the series include corporal punishment, meted out with severity on the part of the first principal, hostage drama; the dunking of a learner's head down a toilet; Baba Nyembe's beating of thugs in *YizoYizo 2*; as well as the murder of KK, Ria and Thebza in *YizoYizo 3*.

Representing the real

Examining issues of genre and 'reality' is particularly important to this discussion as perceptions of violence and gender, for example, are connected to opinions advocating these portrayals reflect reality. Realism is indeed contentious and at the root of mixed emotions. The disparity exists somewhere between opinions advocating that the shock of reflecting serious dysfunction in our schools will, hopefully, trigger corrective behaviour, and opinions about possible copycat actions as well as about violence against characters (Miya, 1999).

Philip Schlesinger *et al.* (1992) confirm the view that there are other social and cultural experiences, which impact on the 'fear' and apprehension of crime and violence. These authors of research on *Women viewing violence* highlight the importance of *personal experience* (of violence) in relation to the fear of violence and crime. To this extent, women subjected to domestic violence were particularly disturbed by representations of similar scenes on television and indicated that 'certain types of media tended to *increase* their anxieties about crime' (Schlesinger 1992, 41). Furthermore,

> when asked to choose from a list of those formats most likely to *increase* fear of crime, women were most likely to choose television news, television dramas and documentaries, television films, and the tabloid press (ibid.).

This view is confirmed by research commissioned by Dr Daan van Vuuren, previous General Manager of Broadcasting Research, SABC, over ten years ago. Some of the findings included:

> *Real life* violence, such as in news programmes, had a greater emotional effect on viewers *who were exposed* to such situations (for example people living in strife-torn areas such as Thokoza) [whereas]

> *Fictional* violence, as depicted in action programmes like *MacGuyver*, had a greater emotional effect on viewers *who did not* experience real-life violence [...] (SABC, 1994: 16).

As suggested earlier in discussions on the meaning of the title of the series, *YizoYizo/ This is it* alludes to the programme's relation to 'reality' or real life depictions of violence and gender relations, for example. The contradictions of having a dramatic text reflect a gritty reality – of fusing factual and fictional – allows the series to assume an 'authoritative perspective'.

Concluding remarks

This article illuminates the nature of *YizoYizo* as edutainment or entertainment-education, emanating from the national public service broadcaster's education wing. It begins with a contextual analysis before turning to some of the messages as well as to key findings of macro research. It draws attention to the graphic approach chosen and to the contradictions of fusing factual and fictional. In positioning the series as an authentic reflection of township high school life, the series assumes an authoritative position, which renders meanings and messages as representative of real experiences of black youth attending township schools. In promoting this authenticity, real life ex-gangsters are used as actors along with colloquial 'street language'.[6]

YizoYizo exists in a very real context of alarming national crime statistics, a HIV/AIDS pandemic and increasing threat of violence against women, amongst others. Most significantly it exists in a context where many forms of violence affect all strata of society where real violence is documented in factual programmes and other media on a daily basis. It therefore remains problematic that the series utilises graphic images as a reflection of this reality, that the reliance on entertainment violence is defended as a reflection of reality. To this extent, I argue the series uses violent images, and the 'gun' in particular, for dramatic intent.

Similarly, it is my contention that within the context of South Africa, specific care and a concerted effort should be made in addressing the realities of HIV/AIDS and gender-based violence – both of which feature as themes in the series but which are not adequately explored.

Representations are symbolic constructions, which stand for the real. It remains important for the national public service broadcaster, to evaluate the use of the graphic approach in engaging educative messages. Furthermore, I contend a certain level of social responsibility is entrusted upon the creators of the series in authenticating real life experiences, especially in representations of violence.

Notes

1. The financial assistance of the National Research Foundation towards an M.A. in Cultural and Media Studies, University of Natal, is hereby acknowledged. Opinions expressed and conclusions arrived at are those of the author and not necessarily attributed to the National Research Foundation.

2. This article is informed by a reception analysis including 27 black, African youths between the ages of 18 and 21 (Smith, 2002).

3. Some of the central characters of the first two series move to the city in search of better opportunities and take up residence at 'San José'. 'San José' is a block of flats/apartments in the inner city, which is run by a corrupt landlady, who employs thugs to intimidate tenants into paying rental and abiding by her rules. San José is a central feature of the final series, with multiple story lines revolving around it.

4. *Kwaito*, a popular local genre, also makes use of what stakeholders refer to as 'street language', which is a mixture of dialects emerging from 'eKassie' (the townships). The series employs subtitles to assist audiences understand the colloquial/slang used by characters.

5. The 'Tirisano Campaign' is the Department of Education's national strategy for improving school effectiveness.

6. The use of slang and indigenous African languages also challenges the hegemony of the English language in telling the stories of and constructing meanings for African language speakers.

Bibliography

Bomb Shelter Productions, http://www.thebomb.co.za

COLTS. 1999. *YizoYizo: A COLTS TV drama series*. Information booklet.

Gibson, A. 2000. Director/Writer of *YizoYizo*. Telephone interview conducted on 10 April 2000.

Mahlatsi, T. 2000. Director/Writer of *YizoYizo*. Interview conducted at Shooting Party on 23 March 2000.

Maslamoney, T. 2000. Programme Manager for Youth, Adult and Public Education. Interview conducted at SABC Education on 18 March 2000.

Perlman, H. 2001. *YizoYizo 2* Magazine: *More than Just TV*.

SABC Education. 1999. *An evaluation of YizoYizo*. The Centre for the Study of Violence and Reconciliation, Co-ordinated Management Consulting (Pty) Ltd., Helene Perold & Associates cc; and The South Africa Institute for Distance Education.

SABC Education. 2002. *YizoYizo 2: The evaluation of its impact on viewers*. Auckland Park: SABC Education (CASE & SAIDE).

SABC Research 1999. Audience Ratings for *YizoYizo*.

SABC Research 2001. Audience Ratings for *YizoYizo 2*.

Tim Modise Show. 2001. Debate (and phone-in programme) including studio guests: ANC MP Lulu Xingwana, Director/Writer of series, Teboho Mahlatsi and writer from the Business Day, Nomavenda Mathiyane. SAfm (19 March, 09:00-10:00).

YizoYizo (Episodes 1-13). 1999. SABC & Laduma Film Factory/Shooting Party.

YizoYizo 2 (Episodes 1-13). 2001. SABC & Bomb productions.

YizoYizo 3 (Episodes 1-13). 2004. SABC & Bomb productions.

YizoYizo 2: Speak Out. 2001. Debate facilitated by Sylvia Volenhoven. SABC1, 20 March, 21:30-22:30.

Secondary sources

Asmal, K. 1999. Call to action: Mobilising citizens to build a South African education and training system for the 21st Century. http://education.pwv.gov.za/Media/Speeches_1999/July99/call_to_action.htm.

Dent, G. (ed.). 1992. *Black popular culture* (A project by Michelle Wallace). Seattle: Bay Press.

Home Affairs Portfolio Committee. 2001. *Film and Publications Board on classification of YizoYizo. 28 March 2001*. http://www.queensu.ca/samp/migdocs/Documents/Minutes/280301.htm.

Fahey, L. 2004. YizoYizo 3 – South Africa. In *The Communication Initiative*. http://www.comminit.com/experiences/pds52004/experiences-1956.html.

Freire, P. 1970 (reprint 1996). *Pedagogy of the oppressed*. London: Penguin.

Gunter, B. & McAleer, J. L. 1990. *Children and television. The one-eyed monster?* London: Routledge.

Hall, S. 1997. *Representation: Cultural representations and signifying practices*. London: Sage/Open University

Hargrave, A. M. 1991. *Taste and decency in broadcasting*. BBSC Annual Review. London: John Libbey.

Kaiser Family Foundation. 2001. Program for Health and Development in South Africa: loveLife. http://www.kff.org/docs/sections/safrica/loveLife.html.

Khumalo, F. 2001. Bring me the telly, I want to smash it to pieces. In *City Press*. 18 March. 20.

Manyaka, E. 2002. *YizoYizo* – the return. In *Interkom*. (186). 20 June-3 July. 10 & 11.

Maslamoney, S. 2004. SABC1 Presentation. Fourth International Entertainment-Education Conference (EE4). Somerset, South Africa. 26-30 September.

Mbatha, S. 2001. Let's get real: the hysteria about *YizoYizo* just shows we're homophobic. In *The Sunday Independent*. 18 March. 1.

Miya, S. 1999. Abezemfundo bathi makubhekwe isifundo esisemdlalweni weTV *iYizo Yizo* yodumo. In *Umafrika*. 9-13 March. 5.

Mowlana, H. 1995. Communication and development: Everyone's problem. In C. Okigbo (ed.). *Media and sustainable development*. Nairobi: Media Congress.

Phalatse, M. 2001. *YizoYizo 2* continues the magic. In *Intercom* (SABC news magazine). 1-14 February. 6.

SABC. 1994. Violence on TV. In *SAUK Radio & TV*, July-September 15-19.

SABC Education Website. 1999. Information on the national education curriculum. http://www.sabceducation.co.za/frameset_educators.html

Sapa. 2002. Shock report on pupil rapes. In *The Natal Witness*, 23 January. 1.

Schlesinger, P., Emerson Dobash, R., Dobash, R. P. & Weaver, C. K. 1992. *Women viewing violence.* London: British Film Institute (BFI).

Singhal, A. & Rogers, E. 1999. *Entertainment-Education: A communication strategy for social change.* Mahwah, New Jersey: Lawrence Erlbaum Associates.

Sithole, M. 2001. Student killed for his trendy *YizoYizo* hat. In *Sunday Tribune.* 17 June. 7.

Smith, R. 2000. *YizoYizo: This is it? Representations and receptions of violence and gender relations.* M.A. Thesis, University of Natal, Durban.

Smith, R. 2002. The social impact of the television series *YizoYizo:* Retaining the local in a global world. Convergence: Technology, culture and social impacts. International Research Seminar.

Smith, R. 2003. YizoYizo as Entertainment-Education: Television and social change. In *Perspectives in Education.* 21 (2). 155-165.

Smith, V. (ed.). 1997. *Representing blackness: Issues in film and video.* London: Athlone Press. 97-122.

Smith, V. 1992. The documentary impulse in contemporary U.S. African-American film. In G. Dent (ed.), 56-64.

Soul City. 1999. *Violence against women in South Africa.* (A resource for journalists). Johannesburg: Soul City Institute for Health and Development Communication.

Thipanyane, T. 1992. Violence and its effects on children. In Centre for Development Studies (ed.), *International Conference on the Rights of the Child.* Bellville: University of the Western Cape. 43-48.

Authors

Eno Akpabio

Ph.D., Lecturer
Department of Mass Communication
University of Lagos
Lagos
Nigeria

Michaella Buck

Ph.D., Psychologist, Associate Professor, Chair
Social Sciences Department
Intercollege
Nicosia
Cyprus

Valerio Fuenzalida

Senior Researcher, Director
Postgraduate Degree Diploma in Audience Studies
Catholic University in Chile
Santiago de Chile
Chile

Christa Gebel

Diplomaed Psychologist
JFF – Institut für Medienpädagogik in Forschung und
Praxis (Institute for Media Research and Media
Education)
München
Germany

Gudmund Gjelsten

Cand. Theol., STM, Director
Bergbo Media
Barstadvik
Norway

John Gultig

Freelance Researcher, Consultant
Toronto
Canada
Formerly Senior Researcher, South African Institute of
Distance Education (SAIDE), Johannesburg, and
Lecturer, University of Natal, Pietermaritzburg
South Africa

Maya Götz

Dr., Head
Internationales Zentralinstitut für das Jugend- und
Bildungsfernsehen (IZI, International Central Institute
for Youth and Educational Television)
München
Germany

Annette Hill

Professor of Media, Research Centre Director
School of Media, Arts and Design
Harrow
United Kingdom

Dorothy Hobson   Dr., Senior Lecturer
                               Media, Communications and Cultural Studies
                               University of Wolverhampton
                               Wolverhampton
                               United Kingdom

Nathalie Hyde-Clarke   Ph.D., Lecturer
                               Media Studies
                               University of the Witwatersrand
                               Johannesburg
                               South Africa

François Jost   Professeur
                               La Sorbonne Nouvelle – University Paris III
                               Directeur, Centre d'Études sur l'image et le son
                               médiatiques (CEISME) (Centre of Study on Media
                               Images and Sounds)
                               Paris
                               France

Alice Y. L. Lee   Dr., Assistant Professor
                               Department of Journalism
                               Hong Kong Baptist University
                               Kowloon Tong, Kowloon
                               Hong Kong

Thaïs Machado-Borges   Dr.
                               Department of Social Anthropology and Latin-
                               American Institute
                               Stockholm University
                               Stockholm
                               Sweden

José Ramón Pérez Ornia   Professor of Audiovisual Communication
                               Universidad Complutense
                               President, GECA (Gabinete de Estudios de la
                               Comunicación Audiovisual)
                               Madrid
                               Spain

Robyn Quin   Professor, Dean
                               Faculty of Communications and Multimedia
                               Edith Cowan University
                               Western Australia

Nayia Roussou   Ph.D., Media Expert, Associate Professor, Chair
                               Communications Department
                               Intercollege
                               Nicosia
                               Cyprus

Doobo Shim	Assistant Professor Information and Communication Management Programme Faculty of Arts and Social Sciences National University of Singapore Singapore
Asbjørn Simonnes	D.M., Ph.D., Associate Professor Volda University College Volda Norway
René Smith	Ph.D. Candidate Culture, Communication & Media Studies University of KwaZulu Natal Durban South Africa
María Dolores Souza	Psychologist, Head of Research Department National Television Council Santiago de Chile Chile
Helga Theunert	Ph.D. JFF - Institut für Medienpädagogik in Forschung und Praxis (Institute for Media Research and Media Education) München Germany
Lorenzo Vilches	Director, Master de Escritura para cine y televisión Facultad CC. de la Comunicación Universidad Autónoma de Barcelona Barcelona Spain